U.S. Special Operations Command

" An Overview of U.S. Special Forces "

Edited by Paul F. Kisak

Contents

Chapter 1

United States special operations forces

United States **Special Operations Forces** (SOF) are components of the Department of Defense's United States Special Operations Command (USSOCOM).

The U.S. military definition of Special Operations Forces according to the *Department of Defense Dictionary of Military and Associated Terms* is "Those Active and Reserve Component forces of the Military Services designated by the Secretary of Defense and specifically organized, trained, and equipped to conduct and support special operations. Also called SOF".[1] The definition in the *DOD Dictionary of Military and Associated Terms* references *Joint Publication 3-05.1 - Joint Special Operations Task Force Operations* (JP 3-05.1) as its source.[1][2]

1.1 List of SOF units

★ Represents a unit led by a Brigadier General or Rear Admiral (lower half)

★★ by a Major General or Rear Admiral (upper half)

★★★ by a Lieutenant General or Vice Admiral

1.1.1 Joint Special Operations Command

Joint Special Operations Command ★★★[3]

- 1st Special Forces Operational Detachment-Delta

- Intelligence Support Activity

- United States Naval Special Warfare Development Group

- 24th Special Tactics Squadron

- US Army Flight Concepts Division

- 427th Special Operations Squadron

- Joint Communications Unit

1.1.2 United States Army

- United States Army Special Operations Command (USASOC) ★★★[3]

Army Rangers during a training course, 2011

- 1st Special Forces Command (Airborne) (Provisional) ★★[3]
    - Special Forces Regiment[3]
        - 1st Special Forces Group[3]
        - 3rd Special Forces Group[3]
        - 5th Special Forces Group[3]
        - 7th Special Forces Group[3]
        - 10th Special Forces Group[3]
        - 19th Special Forces Group (Army National Guard)[3]
        - 20th Special Forces Group (Army National Guard)[3]
    - Military Information Support Operations Command[3]
        - 4th Military Information Support Group[3]
        - 6th Military Information Support Group[3]
    - 95th Civil Affairs Brigade[3]
        - 91st Civil Affairs Battalion[3]
        - 92nd Civil Affairs Battalion[3]
        - 96th Civil Affairs Battalion[3]
        - 97th Civil Affairs Battalion[3]
        - 98th Civil Affairs Battalion[3]
    - 528th Sustainment Brigade[3]
        - 112th Signals Battalion[3]
        - Special Troops Battalion[3]
        - 195th Support Company (National Guard)[3]

- 197th Support Company[3]
- 75th Ranger Regiment[3]
  - 1st Ranger Battalion[3]
  - 2nd Ranger Battalion[3]
  - 3rd Ranger Battalion[3]
  - 75th Ranger Special Troops Battalion[3]
- US Army Special Operations Aviation Command (ARSOAC) ★[3]
  - 160th Special Operations Aviation Regiment (SOAR)[3]
  - Special Operations Aviation Training Battalion[3]
- John F. Kennedy Special Warfare Center and School ★★[3]
  - Special Warfare Training Group (Airborne)[3]
  - Special Warfare Education Group (Airborne)[3]
  - Special Warfare Medical Group (Airborne)[3]

1.1.3 United States Navy

Navy SEALs desert training exercise, 2004

- Naval Special Warfare Command (NSWC) ★★[3]
  - Naval Special Warfare Group 1[3]
    - SEAL Teams 1, 3, 5, 7[3]

- Logistics Support Unit 1[3]
- Naval Special Warfare Unit 1[3]
- Naval Special Warfare Unit 3[3]
- Naval Special Warfare Group 2[3]
  - SEAL Teams 2, 4, 8, 10[3]
  - Logistics Support Unit 2[3]
  - Naval Special Warfare Unit 2[3]
  - Naval Special Warfare Unit 4[3]
  - Naval Special Warfare Unit 10[3]
- Naval Special Warfare Group 3[3]
  - SEAL Delivery Vehicle Team 1[3]
  - Logistics Support Unit 3[3]
  - SEAL Delivery Vehicle Team 1 Detachment 1[3]
- Naval Special Warfare Group 4[3]
  - Special Boat Team 12[3]
  - Special Boat Team 20[3]
  - Special Boat Team 22[3]
  - NAVSCIATTS[3]
- Naval Special Warfare Group 10[3]
  - Support Activity 1[3]
  - Support Activity 2[3]
  - Mission Support Center[3]
  - Cultural Engagement Unit[3]
- Naval Special Warfare Group 11[3]
  - SEAL Teams 17, 18 (Navy Reserve)[3]
- Naval Special Warfare Center[3]
  - Basic Training Command[3]
  - Advanced Training Command[3]
- United States Naval Special Warfare Development Group[3]

1.1.4   United States Air Force

Note, non operations-related squadrons are not included for a condensed list of units

- Air Force Special Operations Command (AFSOC) ★★★[3]
  - 1st Special Operations Wing[3]
    - 1st Special Operations Group[4]
      - 4th Special Operations Squadron[4]
      - 23rd Weather Squadron[4]
      - 8th Special Operations Squadron[4]
      - 9th Special Operations Squadron[4]
      - 15th Special Operations Squadron[4]
      - 34th Special Operations Squadron[4]
      - 319th Special Operations Squadron[4]

- - 24th Special Operations Wing[3]
    - 720th Special Tactics Group[5]
      - 17th Special Tactics Squadron[5]
      - 21st Special Tactics Squadron[5]
      - 22d Special Tactics Squadron[5]
      - 23d Special Tactics Squadron[5]
      - 26th Special Tactics Squadron[5]
    - 724th Special Tactics Group[5]
      - 24th Special Tactics Squadron[5]
      - 724th Intelligence Squadron[5]

- - 27th Special Operations Wing[3]
    - 27th Special Operations Group[6]
      - 3rd Special Operations Squadron[6]
      - 9th Special Operations Squadron[6]
      - 16th Special Operations Squadron[6]
      - 20th Special Operations Squadron[6]
      - 33rd Special Operations Squadron[6]
      - 56th Special Operations Intelligence Squadron[6]
      - 73rd Special Operations Squadron[6]
      - 318th Special Operations Squadron[6]
      - 524th Special Operations Squadron[6]

- - 193d Special Operations Wing (Air National Guard)[3]
    - 193d Special Operations Squadron

- - 919th Special Operations Wing (Air Force Reserve)[3]
    - 919th Special Operations Group[7]
      - 2d Special Operations Squadron (Nellis AFB)[7]
      - 5th Special Operations Squadron[7]
      - 711th Special Operations Squadron[7]

- - 352d Special Operations Wing (Provisional)[3]
    - 7th Special Operations Squadron[8]
    - 67th Special Operations Squadron[8]
    - 321st Special Tactics Squadron[8]

- - 353rd Special Operations Group[3]
    - 1st Special Operations Squadron[9]
    - 17th Special Operations Squadron[9]
    - Detachment 1, 43rd Intelligence Squadron[9]
    - 320th Special Tactics Squadron[9]

- - Air Force Special Operations Air Warfare Center ★★[3]
    - 19th Special Operations Squadron[10]
    - 551st Special Operations Squadron[10]
    - 5th Special Operations Squadron (USAF Reserves)[10]

- 371st Special Operations Combat Training Squadron[10]
- 280th Combat Communications Squadron[10]
- 18th Flight Test Squadron[10]
- 6th Special Operations Squadron[10]
- United States Air Force Special Operations School[10]

1.1.5   United States Marine Corps

Marine Raiders conduct combat operations in eastern Afghanistan

- United States Marine Corps Forces Special Operations Command (MARSOC) ★★[3]
    - Marine Raider Regiment[3]
        - 1st Marine Raider Battalion[3]
        - 2nd Marine Raider Battalion[3]
        - 3rd Marine Raider Battalion[3]
    - Marine Raider Support Group[3]
        - 1st Marine Raider Support Battalion[3]
        - 2nd Marine Raider Support Battalion[3]
        - 3rd Marine Raider Support Battalion[3]
    - Marine Special Operations School[3]

1.2   SOF career fields

1.2.1 United States Army

- Special Forces
- Rangers

Enablers[11]

- Sustainers
- Army Special Operations Aviators
- Military Information Support Operators (Psychological Operations)
- Civil Affairs Soldiers
- Military Intelligence and other Special Operations Support Jobs with enlisted Special Qualification (SQI) Identifier "S" or Officer Personnel Management System (OPMS) Identifier "K9"

1.2.2 United States Marine Corps

- United States Marine Corps Critical Skills Operator (CSO)

Enablers[11]

- Special Operations Capabilities Specialist
- Combat Services Specialist

1.2.3 United States Navy

- Navy SEALs
- Special warfare combatant-craft crewmen (SWCC)
- Special Amphibious Reconnaissance Corpsman (SARC)

Enablers[11]

- United States Navy EOD

1.2.4 United States Air Force

Officers

- Combat Rescue Officer (CRO) - PJ officers
- Special Tactics Officer (STO) - CCT/SOWT officers
- Air Liaison Officer (ALO)* - TACP officers

Enlisted

- Combat Control (CCT)

- Pararescue (PJ)

- Special Operations Weather Technician (SOWT)

- Tactical Air Control Party (TACP)*

* Note: ALO/TACP are not inherently designated SOF, only ALO/TACP belonging to Special Tactics Squadrons which are under AFSOC, the vast majority of TACPs/ALOs are in Air Support Operations Squadrons which belong to Air Combat Command.

1.3   U.S. Special Operations centers, schools, and courses

- International Special Training Center (ISTC) - Pfullendorf, Federal Republic of Germany

- Joint Special Operations University – Hurlburt Field

- Advanced Special Operations Techniques Course (ASOTC) - Fort Bragg

- John F. Kennedy Special Warfare Center and School – Fort Bragg

- Military Free Fall Advanced Tactical Infiltration Course (ATIC) - Yuma Proving Ground, Arizona

- Naval Special Warfare Center – Coronado, California

- Naval Special Warfare Advanced Training Command, Imperial Beach, CA

- Recon and Surveillance Leaders Course (RSLC) - Fort Bening, Georgia

- Special Forces Advanced Urban Combat (SFAUC) - Fort Bragg

- Special Forces Combat Diver Qualification Course - Key West, Florida

- Special Forces Sniper Course (SFSC) - Fort Bragg

- Special Forces Advanced Targeting Reconnaissance Target Analysis Exploitation Techniques (SFARTAETC)

- Special Forces Physical Surveillance Course

- SOF Sensitive Site Exploitation, Technical Exploitation Course

- SOF Sensitive Site Exploitation, Operator Advanced Course

- Special Forces Master Mountaineering Course (Level 1)

- Special Forces Senior Mountaineering Course (Level 2)

- Winter Warfare, Mountain and Cold Weather Operations

- Special Forces Technical Surveillance (SFTSC)

- Marine Special Operations School – Camp Lejeune

  - Marine Corps Special Operations Training Group

- US Army Ranger Assessment and Selection Program (RASP) – Fort Benning, Georgia

- US Army Small Unit Ranger Tactics (SURT) – Fort Benning, Georgia

- USAF Combat Control School – Pope Field, North Carolina

- USAF Pararescue Recovery Specialist Course - Kirtland AFB, NM

- USAF Special Operations School – Hurlburt Field, FL
    - Special Tactics Training Squadron
- Special Operations Terminal Attack Control Course (SOTACC), Yuma Proving Ground, Arizona[12]
- JTAC Advanced Instructor Course – Nellis AFB, NV[13]
- US Navy Rescue Swimmer school, Pensacola, Florida
- US Coast Guard Special Mission Training Center, Camp Lejeune, North Carolina

1.4 Commands

- United States Special Operations Command (SOCOM)[11]
    - Joint Special Operations Command (JSOC)[11]
    - United States Air Force Special Operations Command (AFSOC)[11]
    - United States Marine Corps Forces Special Operations Command (MARSOC)[11]
    - United States Army Special Operations Command (USASOC)[11]
    - United States Naval Special Warfare Command (NSWC)[11]
    - Special Operations Command – Joint Capabilities (SOC-JC)
    - Theater Special Operations Commands
        - Special Operations Command Africa (SOCAFRICA)[11]
        - Special Operations Command Central (SOCCENT)[11]
        - Special Operations Command Europe (SOCEUR)[11]
            - Joint Special Operations Air Component Europe
        - Special Operations Command Pacific (SOCPAC)[11]
        - Special Operations Command South (SOCSOUTH)[11][14]
        - Special Operations Command North (SOCNORTH)[15][11]
        - Special Operations Command Korea (SOCKOR)[11]

1.5 Notes

[1] special operations forces. Dtic.mil. Retrieved on 2014-05-24.

[2] "Joint Special Operations Task Force Operations" (PDF). 26 April 2007. p. GP-15 (Glossary page). Retrieved 2013-09-19.

[3] SOCOM Public Affairs (2015). *SOCOM Fact Book 2015* (PDF). SOCOM Public Affairs.

[4] "1st Special Operations Group fact sheet". July 1, 2015.

[5] "24th Special Operations Wing fact sheet". July 1, 2015.

[6] "27th Special Operations Wing fact sheet". July 1, 2015.

[7] "919th Special Operations Wing fact sheet". July 1, 2015.

[8] "352d Special Operations Wing fact sheet". July 1, 2015.

[9] "353rd Special Operations Group fact sheet". July 1, 2015.

[10] "Air Force Special Operations Air Warfare Center". July 1, 2015.

[11] "SOCOM 2014 Factbook" (PDF). 2014. Retrieved 21 April 2014.

[12] http://www.yumasun.com/news/military_news/air-force-becomes-newest-ypg-tenant/article_86301f97-82f9-57a8-8f72-html

[13] "Enlisted heroes receive graduate-level education at Weapons School". 6 February 2013. Retrieved 21 March 2013.

[14] Special Operations Command South

[15] U.S. Special Operations Command, North (Provisional Command) > U.S. Northern Command > Article View. Northcom.mil (2013-05-16). Retrieved on 2014-05-24.

1.6 References

- United States Department of Defense (5 June 2003). "US DOD Dictionary of Military Terms: Joint Acronyms and Abbreviations". United States Department of Defense. United States of America. Retrieved 11 January 2004.

- CSM Eric Haney (retired, former Delta Force operator and founding member) (2002). *Inside Delta Force: The Story of America's Elite Counterterrorist Unit*. Delacorte Press. ISBN 0-385-33603-9.

- Linda Robinson (2004). *Masters of Chaos: The Secret History of the Special Forces*. PublicAffairs. ISBN 1-58648-249-1.

- Mark Bowden (1999). *Black Hawk Down: A Story of Modern Warfare*. Atlantic Monthly Press. ISBN 0-87113-738-0.

- Sean Naylor (2005). *Not a Good Day to Die: The Untold Story of Operation Anaconda*. The Berkeley Publishing Group. ISBN 0-425-19609-7.

- "Special Forces Units". Retrieved 8 October 2006.

1.7 External links

- David Ignatius: Learning to Fight a War - Washington Post, 2008-02-10

- US Special Operation Forces – 2009 SOCOM Factbook

Chapter 2

Special forces

For specific special forces units, see List of military special forces units and List of defunct special forces units. For Green Berets, a special unit of United States Army, see Special Forces (United States Army). For 2003 film, see Special Forces (2003 film).

"Spec Ops" redirects here. For the video game series, see Spec Ops (series).

For French 2011 film, see Special Forces (2011 film).

Polish GROM special forces troops at Umm Qasr during the 2003 invasion of Iraq

Special forces and **special operations forces** are military units trained to perform unconventional missions.[1] Special forces, as they would now be recognised, emerged in the early 20th century, with a significant growth in the field during the Second World War.

Depending on the country, special forces may perform some of the following functions: airborne operations, counter-insurgency, "counter-terrorism", covert ops, direct action, hostage rescue, high-value targets/manhunting, intelligence operations, mobility operations, and unconventional warfare. The term "special forces" in the US refers to the US Army's forces while the term "special operation forces" refers to all units. In Russian-speaking countries special forces are typically called *spetsnaz*, an acronym for "special purpose". Likewise Russian speakers refer to special forces of other nations as spetsnaz, for example US Special Forces would be referred to as *Amerikanski spetsnaz* in Russian.

2.1   Capabilities

Special forces capabilities include the following:

- Reconnaissance and surveillance in hostile environments

- Training and development of other states' military and security forces

- Offensive action

- Support to counter-insurgency through population engagement and support

- Counter-terrorism operations

- Sabotage and demolition

- Hostage rescue

2.2   History

2.2.1   Early period

Special forces have played an important role throughout the history of warfare, whenever the aim was to achieve disruption by "hit and run" and sabotage, rather than more traditional conventional combat. Other significant roles lay in reconnaissance, providing essential intelligence from near or among the enemy and increasingly in combating irregular forces, their infrastructure and activities.

Chinese strategist Jiang Ziya, in his *Six Secret Teachings*, described recruiting talented and motivated men into specialized elite units with functions such as commanding heights and making rapid long-distance advances.[2] Hamilcar Barca in Sicily (249 BC) had specialized troops trained to launch several offensives per day. In the late Roman or early Byzantine period, Roman fleets used small, fast, camouflaged ships crewed by selected men for scouting and commando missions. Muslim forces also had naval special operations units, including one that used camouflaged ships to gather intelligence and launch raids and another of soldiers who could pass for Crusaders who would use ruses to board enemy ships and then capture and destroy them.[3] In Japan, ninjas were used for reconnaissance, espionage and as assassins, bodyguards or fortress guards, or otherwise fought alongside conventional soldiers.[4] During the Napoleonic wars, rifle and sapper units were formed that held specialised roles in reconnaissance and skirmishing and were not committed to the formal battle lines.

2.2.2   First specialized units

The British Indian Army deployed two special forces during their border wars: the Corps of Guides formed in 1846 and the Gurkha Scouts (a force that was formed in the 1890s and was first used as a detached unit during the 1897–1898 Tirah Campaign).[5]

During the Second Boer War (1899–1902) the British Army felt the need for more specialised units became most apparent. Scouting units such as the Lovat Scouts, a Scottish Highland regiment made up of exceptional woodsmen outfitted in ghillie suits and well practised in the arts of marksmanship, field craft, and military tactics filled this role. This unit was formed in 1900 by Lord Lovat and early on reported to an American, Major Frederick Russell Burnham, the Chief of Scouts under Lord Roberts. After the war, Lovat's Scouts went on to formally become the British Army's first sniper unit.[6] Additionally, the Bushveldt Carbineers, formed in 1901, can be seen as an early unconventional warfare unit.

2.2.3 Modern special forces

Britain

Modern special forces emerged during the Second World War. In 1940, the British Commandos were formed following Winston Churchill's call for "specially trained troops of the hunter class, who can develop a reign of terror down the enemy coast."[7] A staff officer, Lieutenant Colonel Dudley Clarke, had already submitted such a proposal to General Sir John Dill, the Chief of the Imperial General Staff. Dill, aware of Churchill's intentions, approved Clarke's proposal[8] and on 23 June 1940, the first Commando raid took place.[8]

By the autumn of 1940 more than 2,000 men had volunteered and in November 1940 these new units were organised into a Special Service Brigade consisting of four battalions under the command of Brigadier J. C. Haydon.[9] The Special Service Brigade was quickly expanded to 12 units which became known as Commandos.[8] Each Commando had a lieutenant colonel as the commanding officer and numbered around 450 men (divided into 75 man troops that were further divided into 15 man sections).

In December 1940 a Middle East Commando depot was formed with the responsibility of training and supplying reinforcements for the Commando units in that theatre.[10] In February 1942 the Commando training depot at Achnacarry in the Scottish Highlands was established by Brigadier Charles Haydon. Under the command of Lieutenant Colonel Charles Vaughan, the Commando depot was responsible for training complete units and individual replacements.[10] The training regime was for the time innovative and physically demanding, and far in advance of normal British Army training.[10] The depot staff were all hand picked, with the ability to outperform any of the volunteers.

Training and assessment started immediately on arrival, with the volunteers having to complete an 8-mile (13 km) march with all their equipment from the Spean Bridge railway station to the commando depot.[10] Exercises were conducted using live ammunition and explosives to make training as realistic as possible. Physical fitness was a prerequisite, with cross country runs and boxing matches to improve fitness. Speed and endurance marches were conducted up and down the nearby mountain ranges and over assault courses that included a zip-line over Loch Arkaig, all while carrying arms and full equipment. Training continued by day and night with river crossings, mountain climbing, weapons training, unarmed combat, map reading, and small boat operations on the syllabus.

Reaching a wartime strength of over 30 individual units and four assault brigades, the Commandos served in all theatres of war from the Arctic Circle to Europe and from the Mediterranean and Middle East to South-East Asia. Their operations ranged from small groups of men landing from the sea or by parachute to a brigade of assault troops spearheading the Allied invasions of Europe and Asia. The first modern special forces units were established by men who had served with the Commandos, including the Parachute Regiment, Special Air Service, and Special Boat Service. The Commandos were also widely imitated elsewhere: the French Naval commandos, Dutch Korps Commandotroepen, Belgian Paracommando Brigade and United States Army Rangers were all influenced to some degree by the British Commandos.[11][12][13]

The first modern special forces unit was the SAS, formed in July 1941 from an unorthodox idea and plan by Lieutenant David Stirling.[14] In June 1940 he volunteered for the No. 8 (Guards) Commando (later named "Layforce"). After Layforce was disbanded, Stirling remained convinced that due to the mechanised nature of war a small team of highly trained soldiers with the advantage of surprise could exact greater damage to the enemy's ability to fight than an entire platoon. His idea was for small teams of parachute trained soldiers to operate behind enemy lines to gain intelligence, destroy enemy aircraft and attack their supply and reinforcement routes. Following a meeting with the C-in-C Middle East, General Claude Auchinleck, his plan was endorsed by the Army High Command.

The force initially consisted of five officers and 60 other ranks.[15] Following extensive training at Kabrit camp, by the River Nile, L Detachment, SAS Brigade undertook its first operations. Stirling's vision was eventually vindicated after a series of successful operations. In 1942, the SAS attacked Bouerat. Transported by the LRDG, they caused severe damage to the harbour, petrol tanks and storage facilities.[16] This was followed up in March by a raid on Benghazi harbour with limited success but they did damage 15 aircraft at Al-Berka.[16] The June 1942 Crete airfield raids at Heraklion, Kasteli, Tympaki and Maleme significant damage was caused, and raids at Fuka and Mersa Matruh airfields destroyed 30 aircraft.[17]

In the Burma Campaign, the Chindits, whose long range penetration groups were trained to operate from bases deep behind Japanese lines, contained commandos (King's Regiment (Liverpool), 142 Commando Company) and Gurkhas. Their jungle expertise, which would play an important part in many British special forces operations post war, was learned at a great cost in lives in the jungles of Burma fighting the Japanese.

Immediately after the German occupation of Greece in April–May 1941, the Greek government fled to Egypt and started to form military units in exile. Air Force Lt. Colonel G. Alexandris suggested the creation of an Army unit along the lines of the British SAS. In August 1942 the Company of Chosen Immortals (Greek: Λόχος Επιλέκτων Αθανάτων) was formed under Cavalry Major Antonios Stefanakis in Palestine, with 200 men. In 1942, the unit was renamed Sacred Band. In close cooperation with the commander of the British SAS Regiment, Lt. Colonel David Stirling, the company moved to the SAS base at Qabrit in Egypt to begin its training in its new role. Operating under British direction, the special forces unit fought alongside the SAS in the Libyan desert and the Aegean.

Australia

Following advice from the British, Australia began raising special forces.[18] The first units to be formed were independent companies, which began training at Wilson's Promontory in Victoria in early 1941 under the tutelage of British instructors. With an establishment of 17 officers and 256 men, the independent companies were trained as "stay behind" forces, a role that they were later employed in against the Japanese in the South West Pacific Area during 1942–43, most notably fighting a guerilla campaign in Timor, as well as actions in New Guinea.[19] In all, a total of eight independent companies were raised before they were re-organised in mid-1943 into commando squadrons and placed under the command of the divisional cavalry regiments that were re-designated as cavalry commando regiments. As a part of this structure, a total of 11 commando squadrons were raised.

They continued to act independently, and were often assigned at brigade level during the later stages of the war, taking part in the fighting in New Guinea, Bougainville and Borneo, where they were employed largely in long-range reconnaissance and flank protection roles.[20] In addition to these units, the Australians also raised the Z Special Unit and M Special Unit. M Special Unit was largely employed in an intelligence-gathering role, while Z Special Force undertook direct action missions. One of its most notable actions came as part of Operation *Jaywick*, in which several Japanese ships were sunk in Singapore Harbour in 1943. A second raid on Singapore in 1944, known as Operation *Rimau*, was unsuccessful.[21]

United States

The United States formed the Office of Strategic Services (OSS) during World War II under the Medal of Honor recipient William J. Donovan. This organization was the predecessor of the Central Intelligence Agency (CIA) and was responsible for both intelligence and special forces missions. The CIA's elite Special Activities Division is the direct descendant of the OSS.[22]

On February 16, 1942, the U.S. Marine Corps activated a battalion of Marines with the specific purpose of securing beach heads, and other special operations. The battalion became the first special operations force of the U.S. The battalion became known as Marine Raiders due to Admiral Chester Nimitz's request for "raiders" in the Pacific front of the war.

In mid-1942, Major-General Lucian Truscott of the U.S. Army, a liaison officer with the British General Staff submitted a proposal to General George Marshall that an American unit be set up "along the lines of the British Commandos", resulting in the formation of the United States Army Rangers. The United States and Canada also formed a sabotage ski brigade for operations in Norway that became known as the Devil's Brigade, officially known as the First Special Service Force, during their eventual service in Italy.

Merrill's Marauders were modelled on the Chindits and took part in similar operations in Burma. In late November 1943, the Alamo Scouts were formed to conduct reconnaissance and raider work in the Southwest Pacific Theater under the personal command of then Lt. General Walter Krueger, Commanding General, Sixth U.S. Army. Krueger envisioned that the Alamo Scouts, consisting of small teams of highly trained volunteers, would operate deep behind enemy lines to provide intelligence-gathering and tactical reconnaissance in advance of Sixth U.S. Army landing operations. In 1988 the Alamo Scouts were individually awarded the Special Forces Tab for their services in World War II and included in the lineage of today's U.S. Army Special Forces.

Axis powers

The Axis powers did not adopt the use of special forces on the same scale as the British. The German army's Brandenburger Regiment was originally founded as a special forces unit used by the Abwehr for infiltration and long distance reconnaissance in Fall Weiss of 1939 and the Fall Gelb and Barbarossa campaigns of 1940 and 1941.

Later during the war the 502nd SS Jäger Battalion, commanded by Otto Skorzeny, sowed disorder behind the Allied lines by mis-directing convoys away from the front lines. A handful of his men were captured by the Americans and spread a rumor that Skorzeny was leading a raid on Paris to kill or capture General Dwight Eisenhower. Although this was untrue, Eisenhower was confined to his headquarters for several days and Skorzeny was labelled "the most dangerous man in Europe".

In Italy, the Decima Flottiglia MAS was responsible for the sinking and damage of considerable British tonnage in the Mediterranean. Also there were other Italian special forces like A.D.R.A. (*Arditi Distruttori Regia Aeronautica*). This regiment was used in raids on Allied airbases and railways in North Africa in 1943. In one mission they destroyed 25 B-17s.

The Imperial Japanese Army first deployed army paratroops in combat during the Battle of Palembang, on Sumatra in the Netherlands East Indies, on 14 February 1942. The operation was well-planned, with 425 men of the 1st Parachute Raiding Regiment seizing Palembang airfield, while the paratroopers of the 2nd Parachute Raiding Regiment seized the town and its important oil refinery. Paratroops were subsequently deployed in the Burma campaign. The 1st Glider Tank Troop was formed in 1943, with four Type 95 Ha-Go light tanks. The paratroop brigades were organized into the *Teishin Shudan* as the first division-level raiding unit, at the main Japanese airborne base, Karasehara Airfield, Kyūshu, Japan.

However, as with similar airborne units created by the Allies and other Axis powers, the Japanese paratroops suffered from a disproportionately high casualty rate, and the loss of men who required such extensive and expensive training limited their operations to only the most critical ones. Two regiments of *Teishin Shudan* were formed into the 1st Raiding Group, commanded by Major General Rikichi Tsukada under the control of the Southern Expeditionary Army Group, during the Philippines campaign. Although structured as a division, its capabilities were much lower, as its six regiments had manpower equivalent to a standard infantry battalion, and it lacked any form of artillery, and had to rely on other units for logistical support. Its men were no longer parachute-trained, but relied on aircraft for transport.

Some 750 men, mainly from the 2nd Raiding Brigade, of this group were assigned to attack American air bases on Luzon and Leyte on the night of 6 December 1944. They were flown in Ki-57 transports, but most of the aircraft were shot down. Some 300 commandos managed to land in the Burauen area on Leyte. The force destroyed some planes and inflicted numerous casualties, before they were annihilated.

2.3 Post WWII

Admiral William H. McRaven, formerly the ninth commanding officer of the U.S. Special Operations Command (2011-2014), described two approaches to special forces operations in the 2012 posture statement to the U.S. Senate Committee on Armed Services: "the direct approach is characterized by technologically enabled small-unit precision lethality, focused intelligence, and inter-agency cooperation integrated on a digitally-networked battlefield", whereas the "indirect approach includes empowering host nation forces, providing appropriate assistance to humanitarian agencies, and engaging key populations."[23] Elements of national power must be deployed in concert without over-reliance on a single capability, such as special forces, that leaves the entire force unprepared and hollow across the spectrum of military operations.[24]

Throughout the latter half of the 20th century and into the 21st century, special forces have come to higher prominence, as governments have found objectives can sometimes be better achieved by a small team of anonymous specialists than a larger and much more politically controversial conventional deployment. In both Kosovo and Afghanistan, special forces were used to co-ordinate activities between local guerrilla fighters and air power. Typically, guerrilla fighters would engage enemy soldiers and tanks causing them to move, where they could be seen and attacked from the air.

Special forces have been used in both wartime and peacetime military operations such as the Laotian Civil War, 1971

Indo-Pakistan War, Vietnam War, Portuguese Colonial War, South African Border War, Falklands War, The Troubles in Northern Ireland, the Jaffna University Helidrop the first and second Gulf Wars, Afghanistan, Croatia, Kosovo, Bosnia, the first and second Chechen Wars, the Iranian Embassy siege (London), the Air France Flight 8969 (Marseille), Operation Defensive Shield, Operation Khukri, the Moscow theater hostage crisis, Operation Orchard, the Japanese Embassy hostage crisis (Lima), in Sri Lanka against the LTTE, and the raid on Osama Bin Laden's compound in Pakistan.

The U.S. invasion of Afghanistan involved special forces from several coalition nations, who played a major role in removing the Taliban from power in 2001–2002. Special forces have continued to play a role in combating the Taliban in subsequent operations.

2.4   See also

- List of military special forces units

- Commando

- Long Range Reconnaissance Patrol

- Recondo School

- Special operations

- SWAT

2.5   Notes

[1] Richard Bowyer, Dictionary of Military Terms, Bloomsbury Reference (2005-08), ISBN 190497015X / ISBN 9781904970156.

[2] Sawyer, Ralph D. (1993). *The Seven Military Classics of Ancient China*. Boulder: Westview Press, Inc. pp. 39, 98–9. ISBN 0-8133-1228-0.

[3] Christides, Vassilios. "Military Intelligence in Arabo-Byzantine Naval Warfare" (PDF). Institute for Byzantine Studies, Athens. pp. 276–80. Retrieved 2011-08-02.

[4] Turnbull, Stephen (2003). *Ninja AD 1460–1650*. Osprey Publishing. pp. 44–7, 50. ISBN 978-1-84176-525-9.

[5] "The Corps of Guides – the original Indian Army special forces." ..."The Scouts were not subordinate to any brigade or division but were *army* troops – deployed at the discretion of the field force commander." (Bellamy 2011, p. 115)

[6] John Plaster (2006). *The Ultimate Sniper: An Advanced Training Manual For Military and Police Snipers*. Paladin Press. p. 5. ISBN 0-87364-704-1.

[7] Haskew, p. 47

[8] Haskew, Michael E (2007). *Encyclopaedia of Elite Forces in the Second World War*. Barnsley: Pen and Sword. pp. 47–8. ISBN 978-1-84415-577-4.

[9] Joslen, H. F. (1990). *Orders of Battle, Second World War, 1939–1945*. London: Naval & Military Press. p. 454. ISBN 1-84342-474-6.

[10] Moreman, Timothy Robert (2006). *British Commandos 1940–46*. London: Osprey Publishing. pp. 37–49. ISBN 1-84176-986-X.

[11] "Les fusiliers marins et les commandos". Ministère de la Défense. Retrieved 17 April 2010.

[12] "The history of the Commando Foundation". Korps Commandotroepen. Retrieved 17 April 2010.

[13] "Centre d'Entraînement de Commandos". Ministère de la Défense,la Composante Terre. Retrieved 17 April 2010.

[14] London Gazette Issue 34420 published 23 July 1937, p. 10 of 80

[15] Thompson, Leroy (1994). *SAS: Great Britain's elite Special Air Service*. Zenith Imprint. p. 48. ISBN 0-87938-940-0.

[16] Shortt, James; McBride, Angus (1981). *The Special Air Service*. Osprey Publishing. p. 9. ISBN 0-85045-396-8.

[17] Molinari, Andrea (2007). *Desert Raiders: Axis and Allied Special Forces 1940–43*. Osprey Publishing. p. 75. ISBN 978-1-84603-006-2.

[18] Horner 1989, p. 21.

[19] Horner 1989, pp. 22–6.

[20] Horner 1989, p. 26.

[21] Horner 1989, pp. 26–7.

[22] The Office of Strategic Services: America's First Intelligence Agency, Michael Warner, CIA History Staff, Center for the Study of Intelligence, United States Central Intelligence Agency (2000)

[23] "POSTURE STATEMENT OF ADMIRAL WILLIAM H. McRAVEN, USN COMMANDER, UNITED STATES SPECIAL OPERATIONS COMMAND BEFORE THE 112th CONGRESS SENATE ARMED SERVICES COMMITTEE MARCH 6, 2012" (PDF). United States Special Operations Command. Retrieved 3 August 2015.

[24] "Special Operations for the 21st Century: Starting Over" (PDF). Association of the United States Army. Retrieved 3 August 2015.

2.6 References

- Bellamy, Chris (2011). *The Gurkhas: Special Force*. UK: Hachette. p. 115. ISBN 9781848545151.

- Breuer, William B. (2001). *Daring missions of World War II*. John Wiley and Sons. ISBN 978-0-471-40419-4.

- Haskew, Michael E (2007). *Encyclopaedia of Elite Forces in the Second World War*. Barnsley: Pen and Sword. ISBN 978-1-84415-577-4.

- Horner, David (1989). *SAS: Phantoms of the Jungle: A History of the Australian Special Air Service* (1st ed.). St Leonards: Allen & Unwin. ISBN 1-86373-007-9.

- Molinari, Andrea (2007). *Desert Raiders: Axis and Allied Special Forces 1940–43*. Osprey Publishing. ISBN 978-1-84603-006-2.

- Otway, Lieutenant-Colonel T.B.H. (1990). *The Second World War 1939–1945 Army – Airborne Forces*. Imperial War Museum. ISBN 0-901627-57-7.

2.7 External links

Japanese drawing of the archetypical ninja, from a series of
sketches (Hokusai manga) by Hokusai.

British Army scouts in South Africa (1893): Frederick Russell Burnham (middle); Hon. Maurice Gifford (right)

The British Commandos were the prototype for the modern special forces. Volunteers had to undergo an arduous training course.

British Commandos wearing the green beret and carrying the Bergen rucksack during the Normandy landings

British SAS in North Africa (1943), in jeeps with mounted heavy machine guns

United States Army Rangers at D-Day, Pointe du Hoc.

Bundesarchiv, Bild 101I-680-8283A-30A
Foto: Faupel | 10. Oktober 1944

Otto Skorzeny (left) and the former Brandenburger *Adrian von Fölkersam (right), 1944.*

ODA 525 team picture taken shortly before infiltration in Iraq, February 1991

Chapter 3

United States Special Operations Command

See also: United States special operations forces

The **United States Special Operations Command** (**USSOCOM** or **SOCOM**) is the Unified Combatant Command charged with overseeing the various Special Operations Component Commands of the Army, Air Force, Navy and Marine Corps of the United States Armed Forces. The command is part of the Department of Defense and is the only Unified Combatant Command legislated into being by the U.S. Congress. USSOCOM is headquartered at MacDill Air Force Base in Tampa, Florida.

The idea of a unified special operations command had its origins in the aftermath of Operation Eagle Claw, the disastrous attempted rescue of hostages at the American embassy in Iran in 1980. The ensuing investigation, chaired by Admiral James L. Holloway III, the retired Chief of Naval Operations, cited lack of command and control and inter-service coordination as significant factors in the failure of the mission.[4] Since its activation on 16 April 1987, U.S. Special Operations Command has participated in many operations, from the 1989 invasion of Panama to the ongoing Global War on Terrorism.[5][6]

USSOCOM conducts several covert and clandestine missions, such as direct action, special reconnaissance, counter-terrorism, foreign internal defense, unconventional warfare, psychological warfare, civil affairs, and counter-narcotics operations. Each branch has a Special Operations Command that is unique and capable of running its own operations, but when the different special operations forces need to work together for an operation, USSOCOM becomes the joint component command of the operation, instead of a SOC of a specific branch.[7]

3.1 History

The unworkable command and control structure of separate U.S. military special operations forces (SOF), which led to the failure of Operation Eagle Claw in 1980, highlighted the need within the Department of Defense for reform and reorganization. Since the incident, the Army Chief of Staff, General Edward C. "Shy" Meyer, called for a further restructuring of special operations capabilities, eventually helping to create the U.S. Delta Force.[8] Although unsuccessful at the joint level, Meyer nevertheless went on to consolidate Army SOF units under the new 1st Special Operations Command in 1982, a significant step to improve the U.S. Army's SOF.

By 1983, there was a small but growing sense in the Congress for the need for military reforms. In June, the Senate Armed Services Committee (SASC) began a two-year-long study of the Defense Department, which included an examination of SOF spearheaded by Senator Barry Goldwater (R-AZ). With concern mounting on Capitol Hill, the Department of Defense created the Joint Special Operations Agency on 1 January 1984; this agency, however, had neither operational nor command authority over any SOF.[9][10] The Joint Special Operations Agency thus did little to improve SOF readiness, capabilities, or policies, and therefore was insufficient. Within the Defense Department, there were a few staunch SOF supporters. Noel Koch, Principal Deputy Assistant Secretary of Defense for International Security Affairs, and his deputy, Lynn Rylander, both advocated SOF reforms.[11]

Senator Barry Goldwater, Former Chairman of the Senate Armed Services Committee

At the same time, a few on Capitol Hill were determined to overhaul United States Special Operations Forces. They included Senators Sam Nunn (D-GA) and William Cohen (R-ME), both members of the Armed Services Committee, and Representative Dan Daniel (D-VA), the chairman of the United States House Armed Services Subcommittee on Readiness. Congressman Daniel had become convinced that the U.S. military establishment was not interested in special operations, that the country's capability in this area was second rate, and that SOF operational command and control was an endemic problem.[11] Senators Nunn and Cohen also felt strongly that the Department of Defense was not preparing adequately for future threats. Senator Cohen agreed that the U.S. needed a clearer organizational focus and chain of command for special operations to deal with low-intensity conflicts.[9]

In October 1985, the Senate Armed Services Committee published the results of its two-year review of the U.S. military structure, entitled "Defense Organization: The Need For Change."[12] Mr. James R. Locher III, the principal author of this study, also examined past special operations and speculated on the most likely future threats. This influential document led to the Goldwater-Nichols Defense Reorganization Act of 1986.[13][14] By spring 1986, SOF advocates had introduced reform bills in both houses of Congress. On 15 May, Senator Cohen introduced the Senate bill, co-sponsored by Senator Nunn and others, which called for a joint military organization for SOF and the establishment of an office in the Defense Department to ensure adequate funding and policy emphasis for low-intensity conflict and special operations.[15] Representative Daniel's proposal went even further—he wanted a national special operations agency headed by a civilian who would bypass the Joint Chiefs and report directly to the Secretary of Defense; this would keep Joint Chiefs and the Services out of the SOF budget process.[10]

Congress held hearings on the two bills in the summer of 1986. Admiral William J. Crowe Jr., Chairman of the Joint Chiefs of Staff, led the Pentagon's opposition to the bills. He proposed, as an alternative, a new Special Operations Forces command led by a three-star general. This proposal was not well received on Capitol Hill—Congress wanted a four-star general in charge to give SOF more clout. A number of retired military officers and others testified in favor of the need for reform.[11] By most accounts, retired Army Major General Richard Scholtes gave the most compelling reasons for change. Scholtes, who commanded the joint special operations task force in Grenada, explained how conventional force leaders misused SOF during the operation, not allowing them to use their unique capabilities, which resulted in high SOF casualties. After his formal testimony, Scholtes met privately with a small number of Senators to elaborate on the problems that he had encountered in Grenada.[16]

Both the House and Senate passed SOF reform bills, and these went to a conference committee for reconciliation. Senate and House conferees forged a compromise. The bill called for a unified combatant command headed by a four-star general for all SOF, an Assistant Secretary of Defense for Special Operations and Low-Intensity Conflict, a coordinating board for low-intensity conflict within the National Security Council, and a new Major Force Program (MFP-11) for SOF (the so-called "SOF checkbook").[17][18] The final bill, attached as a rider to the 1987 Defense Authorization Act, amended the Goldwater-Nichols Act and was signed into law in October 1986. Congress clearly intended to force DOD and the Administration to face up to the realities of past failures and emerging threats. DOD and the Administration were responsible for implementing the law, and Congress subsequently had to pass two additional bills to ensure proper implementation.[11] The legislation promised to improve SOF in several respects. Once implemented, MFP-11 provided SOF with control over its own resources, better enabling it to modernize the force. Additionally, the law fostered inter-service cooperation: a single commander for all SOF promoted interoperability among the forces assigned to the same command. The establishment of a four-star Commander in Chief and an Assistant Secretary of Defense for Special Operations and Low Intensity Conflict eventually gave SOF a voice in the highest councils of the Defense Department.[17]

Implementing the provisions and mandates of the Nunn-Cohen Act, however, was neither rapid nor smooth. One of the first issues to surface was appointing an ASD (SO/LIC), whose principal duties included monitorship of special operations activities and low-intensity conflict activities of the Department of Defense. The Congress even increased the number of assistant secretaries of defense from 11 to 12, but the Department of Defense still did not fill this new billet. In December 1987, the Congress directed Secretary of the Army John O. Marsh to carry out the ASD (SO/LIC) duties until a suitable replacement was approved by the Senate. Not until 18 months after the legislation passed did Ambassador Charles Whitehouse assume the duties of ASD (SO/LIC).[19]

Meanwhile, the establishment of USSOCOM provided its own measure of excitement. A quick solution to manning and basing a brand new unified command was to abolish an existing command. United States Readiness Command (USREDCOM), with an often misunderstood mission, did not appear to have a viable mission in the post Goldwater-Nichols era, and its Commander in Chief, General James Lindsay, had had some special operations experience. On 23 January 1987, the Joint Chiefs of Staff recommended to the Secretary of Defense that USREDCOM be disestablished to

General James Lindsay the first Commander in Chief, Special Operations Command

provide billets and facilities for USSOCOM. President Ronald Reagan approved the establishment of the new command on 13 April 1987. The Department of Defense activated USSOCOM on 16 April 1987 and nominated General Lindsay to be the first Commander in Chief Special Operations Command (USCINCSOC). The Senate accepted him without debate.[11]

3.1.1 Operation Earnest Will

MH-60 landing on Hercules

USSOCOM's first tactical operation involved SEALs, Special Boat Teams (SBT), and 160th Special Operations Aviation Regiment (Airborne) ("Night Stalkers") aviators working together during Operation Earnest Will in September 1987. During Operation Earnest Will, the United States ensured that neutral oil tankers and other merchant ships could safely transit the Persian Gulf during the Iran–Iraq War. Iranian attacks on tankers prompted Kuwait to ask the United States in December 1986 to register 11 Kuwaiti tankers as American ships so that they could be escorted by the U.S. Navy. President Reagan agreed to the Kuwaiti request on 10 March 1987, hoping it would deter Iranian attacks.[11] The protection offered by U.S. naval vessels, however, did not stop Iran, which used mines and small boats to harass the convoys steaming to and from Kuwait. In late July 1987, Rear Admiral Harold J. Bernsen, commander of the Middle East Force, requested NSW assets. Special Boat Teams deployed with six Mark III Patrol Boats and two SEAL platoons in August.[11] The Middle East Force decided to convert two oil servicing barges, Hercules and Wimbrown VII, into mobile sea bases. The mobile sea bases allowed SOF in the northern Persian Gulf to thwart clandestine Iranian mining and small boat attacks.

On 21 September, Nightstalkers flying MH-60 and Little Birds took off from the frigate USS *Jarrett* to track an Iranian ship, the *Iran Ajr*. The Nightstalkers observed the *Iran Ajr* turn off its lights and begin laying mines. After receiving permission to attack, the helicopters fired guns and rockets, stopping the ship. As the *Iran Ajr's* crew began to push mines over the side, the helicopters resumed firing until the crew abandoned ship. Special Boat Teams provided security while a SEAL team boarded the vessel at first light and discovered nine mines on the vessel's deck, as well as a logbook revealing areas where previous mines had been laid. The logbook implicated Iran in mining international waters.[11]

Within a few days, the Special Operations forces had determined the Iranian pattern of activity; the Iranians hid during the day near oil and gas platforms in Iranian waters and at night they headed toward the Middle Shoals Buoy, a navigation aid for tankers. With this knowledge, SOF launched three Little Bird helicopters and two patrol craft to the buoy. The Little Bird helicopters arrived first and were fired upon by three Iranian boats anchored near the buoy. After a short but intense firefight, the helicopters sank all three boats. Three days later, in mid-October, an Iranian Silkworm missile hit the tanker *Sea Isle City* near the oil terminal outside Kuwait City. Seventeen crewmen and the American captain were injured

One of two Iranian oil platform set ablaze after shelling by American destroyers.

in the missile attack.[11][20] During Operation Nimble Archer, four destroyers shelled two oil platforms in the Rostam oil field. After the shelling, a SEAL platoon and a demolition unit planted explosives on one of the platforms to destroy it. The SEALs next boarded and searched a third platform 2 miles (3 km) away. Documents and radios were taken for intelligence purposes.

On 14 April 1988, 65 miles (100 km) east of Bahrain, the frigate USS Samuel B. Roberts (FFG-58) hit a mine, blowing an immense hole in its hull.[21] Ten sailors were injured. During Operation Praying Mantis the U.S. retaliated fiercely, attacking the Iranian frigate *Sahand* and oil platforms in the Sirri and Sassan oil fields.[20] After U.S. warships bombarded the Sirri platform and set it ablaze, a UH-60 with a SEAL platoon flew toward the platform but was unable to get close enough because of the roaring fire. Secondary explosions soon wrecked the platform.[11] Thereafter, Iranian attacks on neutral ships dropped drastically. On 18 July, Iran accepted the United Nations cease fire; on 20 August 1988, the Iran–Iraq War ended. The remaining SEALs, patrol boats, and helicopters then returned to the United States.[11] Special operations forces provided critical skills necessary to help CENTCOM gain control of the northern Persian Gulf and balk Iran's small boats and minelayers. The ability to work at night proved vital, because Iranian units used darkness to conceal their actions. Additionally, because of Earnest Will operational requirements, USSOCOM would acquire new weapons systems—the patrol coastal ships and the Mark V Special Operations Craft.[11]

3.1.2   Somalia

Special Operations Command first became involved in Somalia in 1992 as part of Operation Provide Relief. C-130s circled over Somali airstrips during delivery of relief supplies. Special Forces medics accompanied many relief flights into the airstrips throughout southern Somalia to assess the area. They were the first U.S. soldiers in Somalia, arriving before U.S. forces who supported the expanded relief operations of Restore Hope.[11][22][23] The first teams into Somalia were CIA Special Activities Division paramilitary officers with elements of JSOC. They conducted very high risk advanced force operations prior to the entry of the follow on forces. The first casualty of the conflict came from this team and was a Paramilitary officer and former Delta Force operator name Larry Freedman. Freedman was awarded the Intelligence Star for *"extraordinary heroism"* for his actions.[24]

The earliest missions during Operation Restore Hope were conducted by Navy SEALs. The SEALs performed several hydro-graphic reconnaissance missions to find suitable landing sites for Marines. On 7 December, the SEALs swam into Mogadishu Harbor, where they found suitable landing sites, assessed the area for threats, and concluded that the port could support offloading ships. This was a tough mission because the SEALs swam against a strong current which left many of them overheated and exhausted. Furthermore, they swam through raw sewage in the harbor, which made them sick.[11] When the first SEALs hit the shore the following night, they were surprised to meet members of the news media. The first Marines came ashore soon thereafter, and the press redirected their attention to them. Later, the SEALs provided personal security for President George Bush during a visit to Somalia.[11][23] In December 1992, Special Forces assets in Kenya moved to Somalia and joined Operation Restore Hope. January 1993, a Special Forces command element deployed to Mogadishu as the Joint Special Operations Forces-Somalia (JSOFOR) that would command and control all special operations for Restore Hope. JSOFOR's mission was to make initial contact with indigenous factions and leaders; provide information for force protection; and provide reports on the area for future relief and security operations. Before redeploying in April, JSOFOR elements drove over 26,000 miles (42,000 km), captured 277 weapons, and destroyed over 45,320 pounds (20,560 kg) of explosives.[11]

Bravo Company, 3rd Battalion of the 75th Ranger Regiment in Somalia, 1993.

In August 1993, Secretary of Defense Les Aspin directed the deployment of a Joint Special Operations Task Force (JSOTF) to Somalia in response to attacks made by General Mohamed Farrah Aidid's supporters upon U.S. and UN forces. The JSOTF, named Task Force (TF) Ranger, was charged with a mission named Operation Gothic Serpent to capture Aidid. This was an especially arduous mission, for Aidid had gone underground, after several Lockheed AC-130 air raids and UN assaults on his strongholds.[11][25][26]

While Marines from the 24th MEU provided an interim QRF (Force Recon Det and helicopters from HMM-263), the task force arrived in the country, and began training exercises. The Marines were asked to take on the Aidid snatch mission, but having the advantage of being in the area for more than two months, decided after mission analysis that the mission was a "no-go" due to several factors, centered around the inability to rescue the crew of a downed helicopter (re: the indigenous forces technique of using RPGs against helicopters and blocking the narrow streets in order to restrict the movement of a ground rescue force). This knowledge was not passed on to the Rangers, due to the Marines operating from the USS Wasp and the Rangers remaining on land. TF Ranger was made up of operators from Delta Force, 75th Ranger Regiment, 160th SOAR, Air Force special tactics units, and SEALs from the Naval Special Warfare Development Group.[11][25] During August and September 1993, the task force conducted six missions into Mogadishu, all of which were successes. Although Aidid remained free, the effect of these missions seriously limited his movements.[26]

On 3 October, TF Ranger launched its seventh mission, this time into Aidid's stronghold the Bakara Market to capture two of his key lieutenants. The mission was expected to take only one or two hours.[25] Helicopters carried an assault and a ground convoy of security teams launched in the late afternoon from the TF Ranger compound at Mogadishu airport. The TF came under increasingly heavy fire, more intense than during previous missions. The assault team captured 24 Somalis including Aidid's lieutenants and were loading them onto the convoy trucks when a MH-60 Blackhawk was hit by a rocket-propelled grenade (RPG).[11][26] A small element from the security force, as well as an MH-6 assault helicopter and an MH-60 carrying a fifteen-man combat search and rescue (CSAR) team, rushed to the crash site.[11][25][26] The battle became increasingly worse. An RPG struck another MH-60, crashing less than 1 mile (1.6 km) to the south of the first downed helicopter. The task force faced overwhelming Somali mobs that overran the crash sites, causing a dire situation.[25] A Somali mob overran the second site and, despite a heroic defense, killed everyone except the pilot, whom they took prisoner. Two defenders of this crash site, Master Sergeant Gary Gordon and Sergeant First Class Randall Shughart, were posthumously awarded the Medal of Honor.[11][25][26] About this time, the mission's quick reaction force (QRF) also tried to reach the second crash site. This force too was pinned by Somali fire and required the fire support of two AH-6 helicopters before it could break contact and make its way back to the base.[11]

The assault and security elements moved on foot towards the first crash area, passing through heavy fire, and occupied buildings south and southwest of the downed helicopter. They fought to establish defensive positions so as not to be pinned down by very heavy enemy fire, while treating their wounded, and worked to free the pilot's body from the downed helicopter. With the detainees loaded on trucks, the ground convoy force attempted to reach the first crash site. Unable to find it amongst the narrow, winding alleyways, the convoy came under devastating small arms and RPG fire. The convoy had to return to base after suffering numerous casualties, and sustaining substantial damage to the their vehicles.

Reinforcements, consisting of elements from the QRF, 10th Mountain Division soldiers, Rangers, SEALs, Pakistan Army tanks and Malaysian armored personnel carriers, finally arrived at 1:55 am on 4 October. The combined force worked until dawn to free the pilot's body, receiving RPG and small arms fire throughout the night.[11] All the casualties were loaded onto the armored personnel carriers, and the remainder of the force was left behind and had no choice but to move out on foot.[25] AH-6 gunships raked the streets with fire to support the movement. The main force of the convoy arrived at the Pakistani Stadium-compound for the QRF-at 6:30 am,[25] thus concluding one of the bloodiest and fiercest urban firefights since the Vietnam War. Task Force Ranger experienced a total of 17 killed in action and 106 wounded. Various estimates placed Somali casualties above 1,000.[25] Although Task Force Ranger's few missions were successes, the overall outcome of Operation Gothic Serpent was deemed a failure because of the Task Force's failure to complete their stated mission, capturing Mohamed Farrah Aidid.[25] Most U.S. forces pulled out of Somalia by March 1994. The withdrawal from Somalia, was completed on March 1995.[11] Even though Operation Gothic Serpent failed, USSOCOM still made significant contributions to operations in Somalia. SOF performed reconnaissance and surveillance missions, assisted with humanitarian relief, protected American forces and conducted riverine patrols. Additionally, they ensured the safe landing of the Marines and safeguarded the arrival of merchant ships carrying food.[11][20]

3.1.3 Iraq

USSOCOM's 10th Special Forces Group, elements of JSOC and CIA/SAD Paramilitary Officers linked up again and were the first to enter Iraq prior to the invasion. Their efforts organized the Kurdish Peshmerga to defeat Ansar Al Islam in Northern Iraq before the invasion. This battle was for control of a territory in Northeastern Iraq that was completely occupied by Ansar Al Islam, an ally of Al Qaeda. This was a very significant battle and led to the termination of a substantial number of terrorists and the uncovering of a chemical weapons facility at Sargat. These terrorists would have been in the subsequent insurgency had they not been eliminated during this battle. Sargat was the only facility of its type discovered in the Iraq war. This battle may have been the Tora Bora of Iraq, but it was a sound defeat for Al Qaeda and their ally Ansar Al Islam. This combined team then led the Peshmerga against Saddam's northern Army. This effort kept Saddam's forces in the north and denied the ability to redeploy to contest the invasion force coming from the south. This effort may have saved the lives of hundreds if not thousands of coalition service men and women.[27]

At the launch of the Iraq War dozens of 12-member Special Forces teams infiltrated southern and western Iraq to hunt for Scud missiles and pinpoint bombing targets. Scores of Navy SEALs seized oil terminals and pumping stations on the southern coast.[28] Air Force combat controllers flew combat missions in MC-130H Combat Talon IIs and established austere desert airstrips to begin the flow of soldiers and supplies deep into Iraq. It was a far cry from the Persian Gulf war of 1991, where Special Operations forces were kept largely on the sidelines. But it would not be a replay of Afghanistan, where Army Special Forces and Navy SEALs led the fighting. After their star turn in Afghanistan, many special operators were disappointed to play a supporting role in Iraq. Many special operators felt restricted by cautious commanders.[29] From that point, USSOCOM has since killed or captured hundreds of insurgents and Al-Qaeda terrorists. It has conducted several foreign internal defense missions successfully training the Iraqi security forces.[30][31]

3.2   Current role

United States Special Operations Command played a pivotal role in fighting the former Taliban government in Afghanistan in 2001[32] and toppling it thereafter, as well as combating the insurgency and capturing Saddam Hussein in Iraq. US-SOCOM in 2004 was developing plans to have an expanded and more complex role in the global campaign against terrorism,[33] and that role continued to emerge before and after the killing of Osama bin Laden in Pakistan in 2011.[34][35] In 2010, "of about 13,000 Special Operations forces deployed overseas, about 9,000 [were] evenly divided between Iraq and Afghanistan."[34]

3.2.1   War in Afghanistan

In the initial stages of the War in Afghanistan, USSOCOM forces linked up with CIA Paramilitary Officers from Special Activities Division to defeat the Taliban without the need for large-scale conventional forces.[36] This was one of the biggest successes of the global War on Terrorism.[37] These units linked up several times during this war and engaged in several furious battles with the enemy. One such battle happened during Operation Anaconda the mission to squeeze life out of a Taliban and Al-Qaeda stronghold dug deep into the Shah-i-Kot mountains of eastern Afghanistan. The operation was seen as one of the heaviest and bloodiest fights in the War in Afghanistan.[38] The battle on an Afghan mountaintop called Takur Ghar featured special operations forces from all 4 services and the CIA. Navy SEALs, Army Rangers, Air Force Combat Controllers, and Pararescuemen fought against entrenched Al-Qaeda fighters atop a 10,000-foot (3,000 m) mountain. Subsequently, the entrenched Taliban became targets of every asset in the sky. According to an executive summary, the battle of Takur Ghar was the most intense firefight American special operators have been involved in since 18 U.S. Army Rangers were killed in Mogadishu, Somalia, in 1993.[39][40][41] During Operation Red Wings on 28 June 2005, four Navy SEALs, pinned down in a firefight, radioed for help. A Chinook helicopter, carrying 16 service members, responded but was shot down. All members of the rescue team and three of four SEALs on the ground died. It was the worst loss of life in Afghanistan since the invasion in 2001. The Navy SEAL Marcus Luttrell alone survived.[42][43] Team leader Michael P. Murphy was awarded the Medal of Honor for his actions in the battle.

3.2.2   Global presence

SOC chief Olson said in 2011 that SOCOM "is a microcosm of the Department of Defense, with ground, air, and maritime components, a global presence, and authorities and responsibilities that mirror the Military Departments, Military Services, and Defense Agencies."[35] In 2010, special operations forces were deployed in 75 countries, compared with about 60 at the beginning of 2009.[34] In 2011, SOC spokesman Colonel Tim Nye (Army[44]) was reported to have said that the number of countries with SOC presence will likely reach 120 and that joint training exercises will have been carried out in most or all of those countries during the year. One study identified joint-training exercises in Belize, Brazil, Bulgaria, Burkina Faso, Germany, Indonesia, Mali, Norway, Panama, and Poland in 2010 and also, through mid-year 2011, in the Dominican Republic, Jordan, Romania, Senegal, South Korea, and Thailand, among other nations. In addition, SOC forces executed the high profile killing of Osama bin Laden in Pakistan in 2011.[35]

Wikileaks' releases of cables from the U.S. Embassy, Pakistan, revealed the presence of a detachment of SOCOM (or possibly United States Army Special Operations Command) referred to as SOC(FWD)-PAK (09ISLAMABAD2449, 9 August 2010). This unit or headquarters may be, in full form, Special Operations Command (Forward)-Pakistan. It seems unlikely that the – symbol refers to the minus sign that sometimes means that the unit or headquarters is operating at less than full strength. The unit or headquarters includes a Military Information Support Team (MIST).[45] Another story that reported on JSOC/Blackwater anti-terrorist operations in Pakistan was Jeremy Scahill's "The Secret U.S. War in Pakistan", in the 7 November 2009, issue of *The Nation*.

In 2010, White House counterterrorism director John O. Brennan said that the United States "will not merely respond after the fact" of a terrorist attack but will "take the fight to al-Qaeda and its extremist affiliates whether they plot and train in Afghanistan, Pakistan, Yemen, Somalia and beyond." Olson said, "In some places, in deference to host-country sensitivities, we are lower in profile. In every place, Special Operations forces activities are coordinated with the U.S. ambassador and are under the operational control of the four-star regional commander."[34]

The conduct of actions by SOC forces outside of Iraq and Afghan war zones has been the subject of internal U.S. debate, including between representatives of the Bush administration such as John B. Bellinger III, on one hand, and the Obama administration on another. The United Nations in 2010 also "questioned the administration's authority under international law to conduct such raids, particularly when they kill innocent civilians. One possible legal justification – the permission of the country in question – is complicated in places such as Pakistan and Yemen, where the governments privately agree but do not publicly acknowledge approving the attacks," as one report put it.[34]

3.3 Subordinate Commands

3.3.1 Joint Special Operations Command

[46] Joint Special Operations Command is a component command of the USSOCOM and is charged to study special operations requirements and techniques to ensure interoperability and equipment standardization, plan and conduct special operations exercises and training, and develop Joint Special Operations Tactics.[1] It was established in 1980 on recommendation of Col. Charlie Beckwith, in the aftermath of the failure of Operation Eagle Claw.[47]

Units

- The U.S. Army's 1st Special Forces Operational Detachment-Delta, popularly known as Delta Force, is the first of the two primary counter-terrorist units of JSOC and SOCOM.[48] Modeled after the British Special Air Service, Delta Force is regarded as one of the premier special operations forces in the world.[49] This is because of Delta's stringent training and selection process. Delta recruits primarily from the most talented and highly skilled operators in the Army Special Forces and the 75th Ranger Regiment although Delta will take anyone and everyone that can pass their screening.[25][49] Recruits must pass a rigid selection course before beginning training. Delta has received training from numerous U.S. government agencies and other tier one SOF and has created a curriculum based on this training and techniques that it has developed.[49] Delta conducts clandestine and covert special operations all over the world.[49] It has the capability to conduct myriad special operations missions but specializes in counter-terrorism and hostage rescue operations.[25][48][50]

- The Naval Special Warfare Development Group (DEVGRU, SEAL Team Six) is the second of the two primary counter-terrorist units of JSOC and SOCOM.[48] DEVGRU is Naval Special Warfare's counterpart to Delta. Like Delta, DEVGRU recruits the best operators from the best units in its branch, the Navy SEALs. DEVGRU is capable of performing any type of special operations mission, but trains especially for counter-terrorist and hostage rescue operations.[25][48]

- The Intelligence Support Activity (ISA, The Activity) is the support branch of JSOC and USSOCOM. Its primary missions are to provide Human Intelligence (HUMINT) and Signal Intelligence (SIGINT) mainly for Delta and

DEVGRU's operations.[48][51] Before the establishing of the Strategic Support Branch in 2001, the ISA needed the permission of the CIA to conduct its operations, which sometimes caused it to be less effective in its support of JSOC's primary units.[48][52][53]

- The Air Force 24th Special Tactics Squadron (24th STS) is the AFSOC component of JSOC. The 24th STS usually operates with Delta and DEVGRU because of the convenience of 24th STS ability to synchronize and control the different elements of air power and enhance air operations deep in enemy territory.[25]

Portions of JSOC units have made up the constantly changing special operations task force, operating in the U.S. Central Command area of operations. The Task Force 11, Task Force 121, Task Force 6-26 and Task Force 145 are creations of the Pentagon's post-11 September campaign against terrorism, and it quickly became the model for how the military would gain intelligence and battle insurgents in the future. Originally known as Task Force 121, it was formed in the summer of 2003, when the military merged two existing Special Operations units, one hunting Osama bin Laden in and around Afghanistan, and the other tracking Sadaam Hussein in Iraq.[54][55]

3.3.2   Special Operations Command – Joint Capabilities

Special Operations Command – Joint Capabilities (SOC-JC) was transferred to USSOCOM from the soon to be disestablished United States Joint Forces Command.[56]

Primary Mission: SOC-JC trains conventional and SOF commanders and their staffs, supports USSOCOM international engagement training requirements, and supports implementation of capability solutions in order to improve strategic and operational Warfighting readiness and joint interoperability. SOC-JC must also be prepared to support deployed Special Operations Joint Task Force (SOJTF) Headquarters (HQ).

As a joint sub-unified command under USSOCOM, SOC-JC's core function is to enhance the interoperability of conventional and Special Operations Forces (SOF) commanders and staffs through robust strategic and operational level joint training. In coordination with the USSOCOM J3, J7/9 and Joint Special Operations University (JSOU), SOC-JC provides excellent training and support to the education for SOF and Conventional Forces (CF) worldwide. Additionally, SOC-JC supports the joint SOF capabilities development process while maintaining the flexibility to support emerging initiatives.

3.3.3   Army

On 1 December 1989 the United States Army Special Operations Command (USASOC) activated as the 16th major Army command. These special operations forces have been America's spearhead for unconventional warfare for more than 40 years. USASOC commands such units as the well known Special Forces (SF, or the "Green Berets") and Rangers, and such relatively unknown units as the Psychological Operations Group (PSYOP) and Civil Affairs Brigade (CA). These are one of the USSOCOM's main weapons for waging unconventional warfare and counter-insurgency. The significance of these units is emphasized as conventional conflicts are becoming less prevalent as insurgent and guerrilla warfare increases.[57][58]

Units

- The 75th Ranger Regiment (U.S. Army Rangers) is the premier light-infantry unit of the United States Army and is headquartered at Fort Benning, Georgia. The 75th Ranger Regiment's mission is to plan and conduct special missions in support of U.S. policy and objectives.[59] The Rangers are a flexible and rapid-deployable force. Each battalion can deploy anywhere in the world within 18 hours notice. The Army places much importance on the 75th Ranger Regiment and its training; it possesses the capabilities to conduct conventional and most special operations missions. Rangers are capable of infiltrating by land, sea, or air and direct action operations such as conducting raids or assaulting buildings or airfields.[60]

- United States Army Special Forces (SF) aka Green Berets perform several doctrinal missions: unconventional warfare, foreign internal defense, special reconnaissance, direct action and counter-terrorism. These missions make Special Forces unique in the U.S. military, because they are employed throughout the three stages of the operational continuum: peacetime, conflict and war.[61] Foreign internal defense operations, SF's main peacetime mission, are designed to help friendly developing nations by working with their military and police forces to improve their technical skills, understanding of human rights issues, and to help with humanitarian and civic action projects. Special Forces unconventional warfare capabilities provide a viable military option for a variety of operational taskings that are inappropriate or infeasible for conventional forces. Special Forces are the U.S. military's premier unconventional warfare force.[62] Foreign internal defense and unconventional warfare missions are the bread and butter of Special Forces soldiers. For this reason SF candidates are trained extensively in weapons, engineering, communications and medicine. SF soldiers are taught to be warriors first and teachers second because they must be able to train their team and be able to train their allies during a FID or UW mission.[61][63] Often SF units are required to perform additional, or collateral, activities outside their primary missions. These collateral activities are coalition warfare/support, combat search and rescue, security assistance, peacekeeping, humanitarian assistance, humanitarian de-mining and counter-drug operations.[64]

- The 160th Special Operations Aviation Regiment (Night Stalkers) headquartered at Fort Campbell, Kentucky provides aviation support to units within USSOCOM. The Regiment consists of MH-6 and AH-6 light helicopters, MH-60 helicopters and MH-47 heavy assault helicopters. The capabilities of the 160th SOAR (A) have been evolving since the early 1980s. Its focus on night operations resulted in the nickname, the "Night Stalkers."[65] The primary mission of the Night Stalkers is to conduct overt or covert infiltration, exfiltration, and resupply of special operations forces across a wide range of environmental conditions.[66]

- 4th Military Information Support Group (Airborne) and 8th Military Information Support Group (Airborne) Soldiers use persuasion to influence perceptions and encourage desired behavior.[67][68] PSYOP soldiers supports national objectives at the tactical, operational and strategic levels of operations. Strategic psychological operations advance broad or long-term objectives; global in nature, they may be directed toward large audiences or at key communicators. Operational psychological operations are conducted on a smaller scale. 4th PSYOP Gp is employed by theater commanders to target groups within the theater of operations. 4th PSYOP Gp purpose can range from gaining support for U.S. operations to preparing the battlefield for combat. Tactical psychological operations are more limited, used by commanders to secure immediate and near-term goals. In this environment, these force-enhancing activities serve as a means to lower the morale and efficiency of enemy forces.[69]

- 95th Civil Affairs Brigade (Airborne) specialists identify critical requirements needed by local citizens in war or disaster situations. They also locate civilian resources to support military operations, help minimize civilian interference with operations, support national assistance activities, plan and execute noncombatant evacuation, support counter-drug operations and establish and maintain liaison with civilian aid agencies and other nongovernmental organizations. In support of special operations, these culturally oriented, linguistically capable Soldiers may also be tasked to provide functional expertise for foreign internal defense operations, unconventional warfare operations and direct action missions.[70]

- Sustainment Brigade (Special Operations) (Airborne) (SBSO(A)) has a difficult mission supporting USASOC. In their respective fields, signal and support soldiers provide supplies, maintenance, equipment and expertise allowing Special Operation Forces to "shoot, move and communicate" on a continuous basis. Because USASOC often uses Special Operations Forces-unique items, soldiers assigned to these units are taught to operate and maintain a vast array of specialized equipment not normally used by their conventional counterparts. SBSO(A) also provides the USASOC with centralized and integrated material management of property, equipment maintenance, logistical automation and repair parts and supplies.[71]

- John F. Kennedy Special Warfare Center (USAJFKSWCS) trains USSOCOM and Army Special Operations Forces through development and evaluation of special operations concepts, doctrines and trainings.[72]

3.3.4 Navy

The United States Naval Special Warfare Command (NAVSPECWARCOM, NAVSOC, or NSWC) was commissioned April 16, 1987, at Naval Amphibious Base Coronado in San Diego as the Naval component to the United States Special Operations Command. Naval Special Warfare Command provides vision, leadership, doctrinal guidance, resources and oversight to ensure component special operations forces are ready to meet the operational requirements of combatant commanders.[73] Today, SEAL Teams and Special Boat Teams comprise the elite combat units of Naval Special Warfare. These teams are organized, trained, and equipped to conduct a variety of missions to include direct action, special reconnaissance, counter-terrorism, foreign internal defense, unconventional warfare and support psychological and civil affairs operations. Their highly trained operators are deployed worldwide in support of National Command Authority objectives, conducting operations with other conventional and special operations forces.

Units

- United States Navy SEALs have distinguished themselves as an individually reliable, collectively disciplined and highly skilled special operations force. The most important trait that distinguishes Navy SEALs from all other military forces is that SEALs are maritime special operations, as they strike from and return to the sea. SEALs (SEa, Air, Land) take their name from the elements in and from which they operate. SEALs are experts in direct action and special reconnaissance missions. Their stealth and clandestine methods of operation allow them to conduct multiple missions against targets that larger forces cannot approach undetected. Because of the dangers inherent in their missions, prospective SEALs go through what is considered by many military experts to be the toughest training regime in the world.[74][75]

- Naval Special Warfare Development Group (DEVGRU), referred to as SEAL Team Six, the name of its predecessor which was officially disbanded in 1987.

- SEAL Delivery Vehicle Teams are SEAL teams with an added underwater delivery capability who use the SDV MK VIII and the Advanced SEAL Delivery System (ASDS), submersibles that provides NSW with an unprecedented capability that combines the attributes of clandestine underwater mobility and the combat swimmer.[76][77]

- Special Warfare Combatant-craft Crewmen (SWCC) operate and maintain state-of-the-art surface craft to conduct coastal patrol and interdiction and support special operations missions. Focusing on infiltration and exfiltration of SEALs and other SOF, SWCCs provide dedicated rapid mobility in shallow water areas where larger ships cannot operate. They also bring to the table a unique SOF capability: Maritime Combatant Craft Aerial Delivery System—the ability to deliver combat craft via parachute drop.[1] Like SEALs, SWCCs must have excellent physical fitness, highly motivated, combat-focused and responsive in high stress situations.[78]

3.3.5 Air Force

Air Force Special Operations Command was established May 22, 1990, with headquarters at Hurlburt Field, Florida. AFSOC is one of the 10 Air Force Major Commands or MAJCOMs, and the Air Force component of United States Special Operations Command. It contains the Twenty-Third Air Force and holds operational and administrative oversight of subordinate special operations wings and groups in the regular Air Force, Air Force Reserve Command and the Air National Guard.

AFSOC provides Air Force special operations forces for worldwide deployment and assignment to regional unified commands. The command's SOF are composed of highly trained, rapidly deployable airmen, conducting global special operations missions ranging from precision application of firepower via airstrikes or close air support, to infiltration, exfiltration, resupply and refueling of SOF operational elements.[79] AFSOC's unique capabilities include airborne radio and television broadcast for psychological operations, as well as aviation foreign internal defense instructors to provide other governments military expertise for their internal development.

The command's core missions include battlefield air operations; agile combat support; aviation foreign internal defense; information operations; precision aerospace fires; psychological operations; specialized air mobility; specialized refueling; and intelligence, surveillance and reconnaissance.[29][80][81]

Units

- Combat Controllers (CCT) are ground combat forces specialized in a traditional pathfinder role while having a heavy emphasis on simultaneous air traffic control, fire support (via airstrikes, close air support and command, control, and communications in covert or austere environments.[82][83]

- Pararescuemen (PJ) are the only Department of Defense specialty specifically trained and equipped to conduct conventional and unconventional personnel recovery operations. A PJ's primary function is as a personnel recovery specialist with emergency trauma medical capabilities in humanitarian and combat environments.

- Special Operations Weather Technicians (SOWT) gather, assess, and interpret weather and environmental intelligence from forward deployed locations, working alongside special operations forces.

Organization

- The 1st Special Operations Wing (1 SOW) is located at Hurlburt Field, Florida. Its mission focus is unconventional warfare: counter-terrorism, combat search and rescue, personnel recovery, psychological operations, aviation assistance to developing nations, "deep battlefield" resupply, interdiction and close air support. The wing's core missions include aerospace surface interface, agile combat support, combat aviation advisory operations, information operations, personnel recovery/recovery operations, precision aerospace fires, psychological operations dissemination, specialized aerospace mobility and specialized aerial refueling.[84] Among its aircraft is the MC-130 Combat Talon II, a low-level terrain following special missions transport that can evade radar detection and slip into enemy territory at a 200-foot (61 m) altitude for infiltration/exfiltration missions, even in zero visibility, dropping off or recovering men or supplies with pinpoint accuracy. It also operates the AC-130 Spooky and Spectre gunships that provide highly accurate airborne gunfire for close air support of conventional and special operations forces on the ground.[48]

- The 24th Special Operations Wing (24 SOW) is located at Hurlburt Field, Florida. It's composed of the 720th Special Tactics Group, 724th Special Tactics Group, Special Tactics Training Squadron and 16 recruiting locations across the United States.[85][86] The Special Tactics Squadrons, under the 720th STG and 724th STG, are made up of Special Tactics Officers, Combat Controllers, Combat Rescue Officers, Pararescuemen, Special Operations Weather Officers and Airmen, Air Liaison Officers, Tactical Air Control Party operators, and a number of combat support airmen which comprise 58 Air Force specialties.[86]

- The 27th Special Operations Wing (27 SOW) is located at Cannon AFB, New Mexico. Its primary mission includes infiltration, exfiltration and re-supply of special operations forces; air refueling of special operations rotary wing and tiltrotor aircraft; and precision fire support. These capabilities support a variety of special operations missions including direct action, unconventional warfare, special reconnaissance, counter-terrorism, personnel recovery, psychological operations and information operations.[87]

- The 193d Special Operations Wing (193 SOW) is an Air National Guard (ANG) unit, operationally gained by AFSOC, and located at Harrisburg International Airport/Air National Guard Station (former Olmsted Air Force Base), Pennsylvania. Under Title 32 USC, the 193 SOW performs state missions for the Governor of Pennsylvania as part of the Pennsylvania Air National Guard. Under Title 10 USC, the 193 SOW is part of the Air Reserve Component (ARC) of the United States Air Force. Its primary wartime and contingency operations mission as an AFSOC-gained unit is psychological operations (PSYOP). The 193 SOW is unique in that it is the only unit in the U.S. Air Force to fly and maintain the Lockheed EC-130J Commando Solo aircraft.

- The 919th Special Operations Wing (919 SOW) is an Air Force Reserve Command (AFRC) unit, operationally gained by AFSOC, and located at Eglin AFB Auxiliary Field #3/Duke Field, Florida. The 919 SOW flies and maintains the MC-130E Combat Talon I and MC-130P Combat Shadow special operations aircraft designed for covert operations.

- The 352d Special Operations Wing (352 SOW) at RAF Mildenhall, United Kingdom serves as the core to United States European Command's standing Joint Special Operations Air Component headquarters. The squadron provides support for three flying squadrons, one special tactics squadron and one maintenance squadron for exercise, logistics, and war planning; aircrew training; communications; aerial delivery; medical; intelligence; security and force protection; weather; information technologies and transformation support and current operations.[88]

- The 353d Special Operations Group (353 SOG) is the focal point for all U.S. Air Force special operations activities throughout the United States Pacific Command (USPACOM) theater. Headquartered at Kadena AB, Okinawa, Japan the group is prepared to conduct a variety of high-priority, low-visibility missions. Its mission is air support of joint and allied special operations forces in the Pacific. It maintains a worldwide mobility commitment, participates in Pacific theater exercises as directed and supports humanitarian and relief operations.[89]

- The United States Air Force Special Operations School (USAFSOS) at Hurlburt Field, Florida is a primary support unit of the Air Force Special Operations Command. The USAFSOS prepares special operations Airmen to successfully plan, organize, and execute global special operations by providing indoctrination and education for AFSOC, other USSOCOM components, and joint/interagency/ coalition partners.[90]

3.3.6   Marine Corps

In October 2005, the Secretary of Defense directed the formation of United States Marine Corps Forces Special Operations Command, the Marine component of United States Special Operations Command. It was determined that the Marine Corps would initially form a unit of approximately 2500 to serve with USSOCOM. On February 24, 2006 MARSOC activated at Camp Lejeune, North Carolina. MARSOC initially consisted of a small staff and the Foreign Military Training Unit (FMTU), which had been formed to conduct foreign internal defense. FMTU is now designated as the Marine Special Operations Advisor Group (MSOAG).[91]

As a service component of USSOCOM, MARSOC is tasked by the Commander USSOCOM to train, organize, equip, and deploy responsive U.S. Marine Corps special operations forces worldwide, in support of combatant commanders and other agencies. MARSOC has been directed to conduct foreign internal defense, direct action and special reconnaissance. MARSOC has also been directed to develop a capability in unconventional warfare, counter-terrorism, and information operations. MARSOC deployed its first units in August 2006, six months after the group's initial activation. MARSOC reached full operational capability in October 2008.[92]

Units

- Marine Raider Regiment (Marine Raiders) consists of a Headquarters Company and three Marine Raider Battalions, the 1st, 2nd and 3rd. The Regiment provides tailored military combat-skills training and advisor support for identified foreign forces in order to enhance their tactical capabilities and to prepare the environment as directed by USSOCOM as well as the capability to form the nucleus of a Joint Special Operations Task Force. Marines and Sailors of the MRR train, advise and assist friendly host nation forces – including naval and maritime military and paramilitary forces – to enable them to support their governments' internal security and stability, to counter subversion and to reduce the risk of violence from internal and external threats. MRR deployments are coordinated by MARSOC, through USSOCOM, in accordance with engagement priorities for Overseas Contingency Operations.

- Marine Intelligence Battalion (MIB) trains, sustains, maintains combat readiness, and provides intelligence support at all operational levels in order to support MARSOF training and operations worldwide with mission-specific intelligence capability.

- Marine Special Operations Support Group (MSOSG) trains, equips, structures, and provides specially qualified Marine forces, including, operational logistics, intelligence, Military Working Dogs, Firepower Control Teams, and communications support in order to sustain worldwide special operations missions as directed by Commander, U.S. Marine Corps Forces Special Operations Command (COMMARFORSOC).

- The Marine Special Operations School (MSOS) performs the screening, recruiting, training, assessment and doctrinal development functions for MARSOC. It includes two subordinate Special Missions Training Branches (SMTBs), one on each coast.

    - The Special Mission Training Branch—East provide special operations training in tactics, techniques and procedures, and evaluation and certification of MARSOC forces to specified conditions and standards for SOF. The Marines of MSOS are operators with the training, experience and mature judgment to plan, coordinate, instruct and supervise development of SOF special reconnaissance and direct action skills.[93]

3.4 List of USSOCOM Combatant Commanders

3.5 USSOCOM medal

The United States Special Operations Command Medal was introduced in 1994 to recognize individuals for outstanding contributions to, and in support of, special operations. Since it was created, there have been more than 50 recipients, four of which are not American. Some of which includes: Generał broni Włodzimierz Potasiński (Poland, 2010, posthumously),[94][95] Kaptein Gunnar Sønsteby (Norway, 2008), Generał brygady Jerzy Gut (Poland, June 2014)[96] and Generał dywizji Piotr Patalong (Poland, October 2014).[97]

3.6 See also

- United States special operations forces

3.7 References

3.7.1 Citations

[1] SOCOM Public Affairs (2013). *SOCOM Fact Book 2013* (PDF). SOCOM Public Affairs.

[2] SOCOM Public Affairs (2015). *SOCOM Fact Book 2015* (PDF). SOCOM Public Affairs.

[3] "U.S. Soldier Dies in Raid to Free Prisoners of ISIS in Iraq". *The New York Times*. 22 October 2015. Retrieved 24 October 2015.

[4] "Biography of Admiral James L. Holloway III, US Navy (Ret.)". June 2006. Retrieved 21 March 2008. |first1= missing |last1= in Authors list (help)

[5] Rother, Larry (6 December 1996). "With a Bang, Panama Is Erasing House of Horrors". *The New York Times*.

[6] Shanker, Thom (12 February 2004). "Regime Thought War Unlikely, Iraqis Tell U.S". *The New York Times*.

[7] "USSOCOM Posture Statement" (PDF). USSOCOM. 2007. Archived from the original (PDF) on 27 February 2008. Retrieved 12 February 2008.

[8] *Delta: America's Elite Counterterrorist Force*. Terry Griswold, D. M. Giangreco. Zenith Imprint, 2005. ISBN 0-7603-2110-8. p. 35

[9] Sloan, Stephen (October 1992). *Beating International Terrorism: An Action Strategy for Preemption and Punishment*. Diane Pub Co. ISBN 1-56806-104-8.

[10] Daniel, W.C. (September 1986). "H.R.5109". *A bill to establish a National Special Operations Agency within the Department of Defense to have unified responsibility for all special operations forces and activities within the Department*.

[11] "USSOCOM Command History" (PDF). Retrieved 12 October 2014.

[12] Goldwater, Barry; Sam Nunn. "S.CON.RES.80". *A concurrent resolution to authorize the printing of 2,000 additional copies of the Committee Print of the Committee on Armed Services (99th Congress, 1st Session) entitled "Defense Organization: The Need for Change"*.

[13] Nichols, Bill; Barry Goldwater (1986). "H.R.3622". *A bill to amend title 10, United States Code, to strengthen the position of Chairman of the Joint Chiefs of Staff, to provide for more efficient and effective operation of the Armed Forces, and for other purposes*.

[14] Lederman, Gordon Nathaniel (November 1999). *Reorganizing the Joint Chiefs of Staff: The Goldwater-Nichols Act of 1986*. Greenwood Press. ISBN 0-313-31085-8.

[15] Cohen, William (May 1986). "S.2453". *A bill to enhance the capabilities of the United States to combat terrorism and other forms of unconventional warfare.*

[16] Taubman, Philip (5 December 1984). "U.S. Military tries to catch up in fighting terror". *New York Times.*

[17] "Special Operations/Low Intensity Conflict & Interdependent Capabilities (ASD SO/LIC & IC)". *DoD.* Retrieved 19 March 2008. |first1= missing |last1= in Authors list (help)

[18] Giles, James E.; Altizer, Harrell B. ; Glass, David V. Parker, Robert W. (March 1989). "Providing Resources for Special Operations Forces: Completing the Transition". Retrieved 19 March 2008. Cite uses deprecated parameter |coauthors= (help)

[19] Lewis, Paul (1 July 2001). "Charles S. Whitehouse, 79, Diplomat and C.I.A. Official". *New York Times.*

[20] Andrew Kelley, Stephen (June 2007). "Better Lucky Than Good: Operation Earnest Will as Gunboat Diplomacy" (PDF). Naval Postgraduate School. Archived from the original (PDF) on 18 March 2009. Retrieved 12 May 2008.

[21] Peniston, Bradley (July 2006). *No Higher Honor: Saving the USS Samuel B. Roberts in the Persian Gulf.* United States Naval Institute Press. ISBN 1-59114-661-5.

[22] "A Big Second Step in Somalia". *New York Times.* 4 May 1993.

[23] "Two Tough Tracks in Somalia". *New York Times.* 10 December 1992.

[24] The Book of Honor: Cover Lives and Classified Deaths at the CIA by Ted Gup, 2000

[25] Bowden, Mark (2001). *Black Hawk Down: A Story of Modern War.* Signet. ISBN 0-451-20393-3.

[26] Eversmann, Matt; Dan Schilling (July 2006). *The Battle of Mogadishu: Firsthand Accounts from the Men of Task Force Ranger.* Presidio Press. ISBN 0-345-46668-3.

[27] Plan of Attack, Bob Woodward, 2004

[28] Dao, James (22 March 2003). "The Commandos; Navy Seals Easily Seize 2 Oil Sites". *New York Times.*

[29] Dao, James (28 April 2003). "Aftereffects: Special Operations Forces; War Plan Drew U.S. Commandos From Shadows". *The New York Times.*

[30] Kruzel, John (26 May 2007). "Navy SEALs share war stories from Anbar province". *American Forces Press Service.*

[31] R. Gordon, Michael (13 June 2003). "After The War: The Allies; In Major Assault, U.S. Forces Strike Hussein Loyalists". *New York Times.*

[32] D. Kozaryn, Linda (14 December 2001). "U.S. Special Operations Forces Change "Face of War"". *American Forces Press Service.*

[33] Thom Shanker, Eric Schmitt (2 August 2004). "The Reach of War: Military; Special Warriors Have Growing Ranks and Growing Pains in Taking Key Antiterror Role". *The New York Times.* Retrieved 11 March 2008.

[34] DeYoung, Karen, and Greg Jaffe, "U.S. 'secret war' expands globally as Special Operations forces take larger role", *Washington Post,* 4 June 2010. Retrieved 5 August 2011.

[35] Turse, Nick, "A Secret War in 120 Countries: The Pentagon's New Power Elite", *CounterPunch,* 4 August 2011. Retrieved 5 August 2011.

[36] *Washington Post* op-ed, John Lehman former Secretary of the Navy, October 2008

[37] Waller, Douglas (3 February 2003). "The CIA Secret Army". *Time Magazine* (Washington). Retrieved 28 September 2009.

[38] "Operation Anaconda". *Time.* 10 March 2002.

[39] Garamone, Jim. "The Battle of Takur Ghar". *American Forces Press Service.*

[40] *Executive Summary of the Battle of Takur Ghar* (PDF). |first1= missing |last1= in Authors list (help)

[41] MacPherson, Malcolm (2006). *Roberts Ridge: A Story of Courage and Sacrifice on Takur Ghar Mountain, Afghanistan.* Dell. ISBN 0-553-58680-7.

[42] Luttrell, Marcus; Patrick Robinson (2007). *Lone Survivor: The Eyewitness Account of Operation Redwing and the Lost Heroes of SEAL Team 10*. Little, Brown and Company. ISBN 0-316-06759-8.

[43] Blumenfield, Laura (11 June 2007). "The Sole Survivor". *Washington Post.*

[44] Naylor, Sean D., "McRaven tapped to lead SOCOM", *Army Times*, 1 March 2011 16:53:04 EST. Retrieved 5 August 2011.

[45] http://www.imgc-global.com/testimonials.html. Retrieved February 2012.

[46] Risen, James (20 September 1998). "The World: Passing the Laugh Test; Pentagon Planners Give New Meaning to 'Over the Top'". *New York Times.*

[47] Emerson 1988, p. 26.

[48] Emerson, Steven (13 November 1988). "Stymied Warriors". *New York Times.*

[49] L. Haney, Eric (August 2005). *Inside Delta Force: The Story of America's Elite Counterterrorist Unit*. Delta. ISBN 0-385-33936-4.

[50] Mark Mazzetti (13 January 2007). "Pentagon Sees Move in Somalia as Blueprint". *New York Times.*

[51] Smith, Michael (2007). *Killer Elite: The Inside Story of America's Most Secret Special Operations Team*. New York, New York: St. Martin's Press. ISBN 0-312-36272-2.

[52] Gellman, Barton (23 January 2005). "Secret Unit Expands Rumsfeld's Domain". *Washington Post.*

[53] Gerth, Jeff; Philip Taubman (8 June 1984). "U.s. military creates secret units for use in sensitive tasks abroad". *New York Times.*

[54] Schmitt, Eric (19 March 2006). "In Secret Unit's 'Black Room,' a Grim Portrait of U.S. Abuse". *New York Times.*

[55] E. Sanger, David (29 February 2004). "New U.S. Effort Steps Up Hunt For bin Laden". *New York Times.*

[56] SOCJFCOM transitions to USSOCOM and becomes Special Operations Command – Joint Capabilities, 2 May 2011

[57] "USASOC overview". Retrieved 8 January 2008.

[58] Schmitt, Eric; Michael R. Gordon (21 September 2001). "A Nation Challenged: The Military: Top Air Chief Sent". *New York Times.*

[59] "75th Ranger Regiment website". Archived from the original on 27 January 2008. Retrieved 12 February 2008.

[60] "75th Ranger Regiment website". Archived from the original on 8 February 2008. Retrieved 12 February 2008.

[61] Couch, Dick (March 2007). *Chosen Soldier: The Making of a Special Forces Warrior*. Three Rivers Press. ISBN 0-307-33939-4.

[62] Shanker, Thom (21 January 2002). "A Nation Challenged: Battlefield; Conduct of War Is Redefined By Success of Special Forces". *New York Times.*

[63] Schmitt, Eric; Thom Shanker (2 March 2008). "U.S. Plan Widens Role in Training Pakistani Forces in Qaeda Battle". *New York Times.*

[64] "USASF mission". Archived from the original on 11 December 2007. Retrieved 8 January 2008.

[65] "Night Stalkers fact sheet". Archived from the original on 17 December 2007. Retrieved 8 January 2008.

[66] "160th SOAR,MH-60 Black Hawk Helicopter Fact Sheet". Retrieved 12 February 2008.

[67] "PSYOP Recruiting website". Archived from the original on 4 February 2008. Retrieved 12 February 2008.

[68] "Army Civil Affairs, Psychological Operations Soldiers Deploy in Support of Tsunami Relief Efforts" (Press release). Department of Defense. 7 January 2005. Retrieved 14 March 2008.

[69] "PSYOP fact sheet". Archived from the original on 3 February 2008. Retrieved 12 February 2008.

[70] "95th Civil Affairs Fact Sheet". Archived from the original on 19 January 2008. Retrieved 21 January 2008.

[71] "SOSCOM Home Page". Archived from the original on 19 January 2008. Retrieved 12 February 2008.

[72] "USAJFKSWCS". Archived from the original on 19 January 2008. Retrieved 19 February 2008.

[73] "NAVSOC info website". Retrieved 8 January 2008.

[74] "Official U.S. Navy SEAL Info Website". Retrieved 11 January 2008.

[75] Couch, Dick (October 2001). *The Warrior Elite: The Forging of SEAL Class 228*. Crown. ISBN 0-609-60710-3.

[76] "Navy SEALs insertion/extraction page". Retrieved 11 January 2008.

[77] Tiron, Roxana (February 2002). "New Mini-Sub Gives SEALs Extra Speed, Range, Payload". *National Defense Magazine*.

[78] "Official U.S. Navy SWCC Info Website". Retrieved 11 January 2008.

[79] Steven Lee Meyers, Thom Shanker (16 October 2001). "A Nation Challenged: The Offensive; Special Operations Gunship Being Used Against Taliban". *New York Times*.

[80] "AFSOC". Retrieved 11 January 2008.

[81] Meyers, Steven Lee; Thom Shanker (17 October 2001). "A Nation Challenged: Air War; Pilots Told to Fire at Will in Some Zones". *New York Times*.

[82] "Combat Control Fact Sheet". *Air Force Special Operations Command*. United States Air Force. Archived from the original on 21 February 2013. Retrieved 13 January 2013.

[83] "Combat Control career description". Retrieved 12 January 2013.

[84] "1st SOW Fact Sheet". AFSOC. Retrieved 20 January 2008.

[85] "Air Force launches first special tactics wing". 2012-06-13. Archived from the original on December 12, 2012. Retrieved January 15, 2013.

[86] "24th SOW Factsheet". Retrieved January 15, 2013.

[87] "N.M. Delegation Welcomes 27th Special Ops. Wing to Cannon" (Press release). 29 August 2007. Retrieved 21 March 2008.

[88] "352nd Fact Sheet". AFSOC. Retrieved 21 January 2008.

[89] "353rd SOG Fact Sheet". AFSOC. Retrieved 21 January 2008.

[90] "USAFOS Fact Sheet". Archived from the original on 9 January 2008. Retrieved 21 January 2008.

[91] Kenyon, Henry (May 2006). "Marine Corps Special Operations Command Hits the Beach". *Signal Magazine*. Retrieved 10 April 2008.

[92] "MARSOC". Retrieved 8 January 2008.

[93] "MARSOC, MSOS Info website". Archived from the original on 9 February 2008. Retrieved 21 January 2008.

[94] USSOCOM Medal recipients

[95] "NEWS | USSOCOM Commander visits POLSOCOM | Dowództwo Wojsk Specjalnych". Wojskaspecjalne.mil.pl. 2010-05-14. Retrieved 2013-04-22.

[96] "Amerykańskie Dowództwo Operacji Specjalnych doceniło polskiego generała". wojsko-polskie.pl. 2014-06-03. Retrieved 2014-06-03.

[97] "Medal USSOCOM dla polskiego generała". mon.gov.pl. 2014-10-29. Retrieved 2014-10-29.

3.7.2 Bibliography

- Briscoe, Charles (2001). *Weapon of Choice: ARSOF in Afghanistan.* Combat Studies Institute Press.

- Couch, Dick (March 2007). *Chosen Soldier: The Making of a Special Forces Warrior.* Three Rivers Press. ISBN 0-307-33939-4.

- Couch, Dick (2006). *Down Range: Navy SEALs in the War on Terrorism.* New York, New York: Three Rivers Press. ISBN 1-4000-8101-7.

- Kelley, Stephen Andrew (June 2007). "Better Lucky Than Good: Operation Earnest Will as Gunboat Diplomacy" (PDF). Naval Postgraduate School. Archived from the original (PDF) on 18 March 2009. Retrieved 12 May 2008.

- Luttrell, Marcus; Patrick Robinson (June 2007). *Lone Survivor: The Eyewitness Account of Operation Redwing and the Lost Heroes of SEAL Team 10.* Little, Brown and Company. ISBN 0-316-06759-8.

- Pirnie, Bruce R. (August 1998). *Assessing Requirements for Peacekeeping, Humanitarian Assistance and Disaster Relief.* RAND Corporation. ISBN 0-8330-2594-5.

- Pushies, Fred (2007). *U.S. Air Force Special Ops.* Osceola, Wisconsin: MBI Publishing Company. ISBN 0-7603-0733-4.

- Smith, Michael (2007). *Killer Elite: The Inside Story of America's Most Secret Special Operations Team.* New York, New York: St. Martin's Press. ISBN 0-312-36272-2.

- Sweetman, Jack (March 1999). *Great American Naval Battles.* Naval Institute Press. ISBN 1-55750-794-5.

- David Tucker, Christopher J. Lamb (2007). *United States Special Operations Forces.* Columbia University Press. ISBN 0-231-13190-9.

- Wise, Harold Lee (May 2007). *Inside the Danger Zone: The U.S. Military in the Persian Gulf, 1987–1988.* US Naval Institute Press. ISBN 1-59114-970-3.

Web

- USDOD. U.S. DOD Dictionary of Military Terms. United States of America: *U.S. Department of Defense.* 5 June 2003.

- USDOD. U.S. DOD Dictionary of Military Terms: Joint Acronyms and Abbreviations. United States of America: *U.S. Department of Defense.* 5 June 2003.

- Talmadge, Eric (27 February 2008). "New US Submarines Trade Nukes for SEALs". Fox News. Associated Press.

- Eric Schmitt, Michael R. Gordon (4 February 2008). "Leak on Cross-Border Chases From Iraq". *New York Times.*

- von Zielbauer, Paul (27 April 2007). "Criminal Charges Are Expected Against Marines, Official Says". *New York Times.*

- Graham, Bradley (2 November 2005). "Elite Marine Unit to Help Fight Terrorism". *Washington Post.* Retrieved 27 May 2010. Check date values in: |year= / |date= mismatch (help)

3.8 External links

- U.S. Special Operations Command

- Air Force Special Operations Command

- U.S. Army Special Operations Command

- U.S. Naval Special Warfare Command

- U.S. Marine Corps Forces Special Operations Command

- Department of Defense

- Joint Special Operations University

The Joint Special Operations Command insignia

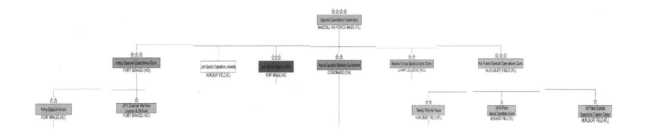

Special Operations Command (SOC)

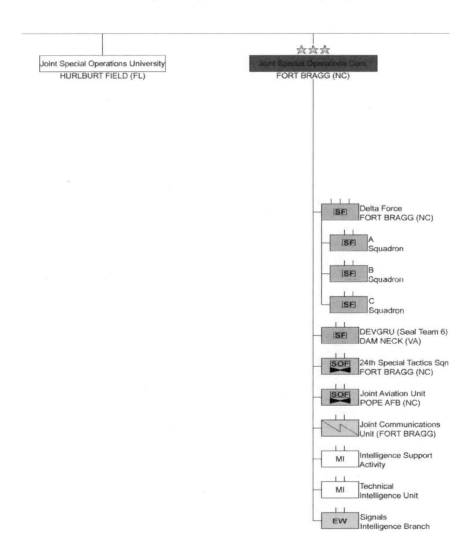

Joint Special Operations Command

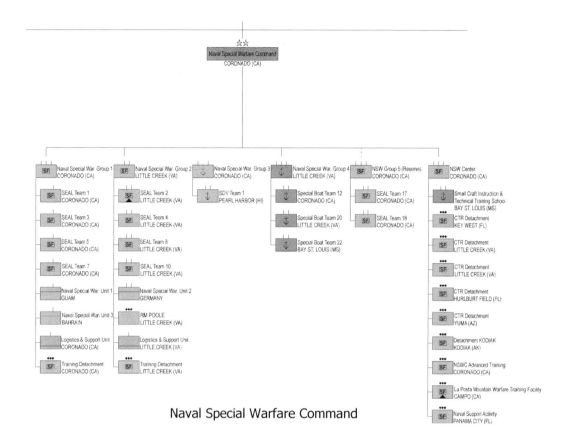

Naval Special Warfare Command

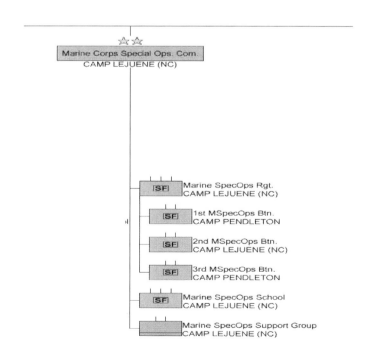

USMC Special Operations Command

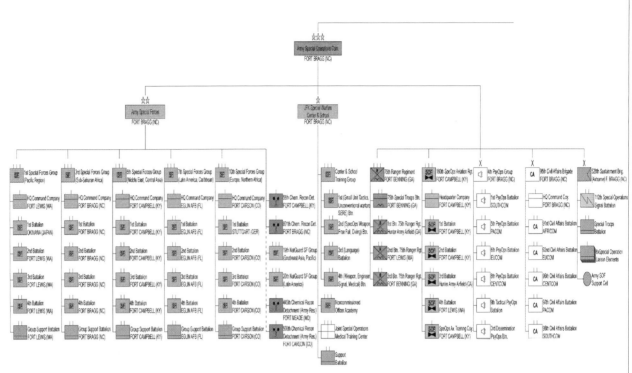

US Army Special Operations Command

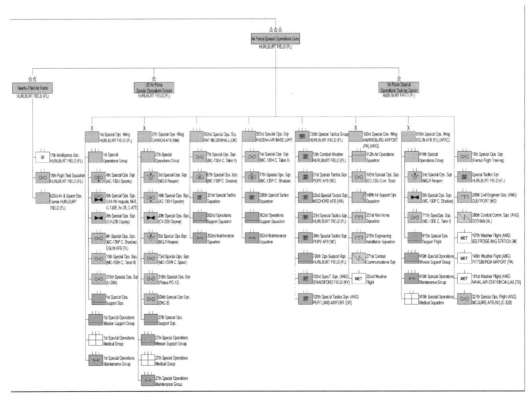

US Air Force Special Operations Command

Special Forces on a patrol in Afghanistan.

United States Naval Special Warfare Command emblem.

SEALs emerge from the water during a demonstration.

Air Force Special Operations Command emblem.

An AC-130U Spooky from the 4th Special Operations Squadron

Combat Controllers from the 21st Special Tactics Squadron conducting close air support training with A-10 pilots in Nevada

United States Marine Corps Forces Special Operations Command emblem

DA/SR Operators from 1st SOB (Special Operations Battalion) respond to enemy fire in Afghanistan

Chapter 4

Department of Defense Dictionary of Military and Associated Terms

The ***Department of Defense Dictionary of Military and Associated Terms*** is a compendium of terminology used by the United States Department of Defense (DOD).

It sets forth standard US military and associated terminology to encompass the joint activity of the Armed Forces of the United States in both US joint and allied joint operations, as well as to encompass the Department of Defense (DOD) as a whole. These military and associated terms, together with their definitions, constitute approved DOD terminology for general use by all components of the Department of Defense. The Secretary of Defense, by DOD Directive 5025.12, 23 August 1989, Standardization of Military and Associated Terminology, has directed its use throughout the Department of Defense to ensure standardization of military and associated terminology.

This publication supplements standard English-language dictionaries with standard terminology for military and associated use. However, it is not the intent of this publication to restrict the authority of the joint force commander (JFC) from organizing the force and executing the mission in a manner the JFC deems most appropriate to ensure unity of effort in the accomplishment of the overall mission.

4.1   See also

- Glossary of military abbreviations

4.2   External links

- The *Department of Defense Dictionary of Military and Associated Terms* online

Chapter 5

Joint Special Operations Command

"JSOC" redirects here. It is not to be confused with JSpOC.

The primary mission of the **Joint Special Operations Command** (**JSOC**) is ostensibly to identify and eliminate terror cells worldwide.[2] JSOC is a component command of the United States Special Operations Command (USSOCOM) and is charged to study special operations requirements and techniques to ensure interoperability and equipment standardization, plan and conduct special operations exercises and training, develop joint special operations tactics and execute special operations missions worldwide. It was established in 1980 on recommendation of Col. Charlie Beckwith, in the aftermath of the failure of Operation Eagle Claw.[3] It is located at Pope Field (Fort Bragg) in North Carolina, USA.

5.1 Overview

The JSOC is the "joint headquarters designed to study special operations requirements and techniques; ensure interoperability and equipment standardization; plan and conduct joint special operations exercises and training; and develop joint special operations tactics".[4] For this task, the Joint Communications Unit (JCU) is tasked to ensure compatibility of communications systems and standard operating procedures of the different special operations units.

5.1.1 Special Mission Units

Further information: Special Mission Unit

The Joint Special Operations Command (JSOC) also commands and controls the Special Mission Units (SMU) of U.S. Special Operations Command (USSOCOM). These units perform highly classified activities.[5][6][7] So far, only four SMUs have been publicly disclosed: The Army's 1st Special Forces Operational Detachment—Delta Force, the Navy's Naval Special Warfare Development Group (DEVGRU) – SEAL Team Six, the Air Force's 24th Special Tactics Squadron,[8] and the Army's Intelligence Support Activity.[9] The Intelligence Support Activity's (ISA) primary role is as a deep reconnaissance, intelligence-gathering SMU, while Delta Force and SEAL Team Six are the primary SMUs for direct action. Units from the Army's 75th Ranger Regiment and 160th Special Operations Aviation Regiment are controlled by JSOC when deployed as part of JSOC Task Forces such as Task Force 121 and Task Force 145.[10][11][12]

JSOC has an operational relationship with the CIA's Special Activities Division (SAD).[13] SAD's Special Operations Group often recruits from JSOC.[14]

5.1.2 Advanced Force Operations

Advanced Force Operations (AFO) is a term used by the U.S. Department of Defense to describe a task force that encompasses personnel from 1st Special Forces Operational Detachment-Delta (1st SFOD-D), DEVGRU and U.S. Army

Intelligence Support Activity (USAISA). Although mainly a term in many cases used to describe a particular sub-set of Delta Force RECCE operators from an even more specialized squadron, the term "AFO" also was later known used to describe mixed Special Mission Unit elements doing long range RECCE/long range target interdiction operations etc. Even in some rare cases including members (or "hangers") from other Coalition SOF units such as the UK SAS/SBS/SRR, Canadian Joint Task Force-2, and others. According to Gen. Michael Repass, who conducted it in the Iraq War and was very familiar with its use in Afghanistan, "AFO consists of U.S. Secretary of Defense-approved military operations such as clandestine operations, source operations, and deployment of enabling forces and capabilities to conduct target-specific preparations prior to the conduct of an actual operation. It is logically part of Operational Preparation of the Battlespace (OPB), which follows the Intelligence Preparation of the Battlespace, a concept well-known in U.S. and NATO doctrine, OPB is seldom used outside of Special Operations Forces channels. OPB is defined by the U.S. Special Operations Command as "Non-intelligence activities conducted prior to D-Day, H-Hour, in likely or potential areas of employment, to train and prepare for follow-on military operations".[15]

An AFO unit reported to JSOC in the Afghanistan War. In the Iraq War, Respass, who first commanded the 10th Special Forces Group, took control of a Joint Unconventional Warfare Task Force, which used the 5th and 10th Groups to conduct AFO. AFO units were heavily involved in Operation Anaconda and Operation Viking Hammer.

5.1.3 JSO Package / Rotational Group

The Joint Special Operations Package / Rotational Group of the United States Special Operations Command (USSOCOM) consist of Tier 1 and Tier 2 U.S. Joint Special Operations Command units that train and deploy together. All Tier 1 and Tier 2 units maintain three separate operational groups within their respective units (The 1st, 2nd, and 3rd Battalions of the 75th Ranger Regiment (United States) as an example).[16] These groups are essentially identical and deploy within their respective JSOC package. The rotational cycle is generally three months. This allows one group to be deployed overseas, another to be on an 18-hour worldwide emergency deployment notice, and the last group to be training, attending military schools, or on "block leave." Tier 1 and Tier 2 units take leave together within their respective JSOC package. This term is called block leave. Given the wartime tasking of JSOC, an additional deployment package is currently being created. This will allow less operational strain on these units.

5.2 Security support

JSOC has provided support to domestic law enforcement agencies during high profile or high risk events such as the Olympics, the World Cup, political party conventions and Presidential inaugurations. Although use of the military for law enforcement purposes in the U.S. is generally prohibited by the Posse Comitatus Act, Title 10 of the U.S. Code expressly allows the Secretary of Defense to make military personnel available to train Federal, State, and local civilian law enforcement officials in the operation and maintenance of equipment; and to provide such law enforcement officials with expert advice.[17] Additionally, civilian and uniformed military lawyers said provisions in several federal statutes, including the Fiscal Year 2000 Defense Department Authorization Act, Public Law 106-65, permits the secretary of defense to authorize military forces to support civilian agencies, including the Federal Bureau of Investigation, in the event of a national emergency, especially any involving nuclear, chemical, or biological weapons.[18]

In January 2005, a small group of commandos were deployed to support security at the Presidential inauguration. They were allegedly deployed under a secret counter-terrorism program named Power Geyser. The *New York Times* quoted a senior military official as saying, "They bring unique military and technical capabilities that often are centered around potential WMD events," A civil liberties advocate who was told about the program by a reporter said that he had no objections to the program as described to him because its scope appeared to be limited to supporting the counterterrorism efforts of civilian authorities.[18]

5.3 Operational history

5.3.1 Operations in Pakistan

According to *The Washington Post*, JSOC's commander Lieutenant General Stanley McChrystal operated in 2006 on the understanding with Pakistan that US units will not enter Pakistan except under extreme circumstances, and that Pakistan will deny giving them permission if exposed.[19]

That scenario happened according to the Islamic Republic News Agency (IRNA), in January 2006, JSOC troops clandestinely entered the village of Saidgai, Pakistan, to hunt for Osama Bin Laden. Pakistan refused entry.[20]

According to a November 2009 report in *The Nation*, JSOC, in tandem with Blackwater/Xe, has an ongoing drone program, along with snatch/grab/assassination operations, based in Karachi and conducted both in and outside of Pakistan.[21][22]

In an October 2009 leak published on the WikiLeaks website, U.S. embassy communication cables from the U.S. Ambassador to Pakistan, Anne W. Patterson, states the Pakistani Army approved the embedding of U.S. Special Operations Forces, including elements from the Joint Special Operations Command, with the Pakistani military to provide support for operations in the country. This goes beyond the original claims of the U.S. that the only role of the Special Forces was in training the Pakistani miliary. The leak further revealed that JSOC elements involved in intelligence gathering and surveillance and use of drone UAV technology.[23]

JSOC is credited with coordination of Operation Neptune Spear that resulted in the death of Osama bin Laden on 1 May 2011.[24][25]

5.3.2 Operations in Afghanistan

According to the movie Dirty Wars, by Jeremy Scahill, JSOC was responsible for a number of raids in Afghanistan. One among them took place in Gardez, initially reported by Jerome Starkey but later in other media as well. The then current commander William Mcraven visited the affected family, offered them a sheep in restitution and apologized for the incident.[25] In the incident,[26] one US trained Police commander and another man were killed, as were 3 women, 2 of whom were pregnant, while going to the men's aid.

How many other raids there were during this time, and before and since, is difficult to count as JSOC only answers to the White House and not the rest of the military. The secrecy around the number of raids could reasonably be counted in the hundreds since they started but only a mere few have been documented as well as the Gardez incident according to Scahill.[27][28]

5.3.3 Operations in Iraq

On 11 January 2007, President Bush pledged in a major speech to "seek out and destroy the networks providing advanced weaponry and training to our enemies in Iraq."[29] The next day, in a meeting of the U.S. Senate Committee on Foreign Relations, Chairman Senator Joseph Biden (Delaware), informed U.S. Secretary of State Condoleezza Rice that the Bush Administration did not have the authority to send U.S. troops on cross-border raids. Biden said, "I believe the present authorization granted the president to use force in Iraq does not cover that, and he does need congressional authority to do that. I just want to set that marker."[30]

Sometime in 2007, JSOC started conducting cross-border operations into Iran from southern Iraq with the CIA. These operations included seizing members of Al-Quds, the commando arm of the Iranian Revolutionary Guard, and taking them to Iraq for interrogation, as well as the pursuit, capture or killing of high-value targets in the war on terror. The Bush administration allegedly combined the CIA's intelligence operations and covert action with JSOC clandestine military operations so that Congress would only partially see how the money was spent.[31]

5.3.4 Operations in Somalia

On 28 October 2013 a drone strike by JSOC on a vehicle near the town of Jilib in Lower Shabelle killed two senior Somali members of Al-Shabaab. Preliminary evidence suggested that one of them was Ibrahim Ali (also known as Anta), an explosives specialist known for his skill in building and using homemade bombs and suicide vests.[32][33] The US administration has been reluctant to use drone strikes in Somalia. The reluctance partly centered on questions of whether Al-Shabaab—which has not tried to carry out an attack on American soil—could legally be the target of lethal operations by the military or the CIA. In May 2013, the White House announced that it would carry out targeted killing operations *only* against those who posed a "continuing and imminent threat to the American people." The strike on 28 Oct. was the first known American operation resulting in a death since that policy was announced and is considered evidence by some observers that views have changed in Washington and that the Obama administration has decided to escalate operations against Al-Shabaab in the aftermath of the group's Westgate shopping mall attack in Nairobi, Kenya, that took place from 21–24 September 2013 and which left some 70 people dead.

5.3.5   Operations in Yemen

Anwar al-Awlaki, a Yemeni-American U.S. citizen, was killed on 30 September 2011, by an air attack carried out by the Joint Special Operations Command. After several days of surveillance of Awlaki by the Central Intelligence Agency, armed drones took off from a new, secret American base in the Arabian Peninsula, crossed into northern Yemen and unleashed a barrage of Hellfire missiles at al-Awlaki's vehicle. Samir Khan, a Pakistani-American al-Qaeda member and editor of the jihadist *Inspire* magazine, also reportedly died in the attack. The combined CIA/JSOC drone strike was the first in Yemen since 2002—there have been others by the military's Special Operations forces—and was part of an effort by the spy agency to duplicate in Yemen the covert war which has been running in Afghanistan and Pakistan.[34][35]

According to *The New York Times* the Yemen government banned military drone operations after a series of botched drone strikes by JSOC, the last of which was a December 2013 drone strike that killed numerous civilians at a wedding ceremony. Despite a ban on military drone operations the Yemen government allowed CIA drone operations to continue.[36]

5.4   List of JSOC commanders

5.5   See also

- 1st Special Forces Operational Detachment – Delta (Delta Force or ACE)

- Central Intelligence Agency's Special Activities Division Special Operations Group (SAD/SOG)

- Intelligence Support Activity (The Activity)

- Naval Special Warfare Development Group (DEVGRU or SEAL Team Six)

- Targeted killing

- U.S. Air Force 24th Special Tactics Squadron (24th STS)

5.6   References

[1] Jim Frederick (2013). "Time: Special Ops". *Time* (Time Inc. Specials). Re-issue of Time's Special Edition: 55.

[2] Feickert, Andrew (17 April 2006). U.S. Special Operations Forces (SOF): Background and Issues for Congress

[3] Emerson, Steven (1988). *Secret Warriors: Inside the Covert Military Operations of the Reagan Era*. New York: G. P. Putnam's Sons. p. 26. ISBN 0-399-13360-7.

[4] "Joint Special Operations Command (JSOC)". GlobalSecurity.org. Retrieved 14 March 2009.

[5] Emerson, Steven (13 November 1988). "Stymied Warriors". *The New York Times*. Retrieved 11 July 2011.

[6] Mazzetti, Mark (13 January 2007). "Pentagon Sees Move in Somalia as Blueprint". *The New York Times*. Retrieved 13 March 2008.

[7] Risen, James (20 September 1998). "The World: Passing the Laugh Test; Pentagon Planners Give New Meaning to 'Over the Top'". *The New York Times*. Retrieved 10 April 2008.

[8] North, Oliver (2010). *American Heroes in Special Operations*. B&H Publishing Group. ISBN 978-0-8054-4712-5.

[9] John Pike. "Joint Special Operations Command (JSOC)".

[10] Naylor, Sean D. (3 Sep 2010). "JSOC task force battles Haqqani militants". *Army Times*. Retrieved 16 May 2011.

[11] Naylor, Sean D. (1 March 2011). "McRaven Tapped to lead SOCOM". *Army Times*. Retrieved 15 May 2011.

[12] Priest, Dana, and William M. Arkin, "'Top Secret America': A look at the military's Joint Special Operations Command", *Washington Post*, 4 September 2011.

[13] Woodward, Bob (18 November 2001). "Secret CIA Units Playing A Central Combat Role". *The Washington Post*. Retrieved 26 October 2008.

[14] Waller, Douglas (3 February 2003). "The CIA's Secret Army". *TIME*. Retrieved 26 October 2008.

[15] Repass, Michael S. (7 April 2003), *Combating Terrorism with Preparation of the Battlespace* (PDF), U.S. Army War College

[16] "75th Ranger Regiment". Retrieved 16 May 2011.

[17] "U.S. Code Title 10, § 373. Training and advising civilian law enforcement officials". Cornell University Law School. Retrieved 16 March 2009.

[18] Schmitt, Eric (23 January 2005). "Commandos Get Duty on U.S. Soil". *New York Times*. Retrieved 16 March 2009.

[19] Priest, Dana and Tyson, Ann Scott (10 September 2006). "Bin Laden Trail 'Stone Cold'". *The Washington Post*. Retrieved 15 March 2009.

[20] "Special U.S. unit can enter Pakistan at will to hunt Osama". GlobalSecurity.org. 11 September 2006. Retrieved 15 March 2009.

[21] Jeremy Scahill (23 November 2009). "Blackwater's Secret War in Pakistan". *The Nation*. Retrieved 27 November 2009d.

[22] James Risen, Mark Mazzeti (20 August 2009). "C.I.A. Said to Use Outsiders to Put Bombs on Drones". *The New York Times*.

[23] Jeremy Scahill (1 December 2010). "The (Not So) Secret (Anymore) US War in Pakistan". *The Nation*.

[24] Ross, Brian; Tapper, Jake; Esposito, Richard; Schifrin, Nick (2 May 2011). "Osama Bin Laden Killed By Navy Seals in Firefight". ABC News. Retrieved 2 May 2011.

[25] Jeremy Scahill (2 May 2011). "JSOC: The Black Ops Force That Took Down Bin Laden". *The Nation*.

[26] ISAF Public Affairs Office (4 April 2010). "Gardez Investigation Concludes". Retrieved 20 October 2013.

[27] Scahill, Jeremy (22 November 2010). "America's Failed War of Attrition in Afghanistan". Retrieved 20 October 2013.

[28] Scahill, Jeremy (18 January 2013). "Dirty Wars". Retrieved 20 October 2013.

[29] "Full Transcript Of Bush's Iraq Speech". CBS News. 10 January 2007. Retrieved 15 March 2009.

[30] "Senators fear Iraq war may spill to Iran, Syria". Reuters. 11 January 2007. Retrieved 15 March 2009.

[31] Reid, Marsha (7 July 2008). "Covert ops in Iran". Geopolitical Monitor. Retrieved 11 September 2014.

[32] "Pentagon Says Shabab Bomb Specialist Is Killed in Missile Strike in Somalia". New York Times. 28 October 2013.

[33] "Drone kills two in Somalia: witnesses: Eyewitnesses say missile came from a drone amid reports dead men are senior members of the al-Shabab armed group". Al Jazeera. 28 October 2013.

[34] "Same US military unit that got Osama bin laden killed Anwar al-Awlaki". *Telegraph.co.uk*. 30 September 2011.

[35] Mark Mazzetti, Eric Schmitt and Robert F. Worth, "Two-Year Manhunt Led to Killing of Awlaki in Yemen", *New York Times* (30 September 2011)

[36] http://www.nytimes.com/2014/04/06/world/delays-in-effort-to-refocus-cia-from-drone-war.html?_r=0

[37] , Flight Sciences Corporation

[38] "Vice Admiral Named JSOC Head". military.com / McClatchy-Tribune Information Services. 14 June 2008. Retrieved 15 March 2009.

[39] "Former JSOC Commander McRaven nominated to lead US Special Ops Command". 6 January 2010.

[40] "Votel nominated to head up Joint Special Operations Command". *Stars and Stripes*. 17 February 2011.

[41] "New commander takes over Joint Special Operations Command at Fort Bragg". *The Fayetteville Observer*. 29 July 2014.

5.7 Further reading

- Berntsen, Gary; Pezzullo, Ralph (27 December 2005). *Jawbreaker: The Attack on Bin Laden and Al-Qaeda: A Personal Account by the CIA's Key Field Commander*. Crown. ISBN 0-307-35106-8.

- Daugherty, William J. (2 June 2006). *Executive Secrets: Covert Action and the Presidency*. University Press of Kentucky. ISBN 0-8131-9161-0.

- Emerson, Steven (1988). *Secret Warriors: Inside the Covert Military Operations of the Reagan Era*. New York: G. P. Putnam's Sons. ISBN 0-399-13360-7.

- Smith, Michael (2006). *Killer Elite: The Inside Story of America's Most Secret Special Operations Team*. London: Cassell. ISBN 0-304-36727-3.

- Steven, Graeme C. S. and Gunaratna, Rohan (14 September 2004). *Counterterrorism: A Reference Handbook*. Contemporary World Issues. ISBN 978-1-85109-666-4.

5.8 External links

- Special Ops say lives were on line in Lynch's rescue, by *The Washington Times*

- US special operations come of age, by *Global Defence Review*

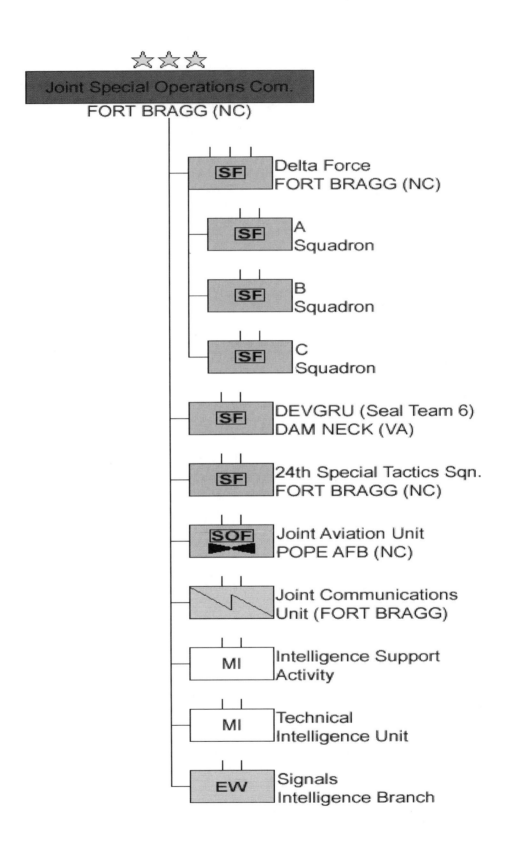

Chapter 6

Delta Force

This article is about the Special Operations Force. For other uses, see Delta Force (disambiguation).

The **1st Special Forces Operational Detachment-Delta** (1st SFOD-D), popularly known as **Delta Force**, is a U.S. Army unit used for hostage rescue and counterterrorism, as well as direct action and reconnaissance against high-value targets. Delta Force and its Navy counterpart, the United States Naval Special Warfare Development Group (or DEVGRU), often referred to as SEAL Team Six, are the United States military's primary counter-terrorism units and fall under the operational control of the Joint Special Operations Command.

It is often referred to in the U.S. media as a Special Mission Unit.[4][5] Along with SEAL Team Six, Delta Force's selection and training is considered one of the most demanding in the world.[6]

6.1 History

Delta Force was formed after numerous, well-publicized terrorist incidents in the 1970s. These incidents led the U.S. government to develop a full-time counter-terrorism unit.

Key military and government figures had already been briefed on a model for this type of unit in the early 1960s. Charlie Beckwith, a Special Forces officer and Vietnam veteran, had served as an exchange officer with the British Army's Special Air Service (22 SAS Regiment) during the Malayan Emergency. Upon his return, Beckwith presented a detailed report highlighting the U.S. Army's vulnerability in not having an SAS-type unit. U.S. Army Special Forces in that period focused on unconventional warfare, but Beckwith recognized the need for "not only teachers, but doers."[7] He envisioned highly adaptable and completely autonomous small teams with a broad array of special skills for direct action and counter-terrorist missions. He briefed military and government figures, who were resistant to creating a new unit outside of Special Forces or changing existing methods.

Finally, in the mid-70s, as the threat of terrorism grew, the Pentagon high command appointed Beckwith to form the unit.[8] Beckwith estimated that it would take 24 months to get his new unit mission-ready. Beckwith's estimate resulted from a conversation he had earlier with Brigadier John Watts while updating his SAS experience in England in 1976. Watts had made it clear to Beckwith that it would take eighteen months to build a squadron, but advised him to tell the Army leadership that it would take two years, and not to "let anyone talk (him) out of this." To justify why it would take two years to build Delta, Beckwith and his staff drafted what they dubbed the "Robert Redford Paper." In it Delta outlined its necessities and historical precedents for a four-phase selection/assessment process.[9]

In the meantime, Colonel Bob "Black Gloves" Mountel of the 5th Special Forces Group was tasked with creating a unit 'to breach the short-term gap' that existed until Delta was ready, dubbed Blue Light.[10]

On 4 November 1979, shortly after Delta had been created, 53 American diplomats and citizens were taken captive and held in the U.S. embassy in Tehran, Iran. The unit was assigned to Operation Eagle Claw and ordered to enter the country covertly and recover the hostages from the embassy by force on the nights of 24 and 25 April in 1980. The operation was aborted due to aviation failures. The review commission that examined the failure found 23 problems with the operation, among them unbriefed weather encountered by the aircraft, command-and-control problems between the multi-service component commanders, a collision between a helicopter and a ground-refueling tanker aircraft, and mechanical problems that reduced the number of available helicopters from eight to five (one fewer than the minimum desired) before the mission contingent could leave the trans-loading/refueling site.[11]

After the failed operation, the U.S. government realized more changes needed to be made. The 160th Special Operations Aviation Regiment (Airborne), also known as the *Night Stalkers*, was created for special operations requiring aviation support. The Navy's Special Warfare Development Group, formerly designated SEAL Team Six, was created for maritime counter-terrorism operations. The Joint Special Operations Command was created for command and control of the various counter-terrorism units of the U.S. military.

6.2 Organization and structure

The unit is under the organization of the US Army Special Operations Command (USASOC) but is controlled by the Joint Special Operations Command (JSOC). Command of 1st SFOD-D is a Colonel's billet. Virtually all information about the unit is highly classified and details about specific missions or operations generally are not available publicly.

Delta Force's structure is similar to the British 22 Special Air Service, the unit that inspired Delta's formation. In *Not a Good Day to Die: The Untold Story of Operation Anaconda*, *Army Times* staff writer Sean Naylor describes Delta as having nearly 1,000 soldiers, of which approximately 250 to 300 are trained to conduct direct action operations. The rest are highly specialized support personnel who are among the very best in their fields.[12]

6.2.1 Recruitment

Since the 1990s, the Army has posted recruitment notices for the 1st SFOD-D.[13] The Army, however, has never released an official fact sheet for the elite force. The recruitment notices in Fort Bragg's newspaper, *Paraglide*, refer to Delta Force by name, and label it "...the U.S. Army's special operations unit organized for the conduct of missions requiring rapid response with surgical application of a wide variety of unique special operations skills..."[14] The notice states that applicants must be male, in the ranks of E-4 through E-8, have at least two and a half years of service remaining in their enlistment, be 21 years or older, and score high enough on the Armed Services Vocational Aptitude Battery test to attend a briefing to be considered for admission.

Delta Force recruits from other branches of the military, including the Marine Corps. During the 2012 Benghazi attack, two Delta operators (one from the Army and one from the Marine Corps) were awarded the Distinguished Service Cross and the Navy Cross, respectively.[15] This was referred to by Delta Force founder Col. Charles Alvin Beckwith in his book *Delta Force*.

On 29 June 2006 during a session of the Committee on Armed Services, General Wayne Downing testified before the U.S. House of Representatives that 70 percent of all Delta operators started their military careers in the 75th Ranger Regiment.[16]

6.2.2 Selection process

Haney's book *Inside Delta Force* described the selection course and its inception in detail. Haney wrote that the selection course began with standard tests including push-ups, sit-ups, and a 2-mile (3.2 km) run, an inverted crawl and a 100-meter swim fully dressed. The candidates are then put through a series of land navigation courses to include an 18-mile (29 km), all-night land navigation course while carrying a 40-pound (18 kg) rucksack. The rucksack's weight and the distance of the courses are increased and the time standards to complete the task are shortened with every march. The physical testing ended with a 40-mile (64 km) march with a 45-pound (20 kg) rucksack over rough terrain that had to be completed in an unknown amount of time. Haney wrote that only the senior officer and NCO in charge of selection are allowed to see the set time limits, but all assessment and selection tasks and conditions were set by Delta training cadre.[17][18]

The mental portion of the testing began with numerous psychological exams. The men then went in front of a board of

Delta instructors, unit psychologists, and the Delta commander, who each ask the candidate a barrage of questions and then dissect every response and mannerism of the candidate with the purpose to mentally exhaust the candidate. The unit commander then approaches the candidate and tells him if he has been selected. If an individual is selected for Delta, he undergoes an intense 6-month Operator Training Course (OTC), to learn counter-terrorism and counter-intelligence techniques, in which the individual maintains little contact with friends and family for the duration. Training includes firearm accuracy and various other munitions training.[18]

In a recent interview, former Delta operator Paul Howe talked about the high attrition rate of his Delta selection course. He said that out of his two classes totaling 240 men, only 12 to 14 candidates completed the course.[19]

6.2.3   Training

According to Eric Haney the unit's **Operator Training Course** is approximately six months long. While the course is constantly changing, the skills taught broadly include the following:

- Marksmanship

  - The trainees shoot without aiming at stationary targets at close range until they gain almost complete accuracy, then progress to moving targets.

  - Once these shooting skills are perfected, trainees move to a shooting house and clear rooms of "enemy" targets – first one only, then two at a time, three, and finally four. When all can demonstrate sufficient skill, "hostages" are added to the "enemies".

- Demolitions and Breaching

  - Trainees learn how to pick many different locks, including those on cars and safes.

  - Advanced demolition, and bomb making using common materials.

- Combined skills. The FBI, FAA, and other agencies were used to advise the training of this portion of OTC. Commercial airliners such as Delta Air Lines would allow Delta to train on their aircraft as well.

  - The new Delta operators use demolition and marksmanship at the shoothouse and other training facilities to train for hostage and counter-terrorist operations with assault and sniper troops working together. They practice terrorist or hostage situations in buildings, aircraft, and other settings.

  - All trainees learn how to set sniper positions around a building containing hostages. They learn the proper ways to set up a TOC and communicate in an organized manner. Although Delta has specialized sniper troops, all members go through this training.

  - The students then go back to the shoothouse and the "hostages" are replaced with other students and Delta Force members. Live ammunition is known to have been used in these exercises, to test the students, and build trust between one another.

- Tradecraft– During the first OTC's and creation of Delta, CIA personnel were used to teach this portion.

  - Students learn different espionage-related skills, such as dead drops, brief encounters, pickups, load and unload signals, danger and safe signals, surveillance and counter-surveillance.

- Executive Protection – During the first OTC's and creation of Delta, the U.S. State Department's Diplomatic Security Service and the United States Secret Service advised Delta.

  - Students take an advanced driving course learning how to use a vehicle or many vehicles as defensive and offensive weapons.

  - They then learn techniques for VIP and diplomatic protection developed by the Secret Service and DSS.

- Culmination Exercise

  - A final test requires the students to apply and dynamically adapt all of the skills that they have learned.

6.3 Uniform

The Pentagon tightly controls information about Delta Force and refuses to comment publicly on the highly secretive unit and its activities. Delta operators are granted an enormous amount of flexibility and autonomy. To conceal their identities, they rarely wear a uniform and usually wear civilian clothing both on and off duty.[18] When military uniforms are worn, they lack markings, surnames, or branch names.[18] Civilian hair styles and facial hair are allowed to enable the members to blend in and avoid recognition as military personnel.[18][20]

6.4 The term *operator*

Inside the United States Special Operations community, an *operator* is a Delta Force member who has completed selection and has graduated OTC (Operators Training Course). *Operator* was first used by Delta Force to distinguish between operational and non-operational personnel assigned to the unit.[18] Other special operations forces use specific names for their jobs (Army *Rangers*, Navy *SEALs*, Air Force *Pararescuemen*); *operator* is the specific term for Delta's operational personnel. However, since the early 2000s other special operations forces have adopted the term. The Central Intelligence Agency's highly secretive Special Activities Division (SAD) and more specifically its elite Special Operations Group (SOG) often works with – and recruits – operators from Delta Force.[21]

SEALs may have unofficially referred to themselves as operators since the Vietnam War. Author and Navy SEAL Gene Wentz makes many references to fellow SEALs as operators in his 1992 book titled "Men In Green Faces," which is about the SEALs in Vietnam.[22] Currently, the official rating used by the Navy to designated SEALs is SO, or "Special Warfare Operator".

6.5 Operations and clandestine operations

Main article: Delta Force Operations and clandestine operations

The majority of the operations assigned to Delta are classified and may never be known to the public. However, details of some operations have become public knowledge. There have been many occasions that Delta has been put on standby and operational plans developed but the unit was stood down for various reasons.

6.6 See also

- Joint Special Operations Command
- SEAL Team Six
- 24th Special Tactics Squadron
- Delta Force in popular culture
- List of Delta Force members
- List of special forces units

6.7 References

[1] Eric L. Haney, *Inside Delta Force: The Story of America's Elite Counterterrorist Unit*, Delacorte Press, 2002

[2] "U.S. conducts raid in Syria, says it kills senior Islamic State leader". *Reuters*. 16 May 2015.

[3] "US-Iraqi rescue operation 'foils IS mass execution'". *BBC News*. 22 October 2015.

[4] Sean D. Naylor (9 May 2011). "Bin Laden raid a triumph for Spec Ops". *Navytimes.com*. Retrieved 16 March 2013.

[5] "SEAL Team Six". *Sealteamsix.americanspecialops.com*. Retrieved 16 March 2013.

[6]

[7] Beckwith, Charlie. *Delta Force*, Avon Books, 2000. (Mass market paperback; original work published 1983.) ISBN 0-380-80939-7. (p. 39)

[8] Beckwith 2000

[9] Beckwith 2000, pp. 142–143

[10] Beckwith 2000, p. 131

[11] Gabriel, Richard A. (1985). *Military Incompetence: Why the American Military Doesn't Win*, Hill and Wang, ISBN 0-374-52137-9, pp. 106–116. Overall, the Holloway Commission blamed the ad hoc nature of the task force and an excessive degree of security, both of which intensified command-and-control problems.

[12] Naylor, Sean (2006). *Not a Good Day to Die: The Untold Story of Operation Anaconda*. Berkeley: Berkley Books. ISBN 0-425-19609-7.

[13] Mountaineer. SFOD-D seeking new members. Fort Carson, Colorado: *Mountaineer* (publication). 16 January 2003. Archived 17 January 2004 at the Wayback Machine

[14] "Fort Bragg's newspaper Paraglide, recruitment notice for Delta Force". Archived from the original on 11 June 2009. Retrieved 17 November 2009.

[15] "Delta Force Marine awarded Navy Cross for fight at CIA annex in Benghazi". Washington Times. Retrieved 2015-12-06.

[16] "Assessing U.S. Special Operations Command's Missions and Roles". Fas.org. Retrieved 11 August 2012.

[17] Beckwith, Charlie A (1983). *Delta Force*. Harcourt.

[18] Haney, Eric L. (2002). *Inside Delta Force*. New York: Delacorte Press. p. 325. ISBN 978-0-385-33603-1.

[19] "Delta Force Tryouts". YouTube.com. Retrieved 18 February 2014.

[20] Bowden, Mark (1999). *Black Hawk Down: A Story of Modern War*. Berkeley: Atlantic Monthly Press. ISBN 0-87113-738-0.

[21] Waller, Douglas (2003-02-03). "The CIA's Secret Army: The CIA's Secret Army". TIME. Retrieved 2015-12-06.

[22] "Navy Special Warfare Operator (SEAL)". *Navycs.com*. Retrieved 15 May 2011.

6.8   Further reading

- Bowden, Mark (2001). *Killing Pablo: The Hunt for the World's Greatest Outlaw*. New York: Atlantic Monthly Press. ISBN 0-87113-783-6. About the hunt for Pablo Escobar.

- Bowden, Mark (2006). *Guests of the Ayatollah: The First Battle in America's War with Militant Islam*. New York: Atlantic Monthly Press. ISBN 0-87113-925-1. OCLC 62738726.

- Bowden, Mark (May 2006). "The Desert One Debacle". *The Atlantic Monthly*.

- Fury, Dalton (2009). *Kill Bin Laden: A Delta Force Commander's Account of the Hunt for the World's Most Wanted Man*. New York: St. Martin's Griffin. ISBN 978-0-312-56740-8. OCLC 317455875.

- Griswold, Terry, and D. M. Giangreco (2002). *DELTA: America's Elite Counterterrorist Force*. Osceola, WI: Motorbooks International. ISBN 0-87938-615-0. OCLC 25549191.

- National Geographic documentary: *Road to Baghdad*.

- Pushies, Fred J., et al. (2002). *U.S. Counter-Terrorist Forces*. St. Paul, Minn.: MBI Publishing Company. ISBN 0-7603-1363-6. OCLC 49391516.

- Schauer, Hartmut (2008). *Delta Force*. Stuttgart: Motorbuch Verlag. ISBN 978-3-613-02958-3.

- Smith, Michael (2007). *Killer Elite: America's Most Secret Special Operations Team*. New York: St. Martin's Press. ISBN 0-312-36272-2. About Delta cooperation with the Intelligence Support Activity.

6.9 External links

- The official website of the United States Department of Defense (DoD)

- The official website of the United States Army

- Special Operations.com Special Forces Article

- Transcript of Sean Naylor's speech to American Enterprise Institute

- 1st Special Forces Operational Detachment (Airborne) DELTA at Global Security

Chapter 7

Intelligence Support Activity

The **United States Army Intelligence Support Activity** (**USAISA**), frequently shortened to **Intelligence Support Activity** or **ISA**, and nicknamed **The Activity**, is a United States Army Special Operations unit originally subordinated to the US Army Intelligence and Security Command (INSCOM). It is tasked to collect actionable intelligence in advance of missions by other US special operations forces, especially 1st SFOD-D and DEVGRU in counter-terrorist operations.

USAISA was the official name of the unit from 1981 to 1989; previously it was known as the Field Operations Group (FOG), created in September 1980. In 1989, the then USAISA commander sent a telex "terminating" the USAISA term and his special access program Grantor Shadow, but the unit continued under a series of different codenames which are changed every two years; known codenames include Centra Spike, Torn Victor, Quiet Enable, Cemetery Wind, and Gray Fox.

7.1 History

7.1.1 Field Operations Group

The Field Operations Group (FOG) was created in summer 1980 in order to take part in a second attempt to rescue the U.S. hostages held in the Tehran embassy after the failure of the Operation Eagle Claw. That operation had highlighted the U.S. shortfall in intelligence gathering,[1] in spite of the attempts by Major Richard J. Meadows, who operated undercover in Tehran during the operation.[2][3]

The Field Operations Group was under command of Colonel Jerry King, and operated in Iran, accomplishing various covert intelligence-gathering missions. The work accomplished by the FOG was successful, however the second attempt (called Operation Credible Sport), never took place because the air assets needed were not available.[4][5]

After the cancellation of Operation Credible Sport, the FOG was not disbanded, but enlarged. The administration saw that ground intelligence contingencies needed to be improved upon if future special operations were to be successful (the CIA did not always provide all the information needed). So, on 3 March 1981, the FOG was established as a permanent unit and renamed US Army Intelligence Support Activity.[4] This activity should not be confused with a later activity known as the Ground Intelligence Support Activity (GISA), as subordinated to the Army G2.

7.1.2 Badge and insignia

The current badge depicts an American bald eagle grasping a claymore, surrounded by a kilt belt, inscribed with Latin translation of "Truth Overcomes All Bonds". In the original crest, the claymore was wrapped in a chain with one of the links broken as a reminder of those killed during the failed Desert Claw mission. This symbol of failure was later deemed no longer appropriate.

The badge was deliberately designed by Jerry King and other founding members of the unit because of their shared

Scottish heritage. The claymore is a greatsword originating from the Scottish Highlands, and the belt surrounding the badge is in the same style as many Scottish clan's badges.

7.1.3   U.S. Army Intelligence Support Activity

Build-up

In 1981 the Intelligence Support Activity began to immediately select new operators, growing from FOG's 50 people to about 100. The ISA remained extremely secret; all of its records were classified under a Special Access Program (at first named OPTIMIZE TALENT). The ISA was given its classified budget of $7 million, a secret headquarters in Arlington, Virginia, and cover name, the Tactical Concept Activity.[4] ISA included three main operations branches (Command, SIGINT and Operations), and an analysis branch, whose name changed over the years (i.e. Directorate of Intelligence, Directorate of Intelligence and Security).[6] Colonel Jerry King became ISA's first commander.[4]

ISA mission was to support top-tier Special Operations Forces (primarily Delta Force and SEAL Team Six) in counter-terrorist operations and other special missions. The ISA would provide actionable intelligence collection, pathfinding, and operational support. The ISA performed several operations mainly in Latin America and Middle East, but also in East Africa, South-East Asia, and Europe.[4]

First missions

The ISA conducted various missions, including giving protection to the Lebanese leader Bachir Gemayel and attempting to buy a Soviet T-72 tank from Iraq (a deal that was finally stopped by the Iraqis).[4]

Dozier kidnapping   On December 17, 1981, the senior U.S. Army officer in NATO Land Forces Southern European Command, Brigadier General James L. Dozier, was kidnapped from his apartment in Verona, Italy, by Italian Red Brigades terrorists. The search for General Dozier saw a massive deployment of Italian and U.S. forces, including thousands of Italian national police, the Carabinieri. The search also featured some unconventional participants, including "remote viewers" from Project Stargate and an international cast of psychics, largely orchestrated by General Albert Stubblebine, then-Commander of U.S. Army Intelligence and Security Command INSCOM, and a great believer in the use of unconventional intelligence-gathering methods. An ISA SIGINT team was sent to Italy, and in conjunction with other Army SIGINT and counter-intelligence units, employed aerial and ground-based SIGINT systems to monitor and geo-locate terrorist communications. ISA and the other Army elements provided useful intelligence, helping Italian police to arrest several Red Brigades terrorists in mid-January 1982. The Italian police and intelligence agencies have never officially disclosed how they located General Dozier in late January 1982. However, U.S. Army participants in the operation have hinted that the mid-January arrests, the interrogation of those arrested, and follow-on investigations led to the eventual location of the Red Brigades hideout where Dozier was being held, in an apartment over a store in Padova. There is little doubt that the successful outcome resulted in part from the contributions of ISA's SIGINT specialists and the other supporting Army intelligence elements. General Dozier was freed unharmed by NOCS operators, also known as "The Leatherheads" for their unique headgear, on January 28, 1982.[4]

Operation Queens Hunter   In early-1982, the ISA was needed to support a SIGINT mission in El Salvador, a mission that the CIA, the NSA and INSCOM were not able to accomplish. The task was submitted to the U.S. Army Special Operations Division (SOD), which started Operation Queens Hunter. Operating from a Beechcraft model 100 King Air flown by SEASPRAY (a clandestine military aviation unit) based in Honduras, ISA SIGINT specialists monitored communications from Salvadoran leftist guerrillas and fascist death squads, providing intelligence which helped the Salvadoran Army defend against guerrilla attacks. The success was such that the operation, planned to last a month, ran for more than three years. More aircraft were deployed, and eventually included eavesdropping on Honduran guerrillas too, as well as Nicaraguan Army units fighting against the Contras.[4]

The POW/MIA affair   The ISA has also conducted an operation to search for U.S. MIAs (soldiers reported as Missing In Action) allegedly held in South-East Asia in secret POWs camps in the 1980s. In 1979, U.S. intelligence thought it had located a POW camp in Laos using aerial and satellite photographs. A ground reconnaissance was needed to determine if people seen on photographs were really American POWs. At the same time, former Special Forces Major James G. "Bo" Gritz planned a private rescue mission with other S.F. veterans. Having informed U.S. government officials about the mission, Bo Gritz was first told to abort his "mission", but was eventually approached by the ISA. Nonetheless, Gritz was not believed to be doing serious work, and Pentagon officials ordered the ISA to terminate their relationship with him when they discovered that ISA had provided him with money and equipment.[4]Operation Grand Eagle aka BOHICA-1987 Scott Barnes ISA OpUS Senate Hearings 1986, 1992

Gray Fox

Gray Fox was the codename used by the ISA at the beginning of the War in Afghanistan. Its members often worked closely with US Special Mission Units.[7]

In 2002, Gray Fox fought alongside Delta Force and DEVGRU in the mountains of Afghanistan.[8] Gray Fox operatives intercepted enemy communications and trekked to observation posts with special operations units. Their efforts may have saved more than a hundred 10th Mountain Division and 101st Airborne Division soldiers fighting near Takur Ghar in Afghanistan's Shahikot Valley during Operation Anaconda.

The unit helped spearhead the search for Saddam Hussein and his family after the U.S.-led invasion of Iraq in 2003. Gray Fox operatives sometimes work under the broader umbrella of "Joint Special Operations Task Force 20," which also includes DEVGRU, the Army's Delta Force, and 160th Special Operations Aviation Regiment. Saddam Hussein was eventually captured during Operation Red Dawn.[7]

Before the standard naming convention of task forces using numbers, Task Force 20 was, and is sometimes still identified, as their original task force name: Task Force Orange.[7]

7.1.4   Under Joint Special Operations Command

In 2003, the Intelligence Support Activity was transferred from the Army to Joint Special Operations Command, where it was renamed the Mission Support Activity.[7]

Since 2005 onward, the ISA does not always operate under a two-worded Special Access Program (SAP) name (Grey Fox, Centra Spike, etc.) In 2009, the unit was referred to as INTREPID SPEAR, until this was revealed to have been leaked in an email to the Pentagon.[7] In 2010 it was referred to as the United States Army Studies and Analysis Activity.[7]

Elements of the former ISA assisted in intelligence collection and analysis operations prior to and during the 2 May 2011 U.S. Special Operations Forces mission which resulted in the death of Osama bin Laden. Elements of DEVGRU, along with the ISA, members of the 160th SOAR, the CIA Special Activities Division, DIA[9] and the NSA combined to execute a raid in Abbottabad, Pakistan, which ultimately killed bin Laden and resulted in the deaths of several family members and associates.

7.2   Recruitment and training

According to Sean Naylor in *Not A Good Day to Die*, most (but certainly not all) Activity operatives come from United States Army Special Forces, due to their self-reliance and specialized skill-set.[8] Candidates go through a rigorous selection process, then once admitted, receive further training in deep surveillance, signals intelligence, etc. Like all units, this special missions unit contains operational detachments as well as support detachments.

7.2.1   HUMINT & SIGINT

Candidates must have previous training in tactics, such as CQB, sniper, counter-sniper, and Source development. Foreign language skills, although highly desired, are not a prerequisite to becoming a member of the ISA, though to be a SIGINT/HUMINT operator in the field with other Special Mission Units, working clandestine operations in non-permissive environments, knowing a minimum of several languages is usually indispensable (i.e Farsi, Arabic, Pashtu etc). Candidates must pass a rigorous assessment and selection course, as well as a lengthy background investigation and psychological testing. After passing assessment and selection, candidates attend and pass Operations Training Course (OTC).

Some of the disciplines focused on in the training course are: infiltration techniques, advanced air operations, professional driving (offensive and off-road), personal defensive measures, and state-of-the-art communications.

7.3 Popular culture

ISA remains a very poorly known force to the public. Some rare mentions of the ISA exist, including:

- Robert Littell's 1991 novel *An Agent in Place*.[10]

- W. E. B. Griffin's The Presidential Agent series, especially its first book, *By Order of the President*, features "Gray Fox" in a major role however they are portrayed as a top secret unit within Delta Force.[11]

- In Dale Brown's *Patrick McLanahan* novels, the ISA operates on the high seas in support of McLanahan's operations. One such was the recovery of Col. David Luger, who was listed as KIA after the events of *Flight of the Old Dog* but was actually captured and interrogated by Russian forces.[12]

- A single reference, "ISA cell phone snipers", is present in the video game *Call of Duty: Modern Warfare 3*. This strongly suggests that the ISA provided the technical intelligence on the location of the daughter of the President of the Russian Federation — as well as the means to communicate with her — when she unsuccessfully tried to escape pursuers in Germany. Members of the ISA only acted in support: they did not actually participate in either of the two rescue attempts.

- ISA are a playable faction in *Call of Duty: Black Ops II*'s multiplayer mode.

- In Mark Bowden's 2001 book *Killing Pablo*, ISA operators ("Centra Spike") play a significant role in the hunt for fugitive drug lord Pablo Escobar of the Medellín Cartel leading to his death in December 1993 at the hands of Search Bloc, a Special Operations unit of the National Police of Colombia.[13]

- In Daniel Suarez's 2012 novel *Kill Decision*, a team of ISA operators is trying to unravel a conspiracy involving autonomous aerial drones.[14]

- In the television series *Person of Interest*, the ISA is mentioned as "an obscure U.S. Army unit that does black ops so dark, technically they don't exist" by former Special Forces soldier, CIA officer and protagonist John Reese (Jim Caviezel). Three operators from the unit serve as antagonists in an episode in which they attempt to assassinate a National Security Agency employee under John's protection. ISA operators are later revealed to be Indigo assets, hunting Relevant threats the Machine has identified. Fellow protagonist Sameen Shaw (Sarah Shahi) is a former ISA operative whom the Government attempts to assassinate after she and her partner inadvertently learn about the Machine.

- Nathan Edmondson's and Mitch Gerads' comic *The Activity*.[15]

- A paramilitary black ops unit called "Cemetery Wind" works for the CIA in the 2014 science fiction action film *Transformers: Age of Extinction*.

- In the anime *Terror in Resonance*, it is mentioned that Five may be a part of the ISA instead of the FBI.

7.4 See also

- United States Joint Special Operations Command

- Naval Special Warfare Development Group (SEAL Team Six)

- 14 Intelligence Company, a similar unit in the United Kingdom Special Forces, superseded by the Special Reconnaissance Regiment

- Swedish Military Intelligence and Security Service, a similar unit in the Swedish Armed Forces.

7.5   References

[1] Memorandum for Director, Defense Intelligence Agency

[2] Clancy, Tom. (2001) *Special Forces*

[3] Meadows biography of Maj Dick Meadows

[4] Richelson, Jeffrey T. *Truth Conquers All Chains*

[5] Brief History of Unit

[6] USAISA 1986 Historical Report and 1987 Historical Report

[7] Marc Ambinder and DB Grady (2012) *The Command: Inside the President's Secret Army*

[8] Sean Naylor (2006) *Not a Good Day to Die: The Untold Story of Operation Anaconda* Berkley Books: Berkeley ISBN 0-425-19609-7

[9] https://fas.org/irp/doddir/army/ar690-950-4.pdf

[10] Littell, Robert (2005). *An Agent in Place*. Penguin Books. ISBN 0143035649.

[11] Griffin, W. E. B. (December 1, 2005). *By Order of the President*. Jove Books. ISBN 0515139777.

[12] Brown, Dale (1987). *Flight of the Old Dog*. D.I. Fine. ISBN 1556110340.

[13] Bowden, Mark (2002). *Killing Pablo: The Hunt for the Richest, Most Powerful Criminal in History*. Atlantic Books. ISBN 1903809487.

[14] Suarez, Daniel (2013). *Kill Decision*. Penguin Group (USA) Inc. ISBN 0451417704.

[15] Truitt, Brian (January 11, 2012). "'The Activity' aims for realism with its government intrigue". *USA Today*. Retrieved July 14, 2014.

7.5.1   Bibliography

- *Secret Warriors: Inside the Covert Military Operations of the Reagan Era*, by Steven Emerson, G.P. Putnam's Sons, New York, 1988 ISBN 0-399-13360-7

- *Truth Conquers All Chains: The U.S. Army Intelligence Support Activity, 1981–1989*, by Jeffrey T. Richelson, article of the *International Journal of Intelligence and CounterIntelligence*, Vol. 12, No. 2, 1999, pp. 168–200, ISSN 0885-0607, available on the InformaWorld

- The Pentagon's Spies: Documents Detail Histories of Once Secret Spy Units, electronic book by Jeffrey T. Richelson, 23 May 2001, on the National Security Archive website. The article collects duplicates of declassified documents about covert US military intelligence units, including the ISA :

  - Memorandum for Director, Defense Intelligence Agency, by Lt. Gen. Philip C. Gast, USAF, 10 December 1980

  - Memorandum to the Deputy Under Secretary for Policy, by Frank Carlucci, 26 May 1982

  - Charter of U.S. Army Intelligence Support Activity, circa mid-1983

  - After Action Report for Operation CANVAS SHIELD, by 902nd Military Intelligence Group, 30 July 1985

  - Brief History of Unit (ISA), circa mid-1986 (presumed)

- United States Army Intelligence Support Activity 1986 Historical Report

  - United States Army Intelligence Support Activity 1987 Historical Report

  - Termination of USAISA and "GRANTOR SHADOW", by Commander, USAISA, 31 March 1989

- *Killing Pablo: the hunt for the world's greatest outlaw*, by Mark Bowden, Atlantic Monthly Press, New York, 2001 ISBN 0-87113-783-6

- *Killer Elite: The Inside Story of America's Most Secret Special Force Unit*, by Michael Smith, Orion Publishing Co, 2005 ISBN 0-304-36727-3 (several editions from 2006 to 2011 with additional material)

Chapter 8

SEAL Team Six

The **United States Naval Special Warfare Development Group** (**NSWDG**), or **DEVGRU**, is a U.S. Navy component of Joint Special Operations Command. It is often referred to as *SEAL Team Six*, the name of its predecessor which was officially disbanded in 1987.[1][2] DEVGRU is administratively supported by Naval Special Warfare Command and operationally commanded by the Joint Special Operations Command. Most information concerning DEVGRU is classified and details of its activities are not usually commented on by either the White House or the Department of Defense.[3] Despite the official name changes, "SEAL Team Six" remains the unit's widely recognized moniker. It is sometimes referred to in the U.S. media as a Special Mission Unit.[4]

DEVGRU and its Army counterpart, Delta Force, are the United States military's primary counter-terrorism units. Although DEVGRU was created as a maritime counter-terrorism unit, it has become a multi-functional special operations unit with several roles that include high-risk personnel/hostage extractions and other specialized missions.

The Central Intelligence Agency's highly secretive Special Activities Division (SAD) and more specifically its elite Special Operations Group (SOG) often works with—and recruits—operators from DEVGRU.[5] The combination of these units led ultimately to the killing of Al-Qaeda leader Osama bin Laden in Operation Neptune Spear.[6][7]

8.1 History

8.1.1 Administrative

The origins of DEVGRU are in SEAL Team Six, a unit created in the aftermath of Operation Eagle Claw.[8][9][10] During the Iran hostage crisis in 1979, Richard Marcinko was one of two U.S. Navy representatives for a Joint Chiefs of Staff task force known as the TAT (Terrorist Action Team). The purpose of the TAT was to develop a plan to free the American hostages held in Iran. In the wake of the disaster at the Desert One base in Iran, the Navy saw the need for a full-time counter-terrorist unit, and tasked Marcinko with its design and development.

Marcinko was the first commanding officer of this new unit. At the time there were two SEAL teams. Marcinko named the unit SEAL Team Six in order to confuse Soviet intelligence as to the number of actual SEAL teams in existence.[10][11][12] The unit's plankowners were hand-picked by Marcinko from throughout the UDT/SEAL community. SEAL Team Six became the U.S. Navy's premier counter-terrorist unit. It has been compared to the U.S. Army's Delta Force.[3][9] Marcinko held the command of SEAL Team Six for three years, from 1980 to 1983, instead of the typical two-year command in the Navy at the time.[10] SEAL Team Six was formally created in October 1980, and an intense, progressive work-up training program made the unit mission-ready just six months later.[12] SEAL Team Six started with 75 shooters. According to

Dick Marcinko, the annual ammunition training allowance for the command was larger than that of the entire U.S. Marine Corps. The unit has virtually unlimited resources at its disposal.[13]

In 1987 SEAL Team Six was dissolved. A new unit named the "Naval Special Warfare Development Group" was formed, essentially as SEAL Team Six's successor.[14][15][16] Reasons for the disbanding are varied,[10] but the name *SEAL Team Six* is often used in reference to DEVGRU.

8.1.2   Operational deployments

Main article: List of operations conducted by SEAL Team Six

8.2   Recruitment, selection and training

In the early stages of creating SEAL Team Six, Marcinko was given six months to get ST6 up and running, or the whole project would come to an end. This meant that there was a timing issue and Marcinko had little time to create a proper selection course, similar to that of Delta Force, and as a result hand-picked the first plankowners of the unit after assessing their Navy records and interviewing each man. It has been said that Marcinko regretted not having enough time to set up a proper selection process and course. All applicants came from the Underwater Demolition Teams (UDTs) and East and West Coast SEAL teams. Marcinko's criteria for recruiting applicants was combat experience so he would know they could perform under fire; language skills were vital, as the unit would have a worldwide mandate to communicate with the local population if needed; union skills, to be able to blend in as civilians during an operation; and finally SEAL skills. Members of SEAL Team Six were selected in part because of the different specialist skills of each man.

Candidates must pass three-days of physical and psychological testing that includes a Physical Screening Test (PST) where candidates must exceed the minimum requirements and perform at their highest level possible. Candidates are then interviewed by an oral review board to deem whether the candidate is suitable to undertake the selection phase.[18] Those who pass the stringent recruitment and selection process will be selected to attend a six- to eight-month Operators Training Course. Candidates will screen with the unit's training wing known as "Green Team". The training course attrition rate is high, usually around 50 percent; during one selection course, out of the original 20 candidates, 12 completed the course.[19] All candidates are watched closely by DEVGRU instructors and evaluated on whether they are suitable to join the individual squadrons. Howard E. Wasdin, a former member of SEAL Team Six said in a recent interview that 16 applied for SEAL Team Six selection course and two were accepted.[20] Those who do not pass the selection phase are returned to their previous assignments and are able to try again in the future.[21]

Like all Special Operations Forces units that have an extremely intensive and high-risk training schedule, there can be serious injuries and deaths. SEAL Team Six/DEVGRU has lost several operators during training, including parachute accidents and close-quarters battle training accidents. It is presumed that the unit's assessment process for potential new recruits is different from what a SEAL operator experienced in his previous career, and much of the training tests the candidate's mental capacity rather than his physical condition, as he will have already completed Basic Underwater Demolitions/SEAL or the Navy EOD training pipeline.

Candidates are put through a variety of advanced training courses led by civilian or military instructors. These can include free-climbing, land warfare, communications, advanced unarmed combat techniques, defensive and offensive driving, advanced diving, and Survival, Evasion, Resistance and Escape (SERE) training. All candidates must perform at the top level during selection, and the unit instructors evaluate the candidate during the training process. Selected candidates are assigned to one of the Tactical Development and Evaluation Squadrons; the others are returned to their previous units. Unlike the other regular SEAL Teams, SEAL Team Six operators were able to go to almost any of the best schools anywhere and train in whatever they wanted depending on the unit's requirements.

8.3   Structure

DEVGRU is divided into color-coded line squadrons.[22]

- **Gold Squadron** (Assault Team)

- **Blue Squadron** (Assault Team)

- **Silver Squadron** (Assault Team)

- **Red Squadron** (Assault Team)

- **Black Squadron** (Reconnaissance & Surveillance Team)

- **Gray Squadron** (Transportation/Divers)

- **Green Squadron** (Selection/Training)

Each assault squadron is divided into three troops (commanded by lieutenant commanders) and these troops are divided into smaller teams.[23] Each line squadron has a specific nickname. Examples being Gold-Knights, Red-Indians, Blue-Pirates.[22][24][25]

8.4 Commanding officers

Command of DEVGRU is a Captain's billet. Ranks listed are the most recent if the officer is still on active duty.

- Commander Richard Marcinko – Nov 1980 to July 1983[26]

- Captain Robert A. Gormly – July 1983 to 1986[22][27]

- Captain Thomas E. Murphy – 1986 to 1987[27]

- Captain Richard T.P. Woolard – 1987 to 1990[28]

- Captain Ronald E. Yeaw – 1990 to 1992[29]

- Captain Thomas G. Moser – 1992 to 1994[30]

- Admiral Eric T. Olson – 1994 to 1997[31]

- Vice Admiral Albert M. Calland III – June 1997 to June 1999[32]

- Vice Admiral Joseph D. Kernan – June 1999 to Aug 2003[32]

- Rear Admiral Edward G. Winters, III – Aug 2003 to Jan 2006[33]

- Rear Admiral Scott P. Moore – 2006 to 2008[34]

- Rear Admiral Brian L. Losey – 2008 to 2010[35]

- Captain Perry F. Van Hooser – 2010 to 2012[36]

8.5 Roles and responsibilities

When SEAL Team Six was first created it was devoted exclusively to counter-terrorism with a worldwide maritime responsibility; its objectives typically included targets such as ships, oil rigs, naval bases, coastal embassies, and other civilian or military bases that were accessible from the sea or inland waterways.

On certain operations small teams from SEAL Team Six were tasked with covertly infiltrating international high risk areas in order to carry out reconnaissance or security assessments of U.S. military facilities and embassies; and to give advice on improvements in order to prevent casualties in an event of a terrorist attack.

Although the unit was created as a maritime counter-terrorism unit, it has become a multi-functional special operations unit with multiple roles that include high-risk personnel/hostage extractions. Such operations include the successful rescue of Jessica Buchanan and Poul Hagen Thisted, the attempted rescue of Linda Norgrove, the successful rescue of American doctor Dilip Joseph[37] and in 1991 the successful recovery of Haitian President Jean-Bertrand Aristide and his family during a coup that deposed him.

After SEAL Team Six was disbanded and renamed, the official mission of the currently operating Naval Special Warfare Development Group is to test, evaluate, and develop technology and maritime, ground, and airborne tactics applicable to Naval Special Warfare forces such as Navy SEALs; however, it is presumed this is a small part of the group's work assignment and more of a cover.

DEVGRU's full mission is classified but is thought to include pre-emptive, pro-active counter-terrorist operations, counter-proliferation (efforts to prevent the spread of both conventional weapons and weapons of mass destruction), as well as the elimination or recovery of high-value targets (HVTs) from unfriendly nations.[38][39] DEVGRU is one of a handful of U.S. Special Mission Units authorized to use pre-emptive actions against terrorists and their facilities.[40]

DEVGRU and the Army's Delta Force train and deploy together on counter-terrorist missions usually as part of a joint special operations task force (JSOTF).[3][12][41][42]

8.6 See also

- Joint Special Operations Command
- Delta Force
- 24th Special Tactics Squadron
- Spetsnaz
- Navy SEALs in popular culture
- List of Navy SEALs
- List of special forces units

8.7 Notes

[1] "Spec ops raids into Pakistan halted". *Navy Times*. Retrieved 14 October 2010.

[2] "Special ops 'surge' sparks debate". *Army Times*. Retrieved 14 October 2010.

[3] Emerson, Steven (13 November 1988). "Stymied Warriors". *The New York Times*. Retrieved 13 March 2008.

[4] "In high demand, Air Force commandos must find new ways to cope with stress of duty". *Gaffney Ledger*. Associated Press. Retrieved 2013-05-04.

[5] Waller, Douglas (3 February 2003). "The CIA's Secret Army". *Time*. http://www.time.com/time/magazine/article/0,9171,1004145-1,00.html

[6] "Osama bin Laden killed in CIA operation". *The Washington Post*. 8 May 2011. Retrieved 19 May 2011.

[7] Naylor, Mark Mazzetti, Nicholas Kulish, Christopher Drew, Serge F. Kovaleski, Sean D.; Ismay, John (2015-06-06). "The Secret History of SEAL Team 6: Quiet Killings and Blurred Lines". *The New York Times*. ISSN 0362-4331. Retrieved 2015-06-06.

[8] Fallows, James (13 December 1981). "Iran from five American viewpoints". *The New York Times*.

[9] Halloran, Richard (26 November 1986). "U.S. moving to expand unconventional forces". *The New York Times*. Retrieved 7 May 2011.

[10] Marcinko, Richard (1992). *Rogue Warrior*. New York: Pocket Books. ISBN 0-671-79593-7.

[11] Pfarrer, Chuck (2011). *SEAL Target Geronimo: The Inside Story of the Mission to Kill Osama Bin Laden*. Macmillan. p. 178. ISBN 978-1-4299-6025-0.

[12] Gerth, Jeff; Philip Taubman (8 June 1984). "U.S. military creates secret units for use in sensitive tasks abroad". *The New York Times*.

[13] Wasdin, Howard (9 May 2011). "'SEAL Team Six' And Other Elite Squads Expanding". NPR. Retrieved 19 May 2011.

[14] von Rosenbach, Alexander (4 May 2011). "Devgru: Bin Laden's ultimate nemesis". *Defence Security Report*. Janes. Retrieved 18 June 2013.

[15] "Naval Special Warfare Development Group (DEVGRU)". Global Security. Retrieved 18 June 2013.

[16] Ambiner, Marc (10 October 2012). "Delta Force Gets a Name Change". *The Atlantic*. Retrieved 18 June 2013.

[17] Abhan, Courtney Messman (30 July 2010). "Special Warfare Development Group seeks Sailors" (PDF). *Naval Station Everett Public Affairs*. Northwest Navigator. p. 3. Retrieved 14 September 2012. NSWDG is located in Virginia Beach, and is a type two sea duty cno priority one major command. The command is an elite counter terrorism unit that conducts research, and develops, tests, and evaluates current and emerging technology. This technology is related to special operations tactics and joint warfare to improve Special Forces war fighting capabilities. ... While at NSWDG, support personnel could have opportunities to earn many special qualifications, their expeditionary warfare specialist (EXW) pin, and Combat Service Support and Combat Support Naval Education Codes (NEC). Special qualifications include parachuting and fast roping, among many others. NSWDG support personnel receive special duty pay, and have some of the highest promotion rates in the Navy.

[18] Anderson Cooper (3 May 2011). "'This is their type of op,' ex-SEAL says". CNN.

[19] Pfarrer, Chuck. *Warrior Soul: The Memoir of a Navy Seal*. New York: Random House. pp. 325 326. ISBN 0-89141-863-6. In one year, the operators of SEAL Six fire more bullets than entire USMC.

[20] "The iron will of Seal Team 6". CBS News. 6 May 2011. Retrieved 19 May 2011.

[21] "LCV Cities Tour: Interview with Howard Wasdin "Seal Team Six: Memoirs of an Elite Navy Seal Sniper"". Global-report.org. 22 June 2011. Retrieved 7 January 2012.

[22] Pfarrer, Chuck. *Warrior Soul: The Memoir of a Navy Seal*. New York: Random House. pp. 325–326. ISBN 0-89141-863-6.

[23] Owen, Mark (2012). *No Easy Day*. Dutton Adult. p. 37. ISBN 9780525953722.

[24] Combs, Cindy C; Slann, Martin W. (2008). *Encyclopedia of Terrorism*. Infobase Publishing. p. 289. ISBN 978-0-8160-6277-5.

[25] Blehm, Eric (2013). *Fearless: The Undaunted Courage and Ultimate Sacrifice of Navy SEAL Team SIX Operator Adam Brown*. WaterBrook Press. ISBN 9780307730701.

[26] Marcinko, Richard (1993). *Rogue Warrior*. Pocket Books. ISBN 978-0671795931.

[27] Mann, Don (2011). *Inside SEAL Team Six: My Life and Missions with America's Elite Warriors*. Little, Brown and Company. p. 142. ISBN 978-0-316-20431-6.

[28] Arostegui, Martin C. (1997). "Get Noriega". *Twilight Warriors: Inside the World's Special Forces*. Macmillan. p. 290. ISBN 978-0-312-30471-3.

[29] Marquis, Susan Lynn (1997). *Unconventional warfare: rebuilding U.S. special operations forces*. Brookings Institution Press. p. 34. ISBN 978-0-8157-5476-3.

[30] Committee on Risk-Based Approaches for Securing the DOE Nuclear Weapons Complex, National Research Council (2011). *Understanding and Managing Risk in Security Systems for the DOE Nuclear Weapons Complex*. National Academies Press. p. 6. ISBN 978-0-309-20884-0.

[31] Butler, Frank K.; John H. Hagmann; David T. Richards (2009). *Tactical Management of Urban Warfare Casualties in Special Operations*. Parabellum Concepts. p. 6.

[32] Naylor, Sean (2006). *Not a Good Day to Die: The Untold Story of Operation Anaconda*. Penguin. p. 253. ISBN 978-0-425-20787-1.

[33] "Rear Admiral Edward G. Winters, III". United States Navy. 30 June 2011. Retrieved 5 February 2012.

[34] Associated Press (15 September 2008). "2 SEALs killed in Afghanistan fighting". *navytimes.com* (Navy Times). Retrieved 2015-10-11. (subscription required (help)). "The deaths of SOCS Marcum and SOC Freiwald are tremendous losses for Naval Special Warfare and the United States," Capt. Scott Moore, commanding officer of Naval Special Warfare Development Group, said in a statement.

[35] "Rear Admiral Brian L. Losey". *navy.mil*. United States Navy. 2014-11-18. Retrieved 2015-10-11.

[36] "Leader in Residence Program". *vmi.edu*. Virginia Military Institute. Retrieved 2015-10-11.

[37] Qadir Sediqi,"U.S. Navy SEAL killed in operation to rescue American doctor in Afghanistan". CNN. 10 December 2012

[38] Shanker, Thom; Risen, James (12 August 2002). "Rumsfeld weighs new covert acts by military units". *The New York Times*. Retrieved 7 May 2011.

[39] "Frequently Asked Questions". *LT Michael P. Murphy USN*. United States Navy. Retrieved 20 May 2008.

[40] *U.S. Special Ops: America's Elite Forces in the 21st Century*, Fred J. Pushies, MBI Publishing Company, 2003.

[41] Couch, Dick (2005). *The Finishing School: Earning the Navy SEAL Trident*. Three Rivers Press. ISBN 0-609-81046-4.

[42] Bowden, Mark (2001). *Black Hawk Down: A Story of Modern War*. Signet. ISBN 0-451-20393-3.

8.8   References

- Marcinko, Richard (1993). *Rogue Warrior*. Pocket Books. ISBN 0-671-79593-7.

- Gormly, Robert A. (1999). *Combat Swimmer: Memoirs of a Navy SEAL*. New York: Penguin Group. ISBN 0-451-19302-4.

- MacPherson, Malcolm (2006). *Roberts Ridge: A Story of Courage and Sacrifice on Takur Ghar Mountain, Afghanistan*. New York: Bantam Dell. ISBN 0-553-58680-7.

- Shipler, David K.; Halloran, Richard (26 November 1985). "Terror: Americans as targets". *The New York Times*. Retrieved 7 May 2011.

8.9   External links

- ShadowSpear.com Special Operations

- Naval Special Warfare Development Group at GlobalSecurity.org

- Mark Mazetti, Nicholas Kulish, Christopher Drew, Serge F. Kowalski, Seasn D. Naylor and John Ismay (June 6, 2015). "*SEAL Team 6: A Secret History of Quiet Killings and Blurred Lines*". The New York Times (The New York Times). According to the New York Times the article probed "the culture of a secretive Special Operations unit, which often acts with limited oversight, and situated it in the context of how today's wars are fought. It implicated the team in troubling failures, like the killing of a British aid worker it was trying to rescue from the Taliban or the deaths of innocent civilians, one a young, unarmed Afghan girl. The article also spotlighted the unit's triumphs apart from the Osama bin Laden raid, such as rescuing Pfc. Jessica Lynch in Iraq, or saving Capt. Richard Phillips from Somali pirates"

- "*Inside SEAL Team 6*" - An undated New York Times article describing the identity, missions, training and dangers of SEAL Team Six.

Richard Marcinko, founder and first Commanding Officer of SEAL Team Six

SEAL Team Six Patch

NSWDG recruiting support personnel,[17] 2007.

Secretary of the Navy, Dr. Donald C. Winter is briefed on the Sentry HP UAV at Dam Neck, 2007.

Chapter 9

24th Special Tactics Squadron

The **24th Special Tactics Squadron** is one of the Special Tactics units of the United States Air Force Special Operations Command (AFSOC). It is the U.S. Air Force component to Joint Special Operations Command.[1][2] It is garrisoned at Pope Field, North Carolina.

9.1 Lineage

- Constituted as **24 Air Corps Interceptor Control Squadron** on 14 October 1941.

  Activated on 21 October 1941.

- Redesignated as **24 Fighter Control Squadron** on 15 May 1942.

  Disbanded on 31 March 1944.

- Reconstituted, and consolidated (1 March 1992) with the **1724 Combat Control Squadron** which was designated, and activated, on 1 May 1987.

- Redesignated as: **1724 Special Tactics Squadron** on 1 October 1987.

- Redesignated as: **24 Special Tactics Squadron** on 31 March 1992.

9.1.1 Assignments

- Fourth Air Force, 21 October 1941

- 24th Pursuit Group, 15 January 1942

- Fourth Air Force, 15 January – 7 July 1942

- IV Fighter Command, 8 July – 14 October 1942

- San Francisco Air Defense (later, San Francisco Fighter) Wing, 15 October 1942 – 31 March 1944

- Twenty-Third Air Force, 1 May 1987;

- 1720th (later, 720th) Special Tactics Group, 1 October 1987 – 29 April 2011

- 724th Special Tactics Group, 29 April 2011 – **Present**[3]

9.1.2 Stations

- Hamilton Field, CA, 21 October – 6 December 1941

- US Army Transport Garfield, 6–10 December 1941

- Hamilton Field, CA, 10 December 1941 – 7 October 1943

- Berkeley, CA, 7 October 1943 – 31 March 1944

- Pope AFB, NC, 1 May 1987 – 1 March 2011

- Pope Field, NC, 1 March 2011 – **Present**

9.1.3 Unit Awards

Other accolades

- Air Commando Association 2012 AFSOC Squadron of the Year[4]

9.2 History

The 24th Special Tactics Squadron participated in the United States invasion of Panama in 1989.[5] The 24th STS deployed 11 personnel including the unit commander, Lt. Col. Jim Oeser, as part of JSOC's Task Force Ranger during Operation Restore Hope in 1993.[6] Due to their actions during the Battle of Mogadishu multiple decorations were awarded to the airmen. Pararescueman (PJ) TSgt Tim Wilkinson received the Air Force Cross and fellow PJ MSgt Scott Fales received the Silver Star, both for providing lifesaving medical care to wounded soldiers.[7] Combat Controller (CCT) SSgt. Jeffrey W. Bray also received the Silver Star for coordinating helicopter attack runs throughout the night around their positions.[7][8][9]

From 15 to 20 September 2000 the 24th STS with the 23rd Special Tactics Squadron took part in the annual Canadian military exercise, Search and Rescue Exercise (SAREX). This was the first time Special Tactics units took part in SAREX.[10][11]

In recent years the squadron has been heavily involved in combat operations in Iraq and Afghanistan where the unit was part of the JSOC groupings Task Force 121, Task Force 6-26 and Task Force 145.[12] In 2003 members of the unit were involved in two combat jumps in the initial phases of the Iraq War alongside the 3rd Ranger Battalion.[13] The first combat jump was on 24 March 2003 near the Syrian border in the Iraqi town of Al Qaim where they secured a small desert landing strip to allow follow-on coalition forces into the area.[13] The second combat jump was two days later near Haditha, Iraq, where they secured the Haditha Dam.[13]

On 8 April 2003 Combat Controller Scott Sather, a member of the 24th STS,[14] became the first airman killed in combat in Operation Iraqi Freedom near Tikrit, Iraq.[15] He was attached to a small team from the 75th Ranger Regimental Reconnaissance Detachment (RRD). The RRD team and Sather were operating alongside Delta Force, under Lieutenant Colonel Pete Blaber, west of Baghdad. They were tasked with deceiving the Iraqi army into believing the main U.S. invasion was coming from the west in order to prevent Saddam Hussein from escaping into Syria.[16] Sather Air Base was named after him.[17]

The 24th STS was a part of JSOC's Task Force 145 which was a provisional grouping specifically charged with hunting down high-value al-Qaeda and Iraqi leadership including Al-Qaeda in Iraq leader, Abu Musab al-Zarqawi, who was killed in June 2006.[18]

The squadron lost three members – PJs John Brown and Daniel Zerbe and CCT Andrew Harvell – in 2011 when the Chinook in which they were flying was shot down in Afghanistan.[19] To honor the three 24th STS members who died in the 2011 Chinook shootdown, 18 members of AFSOC marched 800 miles from Lackland Air Force Base, San Antonio Texas to Hurlburt Field, Florida in their memory.[20]

9.3   Notable members

Colon-Lopez in Afghanistan in 2004 while a member of the 24th STS.

- PJ Tim Wilkinson received the Air Force Cross for his actions during the 1993 Battle of Mogadishu.[21] Wilkinson was portrayed by Ty Burrell in the 2001 film Black Hawk Down which chronicled the events of the Battle of Mogadishu.[22]

- CCT John Chapman was posthumously awarded the Air Force Cross for his actions in the Battle of Takur Ghar during the War in Afghanistan.[23] In 2005 a U.S. Navy Buffalo Soldier-class container ship was renamed the *TSgt John A. Chapman* in Chapman's honor.[24]

- PJ Ramon Colon-Lopez was a member of the 24th STS twice. From February 1999 – January 2005 Colon-Lopez was a Special Tactics Element Leader and April 2009 – April 2011 he was the Squadron's Senior Enlisted Advisor.[25] In 2007 Colon-Lopez was one of the first six recipients of the newly created Air Force Combat Action Medal.[26] He was awarded the AFCAM for a 2004 operation in Afghanistan during which he led an Advance Force Operations Team.[27]

9.4   Commanders

- Jul 2003 – Jul 2005, Lt. Col. Mark F. Stratton[28]

- Jun 2005 – Jun 2007, Lt. Col. Robert G. Armfield - Previous 24th STS assignments: Director of Operations (Jan 1998 - Jul 2002)[29]

- Jun 2009 – Apr 2011, Lt. Col. Matthew Wolfe Davidson - Previous 24th STS assignments: Flight Commander (Aug 1998 - Jan 2002), Deputy Commander (Jun 2008 – Jun 2009)[30]

9.5   See also

- List of United States Air Force special tactics squadrons

9.6   References

This article incorporates public domain material from websites or documents of the Air Force Historical Research Agency.

[1] Priest, Dana (2 September 2011). "'Top Secret America': A look at the military's Joint Special Operations Command – Washington Post". Articles.washingtonpost.com. Retrieved 4 May 2013.

[2] "The Secret US War in Pakistan". The Nation. 23 November 2009. Retrieved 13 May 2013.

[3] "Factsheets : 24th Special Operations Wing" Check |url= value (help). Afsoc.af.mil. Retrieved 4 May 2013.

[4] Mike Martin (2012-10-16). "AFSOC Airmen past, present recognized at 2012 Air Commando Association banquet". Afsoc.af.mil. Retrieved 2014-07-14.

[5] "AFHRA Factsheet: 24 SPECIAL TACTICS SQUADRON (AFSOC)".

[6] Bruce Rolfsen. "The real 'Black Hawk Down'". Air Force Times. Retrieved 10 March 2013.

[7] Frank Oliveri. "Heroes at Mogadishu". *Airman Magazine*. Retrieved 10 March 2013.

[8] "Awards of the Silver Star for Conspicuous Gallantry in Action During Operation Restore Hope in Somalia(1993)". Retrieved 10 March 2013.

[9] Gertz, Bill (3 October 1993). "The Fast Pace of Special Ops". Airforcemag.com. Retrieved 13 May 2013.

[10] "SARSCENE Magazine – Special 2001 edition". Nss.gc.ca. Retrieved 2 May 2013.

[11] John Pike. "23rd Special Tactics Squadron [23rd STS]". Globalsecurity.org. Retrieved 2 May 2013.

[12] Naylor, Sean (2006). *Not a Good Day to Die: The Untold Story of Operation Anaconda*. Berkeley: Berkley Books. ISBN 0-425-19609-7.

[13] John Pike. "United States Combat Jumps". Globalsecurity.org. Retrieved 13 May 2013.

[14] "Air Force Staff Sgt. Scott D. Sather". Projects.militarytimes.com. 8 April 2003. Retrieved 13 May 2013.

[15] Michael Robert Patterson. "Scott D. Sather, Staff Sergeant, United States Air Force". Arlingtoncemetery.net. Retrieved 13 May 2013.

[16] "Our Fallen Heroes: Scott Sather". SOFREP. Retrieved 13 May 2013.

[17] "DVIDS – News – Sather Air Base welcomes new commander". Dvidshub.net. Retrieved 13 May 2013.

[18] "OTS Foundation Portal – The hunt ends". Air Force OTS. 11 September 2001. Retrieved 13 May 2013.

[19] "DoD names troops killed in Chinook shootdown". 11 August 2011. Retrieved 1 May 2013.

[20] "Airmen to walk 800 miles in memorial march for fallen from Bragg". Fayobserver.com. 15 October 2011. Retrieved 13 May 2013.

[21] "The Air Force Cross For Actions in Somalia in 1993". Retrieved 7 September 2012.

[22] "Ty Burrell, left,... – Ty Burrell and Jeremy Piven in 'Black Hawk Down'". Courant.com. Retrieved 13 May 2013.

[23] "The Air Force Cross in the Global War on Terrorism". Retrieved 7 September 2012.

[24] Senior Airman Becky J. LaRaia; Lisa Terry McKeown, 43rd Airlift Wing Public Affairs (8 April 2005). "Ship takes heroic legacy to the fight". US Air Force. Retrieved 15 January 2010.

[25] "USAF Biography: Chief Master Sergeant Ramon Colon-Lopez". Jan 2013. Retrieved 1 May 2013.

[26] Stars and Stripes

[27] Dept of Defense

[28] http://www.37trw.af.mil/library/biographies/bio_print.asp?bioID=14941&page=1

[29] http://www.afsoc.af.mil/AboutUs/Biographies/Display/tabid/141/Article/495021/colonel-robert-g-armfield.aspx

[30] http://www.24sow.af.mil/AboutUs/Biographies/Display/tabid/141/Article/499972/colonel-matthew-wolfe-davidson.aspx

9.7   Further reading

- Col John T. Carney Jr.; Benjamin F. Schemmer (2003). *No Room for Error: The Covert Operations of America's Special Tactics Units from Iran To Afghanistan*. Presidio Press. ISBN 978-0345453358.

9.8   External links

- 24th globalsecurity.org
- findarticles.com

Chapter 10

Flight Concepts Division

The **US Army's Flight Concepts Division** is a special force of the United States Army that executes aviation operations.[1][2]

10.1   References

[1] Emerson, Steven. *Secret Warriors.*

[2] Seymour M. Hersh (22 November 1987). "Who's In Charge Here?". *New York Times.* Retrieved 24 October 2010.

Chapter 11

427th Special Operations Squadron

Not to be confused with 427 Special Operations Aviation Squadron.

The **427th Special Operations Squadron** (427th SOS) is a possible un-adknowledged unit of the United States Air Force. The squadron appears to be a clandestine unit not listed by the Air Force Historical Research Agency.[1] It is reported by the press to be stationed at Pope Air Force Base, North Carolina.[2]

The squadron was originally formed during World War II as the **427th Night Fighter Squadron**. Its planned mission to defend United States Army Air Force bases in the Soviet Union was cancelled when the Soviets did not allow the unit to be based in Ukraine SSR during the Operation Frantic shuttle bombing missions that took place in 1944. It later served in Italy, India, Southern China and Burma as a P-61 Black Widow night fighter interceptor squadron.

The squadron was re-activated during the Vietnam War to train South Vietnamese Air Force pilots in using the Cessna A-37 Dragonfly in counter-insurgency operations. Its most recent activation may involve counter-insurgency and counter-terrorist operations as part of Air Force Special Operations Command.[2]

11.1 Mission

The 427th SOS is a clandestine unit which the Air Force discloses little information about. According to news reports about the organization it may provide Short Takeoff/Landing (STOL) and tactically qualified crews to support training requirements for the US Army Special Operations Forces (SOF) community. It may support the US Army Special Operations Command (USASOC), The US Army Special Forces Command (USASFC), and the John F Kennedy Special Warfare Center (JFKSWCS).[2]

It is believed that the 427th SOS provides US Army SOF personnel the opportunity to train on various types of aircraft for infiltration and exfiltration that they may encounter in the lesser developed countries in which they provide training. If this is factual, then the 427th SOS aircrews must be proficient in smaller types of aircraft in order to familiarize US Army personnel with their characteristics, peculiarities, and capabilities.[2]

The Army's 160th SOAR (A) uses rotary wing platforms (MH-60, MH-47, MH-6/AH-6). AFSOC primarily uses fixed-wing aircraft (MC-130, AC-130, CASA-212) with the exception of its MH-53's & CV-22's. The 427th likely uses non-standard airframes that are usually found in 3d world or former eastern block nations.[2]

11.2 History

The **427th Night Fighter Squadron** was formed at Hammer Field, California, where its crews were trained. The squadron also flew training missions in the Bakersfield area. With their training as a unit completed, personnel of the 427th NFS packed their bags and left California's sunny San Joaquin Valley in mid-July 1944. Initially traveling by ship from the east coast to Casablanca, French Morocco. Once the squadrons' planes were assembled and checked out, the unit flew east to Cairo, Egypt, where they expected orders for Poltava Airfield, Ukraine on the Soviet Eastern Front.[3]

11.2.1 The Russian Front and the Mediterranean

The expected mission on the Russian Front was to provide night fighter escort and air defense for Eighth and Fifteenth Air Force B-17 Flying Fortress bombers on "shuttle" missions from their bases in England and Italy to targets in Eastern Europe as part of Operation Frantic. However, a Luftwaffe night attack on the Soviet Air Force bases where the bombers landed in Ukraine on 21 June 1944 created mass havoc and destroyed many aircraft on the ground. The Soviets refused to allow USAAF night fighters to defend the bomber bases, insisting that air defense was their responsibility, the 427th's orders to Poltava were scrubbed.[3]

Instead, the 427th NFS was to join the four Bristol Beaufighter-equipped night fighter squadrons of the Twelfth Air Force in the Mediterranean area. After about a week's stay in Cairo, the air echelon departed and arrived at the 19th Replacement Depot outside Naples, Italy. Their new assignment was to provide night air defense from Pomigliano Airfield, which started upon their arrival on 3 September. Their stay was short, as on 20 September the 427th was given orders to relocate to the China-Burma-India Theater of Operations and join the Tenth Air Force in India.[3]

Although the 427th was in operation in the Naples area for less than three weeks, it was able to fly a number of missions and had contacts with Luftwaffe reconnaissance aircraft from northern Italy. On one of these missions, a radar malfunction experienced just before coming into firing range prevented possible destruction of the German aircraft. On the other mission in which contact was made, the attack was cut short when the Naples antiaircraft defenses tried to help and nearly shot down the 427th's P-61.[3]

11.2.2 China-Burma-India Theater

427th Night Fighter Squadron P-61 Black Widows arriving at Calcutta, India, 1944

Arriving in India, the squadron cooperated closely with the 426th NFS. The 426th, with only four operational Black Widows, needed additional aircraft for their Chengtu, China operations. A deal was struck between the COs of the two squadrons in which the 427th would give the 426th eight of its twelve aircraft in exchange for the 426th's aircraft at the depot at Karachi, where two were assembled and six were being assembled. At this time the 427th was assigned to Pandaveswar Airfield in West Bengal.[3]

On 28 November another contingent of the 427th NFS arrived at Myitkyina Airfield, Burma. More of the squadron arrived during December, basically by truck over the Ledo Road from their headquarters in India to prepare Myitkyina as the squadron's new headquarters where they would remain until May 1945.[3]

During December, the 427th's small detachment of three P-61s at Myitkyina saw all there was of aerial "action." They participated in seventeen combat missions. Three were patrols ordered by higher headquarters, two were due to enemy aircraft in the area.[3]

Northrop P-61A-10-NO Black Widow 42-5628 of the 427th Night Fighter Squadron in flight over Northern Burma, 1944

On 25 December 1944 a detachment of the 427th NFS arrived at Kunming airport, China, relieving the 426th's detachment, although the bulk of the squadron remained in Burma. During January 1945, they flew patrols over Myitkyina and Bhamo and twelve local tactical interceptions. No enemy aircraft was encountered. Unfortunately for the 427th, one of those misfortunes of war occurred. On 22 January one of its aircraft in the China detachment operating out of Suichwan Airfield in southeast China shot down a US C-87 (a transport version of the Liberator bomber) with a crew of nine. The C-87 was in a prohibited area and made no radio calls, which led to the conclusion that it was hostile.[3]

From this point on, Japanese night flying nearly ceased. The 427th flew more and more night intruder missions. It modified its aircraft to carry a three-tube bazooka-type rocket launcher under each wing. With its rocket-carrying P-61s, it operated against Japanese forces from its bases at Myitkyina in Burma as well as Kunming in China.[3]

The 427th NFS intruder missions started on 22 February with a sweep of the road network south of Lashio, Burma. The squadron flew seven night intruder sorties that month. In mid-March, day and night offensive reconnaissance missions covering Pangkeyhtu/Loi-lem/Ho-pong/Namsang road network. Thirty-three-day and night patrols were accomplished that month. Missions planned to originate from Kunming and Chihkiang Airfield were curtailed in April because of a shortage of fuel.[3]

Squadron headquarters moved from Burma to Kisselbarri, near Dinjan, India, in late May. The detachment at Kunming China remained there, operating elements from Dinjan Airfield, India; Chengkung and Nanning Airport in China until the war's end. Activity increased in July, with the squadron claiming 155 sampans destroyed and fifty-two damaged in addition to numerous warehouses, barges, trains and trucks destroyed. Besides flying day and night intruder sorties, two special medical supply airdrop sorties were flown in a BT-13 Valiant aircraft.[3]

On 13 August 1945, the 427th was ordered to move to Liuchow Airfield, China. The air echelon flew there immediately while the ground echelon began the movement by road. With the war over, the air echelon was ordered to fly to Yangkai Airfield, China, to turn in their aircraft for 'pickling' (preparation for storage) and start processing home. All aircraft were turned in at Yangkai on 29 August. The 427th Night Fighter Squadron was inactivated on 13 October 1945.[3]

11.2.3   Vietnam War

Cessna OA-37B

The **427th Special Operations Training Squadron** was with Tactical Air Command, being assigned to England Air Force Base, Louisiana on 1 July 1970. The squadron's mission was to provide transition training to South Vietnamese Air Force pilots for the OA-37B Dragonfly counterinsurgency aircraft to combat guerrilla type activity. The standard A-37 aircraft was fitted with a refueling probe in the nose; reticulated foam was added to the self-sealing fuel tanks to protect against fire or explosions if hit by incendiary anti-aircraft rounds. The cockpit was armor-plated and the undercarriage was strengthened to carry greater weight and to enable the aircraft to operate off rough remote airstrips.[4]

The squadron was inactivated on 15 July 1972.[5]

11.2.4 Lineage

Emblem of the 427th Night Fighter Squadron, World War II

- Constituted as the **427th Night Fighter Squadron** on 19 January 1944

  Activated on 1 February 1944
  Inactivated on 29 October 1945[5]

- Activated and Re-designated as the **427th Special Operations Training Squadron** on 1 July 1970

  Inactivated 15 July 1972

- Activated and Re-designated as the **427th Special Operations Squadron**, undetermined

11.2.5 Assignments

- Fourth Air Force

  IV Fighter Command

    Attached to 481st Night Fighter Operational Training Group, 1 February 1944

- Tenth Air Force, 11 June 1944
- Twelfth Air Force

  Attached to 62nd Fighter Wing, September 1944

- Army Air Forces India-Burma Sector, 2 October 1944
- Tenth Air Force, 13 December 1944
- Fourteenth Air Force, 24 August – 29 October 1945[5]
- Tactical Air Command

  4410th Special Operations Training Group, 1 July 1970 – 15 July 1972

- Air Force Special Operations Command, (date undetermined)

11.2.6 Stations

11.2.7 Aircraft

11.3 See also

- 481st Night Fighter Operational Training Group

11.4 References

This article incorporates public domain material from websites or documents of the Air Force Historical Research Agency.

[1] Email from AFHRA 2 June 2014 stating their office has no record of the 427th Special Operations Squadron

[2] The USAF's Most Secretive Squadron 427th Special Operations Squadron

[3] Northrop P-61 Black Widow—The Complete History and Combat Record, Garry R. Pape, John M. Campbell and Donna Campbell, Motorbooks International, 1991.

[4] Darling. Kevin (2005) Tweet and the Dragonfly the Story of the Cessna A-37 and T-37, Lulu.com, ISBN 1411647483

[5] Maurer, Maurer, ed. (1982) [1969]. *Combat Squadrons of the Air Force, World War II* (PDF) (reprint ed.). Washington, DC: Office of Air Force History. ISBN 0-405-12194-6. LCCN 70605402. OCLC 72556.

11.5 External links

Chapter 12

Joint Communications Unit

The **Joint Communications Unit** (JCU) is a technical unit of the SOCOM charged to standardize and ensure interoperability of communication procedures and equipment of the Joint Special Operations Command (JSOC) and its subordinate units. The JCU was activated at Ft. Bragg, NC in 1980, after the failure of Operation Eagle Claw. The JCU has earned the reputation of "DoD's Finest Communicators."

12.1   External links

- Joint Communications Unit;

- JSOC's Joint Communication Unit (JCU) on SpecWarNet

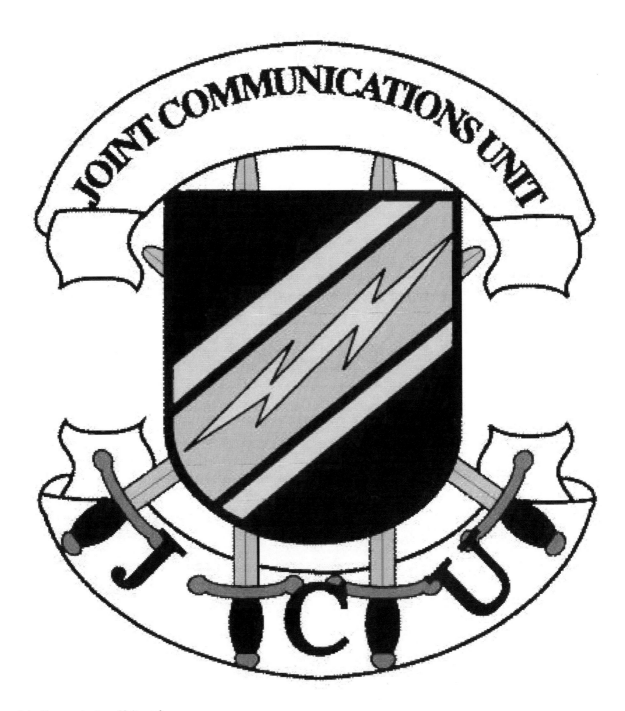

Joint Communications Unit patch

Chapter 13

United States Army Special Operations Command

Not to be confused with United States Special Operations Command or United States Army Special Forces Command.

The **United States Army Special Operations Command** (Airborne) (**USASOC**) is the command charged with overseeing the various special operations forces of the United States Army. Headquartered at Fort Bragg, NC, it is the largest component of the United States Special Operations Command. Its mission is to organize, train, educate, man, equip, fund, administer, mobilize, deploy and sustain Army special operations forces to successfully conduct worldwide special operations.

13.1 Subordinate units

13.1.1 U.S. Army Special Forces Command (Airborne)

Established in 1952, the United States Army Special Forces Command (Airborne), also known as the Green Berets, are a special operations force of the United States Army tasked with five primary missions: unconventional warfare, foreign internal defense, special reconnaissance, direct action, and counter-terrorism. These missions make Special Forces unique in the U.S. military, because they are employed throughout the three stages of the operational continuum: peacetime, conflict and war.[4]

Special Forces Command's unconventional warfare capabilities provide a viable military option for a variety of operational taskings that are inappropriate or infeasible for conventional forces, making it the U.S. military's premier unconventional warfare force.[4]

Foreign Internal Defense operations, SF's main peacetime mission, are designed to help friendly developing nations by working with their military and police forces to improve their technical skills, understanding of human rights issues, and to help with humanitarian and civic action projects.[4]

Often SF units are required to perform additional, or collateral, activities outside their primary missions. These collateral activities are coalition warfare/support, combat search and rescue, security assistance, peacekeeping, humanitarian assistance, humanitarian de-mining and counter-drug operations.[4]

Coalition warfare/support emerged as a result of Operation Desert Shield/Desert Storm and continues today in both Operation Iraqi Freedom and Operation Enduring Freedom. This activity ensures the ability of a wide variety of foreign troops to work together effectively in a wide variety of military exercises or operations.[4]

13.1.2 75th Ranger Regiment

The 75th Ranger Regiment, also known as the Rangers, is a light infantry special operations force. The regiment is headquartered at Fort Benning, Georgia and is composed of one special troops battalion and three light infantry special operations battalions with specialized skills that enable them to perform a variety of special operations missions.

The 75th Ranger Regiment is capable of executing a myriad of complex, joint special operations missions in support of U.S. policy and objectives. Their capabilities include air assault and direct action raids seizing key terrain such as airfields, and destroying strategic facilities. Rangers are capable of conducting squad through regimental size operations using a variety of infiltration techniques including airborne, air assault and ground platforms. The regiment is an all-volunteer force with an intensive screening and selection process followed by combat-focused training. Rangers are resourced to maintain exceptional proficiency, experience and readiness.[5]

13.1.3 U.S. Army Special Operations Aviation Command

The U.S. Army Special Operations Aviation Command (ARSOAC), activated on 25 March 2011, organizes, mans, trains, resources and equips Army special operations aviation units to provide responsive, special operations aviation support to Special Operations Forces (SOF) and is the USASOC aviation staff proponent.[6]

During the past decade of persistent engagement by SOF, USASOC aviation experts recognized a need for separating the combat role of Army SOF aviation from the resourcing responsibilities. This structure provides the appropriate command and control, manning and visibility for the complex and sensitive tasks required of Army SOF aviation units and organizations. ARSOAC is a one-star, subordinate command to USASOC.[6]

The 160th Special Operations Aviation Regiment (Airborne), ["Death Waits In The Dark"] newly subordinate to ARSOAC,[7] provides aviation support to special operations forces. Known as Night Stalkers, these soldiers are recognized for their proficiency in nighttime operations. Soldiers of the 160th pioneered the Army's nighttime flying techniques. The unit became known as the Night Stalkers because of its capability to strike undetected during the hours of darkness and its unprecedented combat successes. Today, Night Stalkers continue to develop and employ new technology and tactics, techniques and procedures for the battlefield. They employ highly modified Chinook, Black Hawk and assault and attack configurations of Little Bird helicopters.[8]

The 160th SOAR(A) is composed of a regiment headquarters, four battalions and a dedicated training company. The regiment headquarters is collocated with the 1st and 2nd Battalions and the Special Operations Aviation Training Company at Fort Campbell, Kentucky; 3rd Battalion is located at Hunter Army Airfield, Georgia; and 4th Battalion is located at Fort Lewis, Washington. This strategic organizational structure postures the regiment to support special operations forces mission and training requirements well into the future.[8] NSDQ - "Night Stalkers Don't Quit"

Soldiers of the 160th have been actively and continuously engaged in the combat operations since October 2001. Today, the 160th Special Operations Aviation Regiment (Airborne) continues a sustained and active forward presence in the U.S. Central Command area of operations at multiple locations in support of operations Enduring Freedom. Crews also provide support to U.S. Southern, Pacific, Africa, and European commands.[8]

13.1.4 Military Information Support Operations Command (Airborne) (Provisional)

The mission of the Military Information Support Operations Command (Airborne) (Provisional) (MISOC) Psychological Operations (PSYOP) units is to provide fully capable strategic influence forces to Combatant Commanders, U.S. Ambassadors, and other agencies to synchronize plans and execute inform and influence activities (IIA) across the range of military operations. PSYOP is composed of two subordinate groups, the 4th Psychological Operations Group (Airborne), the 8th Military Psychological Operations Group (Airborne), and the 3rd Psychological Operations Battalion (Airborne); which provides state of the art trans media reach back support to the other two PSYOP groups.[9]

Psychological Operations is a part of the broad range of U.S. political, military, economic and ideological activities used by the U.S. government to secure national objectives. Used during peacetime, contingencies and declared war these activities are not forms of force, but are force multipliers that use nonviolent means in often violent environments. Persuading rather than compelling physically, they rely on logic, fear, desire or other mental factors to promote specific emotions, attitudes or behaviors.[9]

The ultimate objective of U.S. PSYOP is to convince enemy, neutral, and friendly nations and forces to take action favorable to the United States and its allies. The ranks of the PSYOP include regional experts and linguists who understand political, cultural, ethnic and religious subtleties and use persuasion to influence perceptions and encourage desired behavior. With functional experts in all aspects of tactical communications, PSYOP offers joint force commanders unmatched abilities to influence target audiences as well as strategic influence capabilities to U.S. diplomacy.[9]

In addition to supporting commanders, PSYOP units provide interagency strategic influence capabilities to other U.S. government agencies. In operations ranging from humanitarian assistance to drug interdiction, PSYOP enhances the impact of those agencies' actions. Their activities can be used to spread information about ongoing programs and to gain support from the local populace.[9]

13.1.5   95th Civil Affairs Brigade (Airborne)

The 95th Civil Affairs Brigade (Airborne) enable military commanders and U.S. Ambassadors to improve relationships with various stakeholders in a local area to meet the objectives of the U.S. government. 95th Civil Affairs Brigade (Airborne) teams work with U.S. Department of State country teams, government and nongovernmental organizations at all levels and with local populations in peaceful, contingency and hostile environments. 95th Civil Affairs Brigade (Airborne) units can rapidly deploy to remote areas with small villages, as well as to larger population centers around the world.[10]

They help host nations assess the needs of an area, bring together local and non-local resources to ensure long-term stability, and ultimately degrade and defeat violent extremist organizations and their ideologies. They may be involved in disaster prevention, management, and recovery, and with human and civil infrastructure assistance programs.[10]

95th Civil Affairs Brigade (Airborne) soldiers are soldiers first, but are adept at working in foreign environments and conversing in one of about 20 foreign languages with local stakeholders. Brigade teams may work for months or years in remote areas of a host nation. Their low profile and command structure allow them to solidify key relationships and processes, to address root causes of instability that adversely affect the strategic interests of the United States.[10]

13.1.6   528th Sustainment Brigade (Airborne)

The 528th Sustainment Brigade (Airborne) is responsible for providing logistical, medical and signal support for Army special operations forces worldwide in support of contingency missions and war fighting commanders.[11]

Headquartered at Fort Bragg, North Carolina, the 528th Sustainment Brigade (Airborne) sets the operational level logistics conditions to enable Army Special Operation Forces (ARSOF) operations worldwide using three ARSOF Support Operations Teams (ASPOs), three Special Operations Resuscitation Teams (SORT), five ARSOF Liaison Elements (ALE), two Medical Level II teams and 112th Special Operations Signal Battalion (Airborne). Together the units of the brigade ensure that U.S. Army Special Operations Forces are equipped to perform their missions.[11]

The brigade has the capability of providing technical control to multiple Special Forces group support battalions in the planning and execution of ARSOF combat service support and combat health support. The 528th Sustainment Brigade (Airborne) is capable of deploying three Army Support Operations Teams in support of three ARSOF-based Special Operations Task Forces or a SOF-based JTF. The Support Operations Team initially co-locates with the group support battalion or a Ranger support operations detachment and provides ARSOF with an in-theater presence providing centralized and integrated material management of property, equipment maintenance, logistical automation and repair parts and supplies.[11]

ARSOF Liaison Elements soldiers are embedded in Army regional theaters' staff. They plan and coordinate with theater Army, Special Operations Command and Army Special Operations Command to ensure support during operations and training. As a theater Army staff member, these officers and non-commissioned officers' knowledge of theater-specific requirements and capabilities assist units in coordination with the theater.[11]

The medical section provides Level II medical support as USASOC asset managed by the brigade surgeon and constitutes the nucleus of the capability of receiving a conventional Army Forward Surgical Team. The medical section is robust enough to provide combat health support on an area basis for approximately 450 personnel. The support includes unit-level medical support and health services, logistics, emergency medical and resuscitative treatment for all classes of patients; emergency dental treatment, physical therapy and preventive medicine support, while maintaining Standard Army Management Information Systems and providing veterinary support.[11][12]

Members of the 112th Special Operations Signal Battalion (Airborne) specialize in communication and force sustainment skills, employing innovative telecommunications technologies to provide Army Special Operations Task Force commanders with secure and nonsecure voice, data and video services. In their respective fields, signal and support soldiers provide oversight of material distribution management, synchronization, and integrated material management of property accountability, maintenance management and logistics automation for deployed ARSOF. Communications expertise allows ARSOF to "shoot, move and communicate" on a continuous basis. Soldiers assigned to ARSOF units are taught to operate and maintain a vast array of unique equipment not normally used by their conventional counterparts. To meet the needs of ARSOF, the Sustainment Brigade has developed logistical and signal packages that are rapidly deployable on a moment's notice. Soldiers assigned to these units are airborne qualified.[11]

The 528th Sustainment Brigade embodies its motto of "We Support to the Utmost," providing the means to effectively and efficiently execute logistics in support of ARSOF operations.[11]

13.1.7   U.S. Army John F. Kennedy Special Warfare Center and School

The U.S. Army John F. Kennedy Special Warfare Center and School (SWCS) at Fort Bragg, North Carolina, is one of the Army's premier education institutions, managing and resourcing professional growth for soldiers in the Army's three distinct special-operations branches: Special Forces, Civil Affairs and Psychological Operations. The soldiers educated through SWCS programs are using cultural expertise and unconventional techniques to serve their country in far-flung areas across the globe. More than anything, these soldiers bring integrity, adaptability and regional expertise to their assignments.[13]

On any given day, approximately 3,100 students are enrolled in SWCS training programs. Courses range from entry-level training to advanced warfighter skills for seasoned officers and NCOs. The 1st Special Warfare Training Group (Airborne) qualifies soldiers to enter the special-operations community, and teaches them advanced tactical skills as they progress through their careers. The Joint Special Operations Medical Training Center, operating under the auspices of the Special Warfare Medical Group, is the central training facility for Department of Defense special-operations combat medics. Furthermore, SWCS leads efforts to professionalize the Army's entire special-operations force through the Special Forces Warrant Officer Institute and the David K. Thuma Noncommissioned Officer Academy. While most courses are conducted at Fort Bragg, SWCS enhances its training by maintaining facilities, and relationships with outside institutions, across the country.[13]

13.2   List of commanders

- LTG Peter Schoomaker, October 1996 – 1997[14]

- LTG William Tangney, 1997 – 11 October 2000

- LTG Bryan D. Brown, 11 October 2000 – 29 August 2002

- LTG Philip R. Kensinger, Jr., 29 August 2002 – 8 December 2005

- LTG Robert W. Wagner, 8 December 2005 – 7 November 2008

- LTG John F. Mulholland, Jr., 7 November 2008 – 24 July 2012[15]

- LTG Charles T. Cleveland, 24 July 2012 – 1 July 2015

- LTG Kenneth E. Tovo, 1 July 2015 – present[16]

13.3   References

[1] *SOCOM Fact Book 2014* (PDF). SOCOM Public Affairs. 2014. Retrieved 2015-12-17.

[2] *SOCOM Fact Book 2015* (PDF). SOCOM Public Affairs. 2015. Retrieved 2015-12-17.

[3]

[4] *U.S. Army Special Forces Command*. *Soc.mil*. Retrieved 2015-12-17.

[5] *75th ranger Regiment*. *Soc.mil*. Retrieved 2015-12-17.

[6]

[7] "Night Stalkers mark new lineage with donning of USASOAC patch | Article | The United States Army". *Army.mil*. 2013-10-03. Retrieved 2015-12-17.

[8] *160th SOAR(A) Overview*. *Soc.mil*. Retrieved 2015-12-17.

[9] "MISOC Units Re-designate as PSYOP – ShadowSpear Special Operations". *Shadowspear.com*. 2015-12-13. Retrieved 2015-12-17.

[10] *95th Civil Affairs Brigade*. *Soc.mil*. Retrieved 2015-12-17.

[11] *528th Sustainment Brigade*. *Soc.mil*. Retrieved 2015-12-17.

[12] Jamie Riesberg (2009). "The Special Operations Resuscitation Team: Robust Role II Medical Support for Today's SOF Environment" (PDF). *Journal of Special Operations Medicine* **9**. Retrieved 2014-01-26.

[13] *About SWCS*. *Soc.mil*. Retrieved 2015-12-17.

[14] "Peter Jan Schoomaker". *History.army.mil*. Retrieved 2015-12-17.

[15]

[16] "USASOC welcomes Tovo as Commanding General". *Army.mil*. 2 July 2015l. Retrieved 2015-12-17.

13.4   External links

- U.S. Army Special Operations Command—official site

U.S. Army Special Forces Shoulder Sleeve Insignia (SSI)

75th Ranger Regiment Shoulder Sleeve Insignia

ARSOAC SSI

USASOC patch.

95th Civil Affairs Brigade (Airborne) SSI

528th Sustainment Brigade (Airborne) SSI

SWCS SSI

Chapter 14

Special Forces (United States Army)

"Green Berets" redirects here. For other uses, see Green Berets (disambiguation).

The **United States Army Special Forces,** known as the **Green Berets** because of their distinctive service headgear, are a special operations force tasked with five primary missions: unconventional warfare (the original and most important mission of Special Forces), foreign internal defense, special reconnaissance, direct action, and counter-terrorism. The first two emphasize language, cultural, and training skills in working with foreign troops. Other duties include combat search and rescue (CSAR), counter-narcotics, counter-proliferation, hostage rescue, humanitarian assistance, humanitarian demining, information operations, peacekeeping, psychological operations, security assistance, and manhunts; other components of the United States Special Operations Command (USSOCOM) or other U.S. government activities may also specialize in these secondary areas.[3] Many of their operational techniques are classified, but some nonfiction works[4] and doctrinal manuals are available.[5][6][7]

As special operations units, Special Forces are not necessarily under the command authority of the ground commanders in those countries. Instead, while in theater, SF units may report directly to a geographic combatant command, USSOCOM, or other command authorities. The Central Intelligence Agency's (CIA) highly secretive Special Activities Division (SAD) and more specifically its Special Operations Group (SOG) recruits from the Army's Special Forces.[8] Joint CIA-Army Special Forces operations go back to the MACV-SOG branch during the Vietnam War.[9] The cooperation still exists today and is seen in the War in Afghanistan.[10][11]

14.1 Mission

The primary mission of the Army Special Forces is to train and lead unconventional warfare (UW) forces, or a clandestine guerrilla force in an occupied nation. The 10th Special Forces Group was the first deployed SF unit, intended to train and lead UW forces behind enemy lines in the event of a Warsaw Pact invasion of Western Europe. As the U.S. became involved in Southeast Asia, it was realized that specialists trained to lead guerrillas could also help defend against hostile guerrillas, so SF acquired the additional mission of Foreign Internal Defense (FID), working with Host Nation (HN) forces in a spectrum of counter-guerrilla activities from indirect support to combat command.

Special Forces personnel qualify both in advanced military skills and the regional languages and cultures of defined parts of the world. While they are best known for their unconventional warfare capabilities, they also undertake other missions that include direct action raids, peace operations, counter-proliferation, counter-drug advisory roles, and other strategic missions.[12] As strategic resources, they report either to USSOCOM or to a regional Unified Combatant Command. To enhance their DA capability, specific Commanders In-Extremis Force (CIF) teams were created with a focus on the direct action side of special operations.[13]

SF team members work closely together and rely on one another under isolated circumstances for long periods of time, both during extended deployments and in garrison. Because of this, they develop clannish relationships and long-standing personal ties. SF non-commissioned officers (NCO) often spend their entire careers in Special Forces, rotating among

U.S. Army Special Forces soldiers from the 3rd Special Forces Group patrol a field in the Gulistan district of Farah, Afghanistan

assignments to detachments, higher staff billets, liaison positions, and instructor duties at the U.S. Army John F. Kennedy Special Warfare Center and School (USAJFKSWCS). They are then required to move to staff positions or to higher command echelons. With the creation of USSOCOM, SF commanders have risen to the highest ranks of U.S. Army command, including command of USSOCOM, the Army's Chief of Staff, and the Chairman of the Joint Chiefs of Staff.[14]

14.2 History

Main article: History of the United States Army Special Forces
Special Forces traces its roots as the Army's premier proponent of unconventional warfare from purpose-formed special operations units like the Alamo Scouts, Philippine guerrillas, First Special Service Force, and the Operational Groups (OGs) of the Office of Strategic Services. Although the OSS was not an Army organization, many Army personnel were assigned to the OSS and later used their experiences to influence the forming of Special Forces.

During the Korean War, individuals such as former Philippine guerrilla commanders Col. Wendell Fertig and Lt. Col. Russell W. Volckmann used their wartime experience to formulate the doctrine of unconventional warfare that became the cornerstone of the Special Forces.[15][16]

In 1951, Major General Robert A. McClure chose former OSS member Colonel Aaron Bank as Operations Branch Chief of the Special Operations Division of the Psychological Warfare Staff (OCPW) in the Pentagon.[17]

In June 1952, the 10th Special Forces Group (Airborne) was formed under Col. Aaron Bank, soon after the establishment of the Psychological Warfare School, which ultimately became today's John F. Kennedy Special Warfare Center and School. The 10th Special Forces Group (Airborne) deployed to Bad Tolz, Germany, in September 1953. The remaining cadre at Fort Bragg formed the 77th Special Forces Group, which in May 1960 became today's 7th Special Forces Group.[18]

Since their establishment in 1952, Special Forces soldiers have operated in Vietnam, El Salvador, Panama, Haiti, Somalia, Bosnia, Kosovo, Afghanistan, Iraq, the Philippines, and, in an FID role, Operation Enduring Freedom – Horn of Africa, which was transferred to United States Africa Command in 2008.

ODA 525 team picture taken shortly before infiltration in Iraq, February 1991

14.3   Organizational structure

14.3.1   Special Forces groups

In 1957 the two original special forces groups (10th and 77th) were joined by the 1st, stationed in the Far East. Additional groups were formed in 1961 and 1962 after President John F. Kennedy visited the Special Forces at Fort Bragg in 1961. Nine groups were organized for the reserve components in 1961. (Tsouras, 1994, 91). Among them were the 16th and 17th Special Forces Groups. However, 17th Special Forces Group, a National Guard formation with elements in Washington, was disestablished on 31 January 1966.

In the early twenty-first century, Special Forces are divided into five active duty (AD) and two Army National Guard (ARNG) Special Forces groups. Each Special Forces Group (SFG) has a specific regional focus. The Special Forces soldiers assigned to these groups receive intensive language and cultural training for countries within their regional area of responsibility (AOR).[19] Due to the increased need for Special Forces soldiers in the War on Terror, all Groups— including those of the National Guard (19th and 20th SFGs)—have been deployed outside of their areas of operation (AOs), particularly to Iraq and Afghanistan. A recently released report showed Special Forces as perhaps the most deployed SOF under USSOCOM, with many soldiers, regardless of Group, serving up to 75% of their careers overseas, almost all of which had been to Iraq and Afghanistan.

Until recently an SF group has consisted of three battalions, but since the Department of Defense has authorized U.S. Army Special Forces Command to increase its authorized strength by one third, a fourth battalion was activated in each active component group by 2012.

- Current structure of the 1st SFG(A)

- Current structure of the 3rd SFG(A)

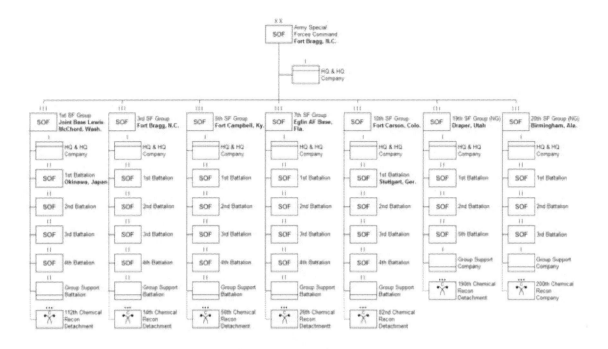

Structure of United States Army Special Forces Command

Soldiers from each of the Army's seven Special Forces groups at the gravesite of President John F. Kennedy in November 2011.

- Current structure of the 5th SFG(A)

Soldiers from the 7th Special Forces Group

- Current structure of the 7th SFG(A)

- Current structure of the 10th SFG(A)

- Current structure of the 20th NG SFG(A)

A Special Forces group is historically assigned to a Unified Combatant Command or a theater of operations. The Special Forces Operational Detachment C or C-detachment (SFODC) is responsible for a theater or a major subcomponent, which can provide command and control of up to 18 SFODAs, three SFODB, or a mixture of the two. Subordinate to it are the Special Forces Operational Detachment Bs or B-detachments (SFODB), which can provide command and control for six SFODAs. Further subordinate, the SFODAs typically raise company- to battalion-sized units when on unconventional warfare missions. They can form 6-man "split A" detachments that are often used for special reconnaissance.

14.3.2   Battalion HQ Element – SF Operational Detachment-C (SFODC) composition

The SFODC, or "C-Team", is the headquarters element of a Special Forces battalion. As such, it is a command and control unit with operations, training, signals and logistic support responsibilities to its three subordinate line companies. A lieutenant colonel (O-5) commands the battalion and the C-Team and the battalion Command Sergeant Major (E-9) is the senior NCO of the battalion and the C-Team. There are an additional 20–30 SF personnel who fill key positions in operations, logistics, intelligence, communications and medical. A Special Forces battalion usually consists of four companies: "A", "B", "C", and Headquarters/Support.

A Special Forces company commander meets with village elders and members of the 209th ANA Corps in Helmand Province, Afghanistan, 2007.

14.3.3 Company HQ Element – SF Operational Detachment-B (SFODB) composition

The ODB, or "B-Team", is the headquarters element of a Special Forces company, and it is usually composed of 11–13 soldiers. While the A-team typically conducts direct operations, the purpose of the B-Team is to support the company's A-Teams both in garrison and in the field. When deployed, in line with their support role, B-Teams are usually found in more secure rear areas. However, under some circumstances a B-Team will deploy into a hostile area, usually to coordinate the activities of multiple A-Teams.

The ODB is led by an 18A, usually a major, who is the company commander (CO). The CO is assisted by his company executive officer (XO), another 18A, usually a captain. The XO is himself assisted by a company technician, a 180A, generally a chief warrant officer three, who assists in the direction of the organization, training, intelligence, counter-intelligence, and operations for the company and its detachments. The company commander is assisted by the company sergeant major, an 18Z, usually a Sergeant Major. A second 18Z acts as the operations sergeant, usually a Master Sergeant, who assists the XO and technician in their operational duties. He has an 18F assistant operations sergeant, who is usually a Sergeant First Class. The company's support comes from an 18D medical sergeant, usually a Sergeant First Class, and two 18E communications sergeants, usually a Sergeant First Class and a Staff Sergeant.

The following jobs are outside of the Special Forces 18-series career management field (CMF), but hold positions on a Special Forces B-Team. Soldiers in these positions are not "Special Forces qualified", as they have not completed the Special Forces Qualification Course (SFQC or "Q" Course); however, they do have the potential to be awarded the Special Qualification Identifier (SQI) "S" (Special Operations / Special Operations Support) once they complete the appropriate unit level training, 24 months with their Special Forces unit, and Basic Airborne School:

- The supply NCO, usually a Staff Sergeant, the commander's principal logistical planner, works with the battalion S-4 to supply the company.

- The Chemical, Biological, Radiological, Nuclear (CBRN defence) NCO, usually a Sergeant, maintains and operates the company's NBC detection and decontamination equipment, and assists in administering NBC defensive measures.[20]

- Other jobs can also exist depending on the B-Team structure. Specialist team members can include I.T. (S-6) personnel, and Military Intelligence Soldiers, including Intelligence Analysts (35F), Human Intelligence Collectors (35M), Signals Intelligence (35 N/P - also known as SOT-A and SOT-B as related to their positions on SFODA and SFODB teams), Intelligence Officers (35 D/E/F), and Counterintelligence Special Agents (35L/351L).

14.3.4 Basic Element – SF Operational Detachment-A (SFODA) composition

A Special Forces company normally consists of six ODAs (Operational Detachments-Alpha) or "A-Teams".[21][22] Each ODA specializes in an infiltration skill or a particular mission-set (e.g. Military Freefall (HALO), combat diving, mountain warfare, maritime operations, etc.). An ODA is identified by its group, battalion, company, and the team itself. For example, ODA 1234 would be the fourth team in the third company of the second battalion of 1st Special Forces Group.

An ODA consists of 12 men, each of whom has a specific function (MOS or Military Occupational Specialty) on the team, however all members of an ODA conduct cross-training. The ODA is led by an 18A (Detachment Commander), a Captain, and a 180A (Assistant Detachment Commander) who is his second in command, usually a Warrant Officer One or Chief Warrant Officer Two. The team also includes the following enlisted men: one 18Z (Operations Sergeant) (known as the "Team Sergeant"), usually a Master Sergeant, one 18F (Assistant Operations and Intelligence Sergeant), usually a Sergeant First Class, and two each, 18Bs (Weapons Sergeant), 18Cs (Engineer Sergeant), 18Ds (Medical Sergeant), and 18Es (Communications Sergeant), usually Sergeants First Class, Staff Sergeants or Sergeants. This organization facilitates 6-man "split team" operations, redundancy, and mentoring between a senior NCO and his junior assistant.

14.4 Qualifications

The basic eligibility requirements to be considered for entry into the Special Forces are:

- Be a male, age 20–30.[23]
- Be a U.S. citizen.
- Be a high school graduate.
- Score a General Technical score of 110 or higher and a combat operation score of 98 on the Armed Services Vocational Aptitude Battery.
- Airborne qualified or volunteer for Airborne training
- Achieve a minimum of 60 points on each event and overall minimum score of 240 on the Army Physical Fitness Test.
- Meet medical fitness standards as outlined in SF Physical IAW AR 40-501
- Must successfully complete the Pre-Basic Task list.
- Eligible for a "SECRET" security clearance
- Swim 50m wearing boots and ACUs prior to SFQC
- Must have 20/20 or corrected to 20/20 in both near and distant vision in both eyes.
- One year of college is preferred, but it is not mandatory for enlistment.

14.5 Selection and training

Main article: United States Army Special Forces selection and training
 The Special Forces soldier trains on a regular basis over the course of their entire career. The initial formal training program for entry into Special Forces is divided into four phases collectively known as the Special Forces Qualification

Two Army National Guardsmen from the 2nd Battalion, 19th Special Forces Group check their course with compasses during a training exercise in 2011

Course or, informally, the "Q Course". The length of the Q Course changes depending on the applicant's primary job field within Special Forces and their assigned foreign language capability but will usually last between 55 to 95 weeks. After successfully completing the Special Forces Qualification Course, Special Forces soldiers are then eligible for many advanced skills courses. These include, but are not limited to, the Military Free Fall Parachutist Course (MFF), the Combat Diver Qualification Course and the Special Forces Sniper Course (SFSC).

14.6 Special Forces MOS descriptions

- 18A – Special Forces Officer[24]

- 180A – Special Forces Warrant Officer[25]

- 18B – Special Forces Weapons Sergeant[26]

- 18C – Special Forces Engineer Sergeant[27]

- 18D – Special Forces Medical Sergeant[28]

- 18E – Special Forces Communications Sergeant[29]

- 18F – Special Forces Intelligence Sergeant

- 18X – Special Forces Candidate (Active Duty Enlistment Option)[30]

- 18Z – Special Forces Operations Sergeant

A Special Forces candidate conducts a pre-mission rehearsal with Army ROTC cadets role playing guerilla fighters during ROBIN SAGE.

14.7   Uniforms and insignia

14.7.1   The Green Beret

U.S. Army Special Forces adopted the Green Beret unofficially in 1954 after searching for a piece of headgear that would set them visually apart. Members of the 77th SFG began searching through their accumulated berets and settled on the Rifle Green color of British Rifle Regiments (as opposed to the Lovat Green of the Commandos) from Captain Miguel de la Peña's collection. Captain Frank Dallas had the new beret designed and produced in small numbers for the members of the 10th & 77th Special Forces Groups.[31]

Their new headdress was first worn at a retirement parade at Fort Bragg on 12 June 1955 for Lieutenant General Joseph P. Cleland, the now-former commander of the XVIII Airborne Corps. Onlookers thought that the commandos were a foreign delegation from NATO. In 1956 General Paul D. Adams, the post commander at Fort Bragg, banned the wearing of the distinctive headdress,[32] (although members of the Special Forces continued to wear it surreptitiously [33]). This was reversed on September 25, 1961 by *Department of the Army Message 578636*, which designated the green beret as the exclusive headdress of the Army Special Forces.[34]

In 1961, President John F. Kennedy authorized them for use exclusively by the U.S. Special Forces. Preparing for an 12 October visit to the Special Warfare Center at Fort Bragg, North Carolina, the President sent word to the Center's commander, Colonel William P. Yarborough, for all Special Forces soldiers to wear green berets as part of the event. The President felt that since they had a special mission, Special Forces should have something to set them apart from the

A 7th SFG Special Forces medic in Kandahar Province in September 2008.

rest. In 1962, he called the green beret "a symbol of excellence, a badge of courage, a mark of distinction in the fight for freedom".[31]

Forrest Lindley, a writer for the newspaper *Stars and Stripes* who served with Special Forces in Vietnam said of Kennedy's authorization: "It was President Kennedy who was responsible for the rebuilding of the Special Forces and giving us back our Green Beret. People were sneaking around wearing [them] when conventional forces weren't in the area and it was sort of a cat and mouse game. Then Kennedy authorized the Green Beret as a mark of distinction, everybody had to scramble around to find berets that were really green. We were bringing them down from Canada. Some were handmade, with the dye coming out in the rain".[35]

Special Forces have a special bond with Kennedy, going back to his funeral. At the commemoration of the 25th anniver-

Army Special Forces Soldiers wearing their green berets

sary of JFK's death, General Michael D. Healy, the last commander of Special Forces in Vietnam, spoke at Arlington Cemetery. Later, a wreath in the form of the Green Beret would be placed on the grave, continuing a tradition that began the day of his funeral when a sergeant in charge of a detail of Special Forces men guarding the grave placed his beret on the coffin.[35]

14.7.2   Insignia

On a wreath of the colors (Argent and Sable), two arrows saltire-wise Argent – that is, two silver arrows crossed with a dagger, also silver, above them, surrounded by a black ribbon.

- The beret crest is taken from the gold crossed arrow collar (branch) beret insignia of the First Special Service Force, an American-Canadian commando unit organized in 1942 for World War II. The crest was changed to silver to create visual harmony with the shield, as well as to make a difference from the collar insignia.

- A silver color metal and enamel device 1 $\frac{1}{8}$ inches (2.9 cm) in height consisting of a pair of silver arrows in saltire, points up and surmounted at their junction by a silver dagger with black handle point up; all over and between a black motto scroll arcing to base and inscribed "DE OPPRESSO LIBER" in silver letters. The motto, De oppresso liber, is traditionally but incorrectly thought to mean "To Free the Oppressed". Its actual translation is uncertain.

This distinctive unit insignia was approved on 8 July 1960. The insignia of the 1st Special Forces was authorized to be worn by enlisted personnel of the U.S. Army Special Forces Command (Airborne) and its subordinate units since at least 1965.

Special Forces distinctive unit insignia

14.7.3 The Tab

Introduced in June 1983, the Special Forces Tab is a service school qualification tab awarded to soldiers who complete one of the Special Forces Qualification Courses. Unlike the Green Beret, soldiers who are awarded the Special Forces Tab are authorized to wear it for the remainder of their military careers, even when not serving with Special Operations units. The cloth tab is an olive drab arc tab 3 1/4 inches (8.26 cm) in length and 11/16 inch (1.75 cm) in height overall, the designation "SPECIAL FORCES" in black letters 5/16 inch (.79 cm) in height and is worn on the left sleeve of utility uniforms above a unit's Shoulder Sleeve Insignia and below the President's Hundred Tab (if so awarded). The metal Special Forces Tab replica comes in two sizes, full and dress miniature. The full size version measures 5/8 inch (1.59 cm) in height and 1 9/16 inches (3.97 cm) in width. The miniature version measures 1/4 inch (.64 cm) in height and 1 inch (2.54 cm) in width. Both are teal blue with yellow border trim and letters and are worn above or below ribbons or medals on the Army Service Uniform.[36][37][38]

Award Eligibility:[36][37]

1. Basic Eligibility Criteria. Any person meeting one of the criteria below may be awarded the Special Forces (SF)

Special Forces Qualification Tab

tab:

    (a) Successful completion of U.S. Army John F. Kennedy Special Warfare Center and School (USAJFKSWCS) approved Active Army (AA) institutional training leading to SF qualification.

    (b) Successful completion of a USAJFKSWCS approved Reserve Component (RC) SF qualification program.

    (c) Successful completion of an authorized unit administered SF qualification program.

2. Active Component institutional training. The SF Tab may be awarded to all personnel who meet the following:

    (a) For successful completion of the Special Forces Qualification Course or Special Forces Detachment Officer Qualification Course (previously known as the Special Forces Officer Course). These courses are/were conducted by the USAJFKSWC (previously known as the U.S. Army Institute for Military Assistance).

    (b) Prior to 1 January 1988, for successful completion of the then approved program of instruction for Special Forces qualification in a Special Forces Group, who were subsequently awarded, by competent authority, SQI "S" in Career Management Field 18 (enlisted), or SQI "3" in Functional Area 18 (officer).

3. Reserve Component (RC) SF qualification programs. The SF Tab may be awarded to all personnel who successfully complete a RC SF qualification program according to TRADOC Regulation 135-5, dated 1 June 1988 or its predecessors and who were subsequently awarded, by competent authority, SQI "S" or "3" in MOS 11b, 11C, 12B, 05B, 91B, or ASI "5G" or "3." The USAJFKSWCS will determine individual entitlement for award of the SF Tab based on historical review of Army, Continental Army Command (CONRAC), and TRADOC regulations prescribing SF qualification requirements in effect at the time the individual began an RC SF qualification program.

4. Unit administered SF qualification programs. The SF Tab may be awarded to all personnel who successfully completed unit administered SF qualification programs as authorized by regulation. The USAJFKSWCS will determine individual entitlement to award of the SF Tab based upon historical review of regulations prescribing SF qualification requirements in effect at the time the individual began a unit administered SF qualification program.

5. Former wartime service. The Special Forces Tab may be awarded retroactively to all personnel who performed the following wartime service:

    (a) 1942 through 1973. Served with a Special Forces unit during wartime and were either unable to or not required to attend a formal program of instruction but were awarded SQI "S", "3", "5G" by competent authority.

    (b) Prior to 1954. Service for at least 120 consecutive days in one of the following organizations:

        i. 1st Special Service Force, August 1942 to December 1944.

        ii. OSS Detachment 101, April 1942 to September 1945.

        iii. OSS Jedburgh Detachments, May 1944 to May 1945.

iv. OSS Operational Groups, May 1944 to May 1945.

v. OSS Maritime Unit, April 1942 to September 1945.

vi. 6th Army Special Reconnaissance Unit (Alamo Scouts), February 1944 to September 1945.

vii. 8240th Army Unit, June 1950 to July 1953.

viii. 1954 through 1975. Any company grade officer or enlisted member awarded the CIB or CMB while serving for at least 120 consecutive days in one of the following type organizations:

A. SF Operational Detachment-A (A-Team).

B. Mobile Strike Force.

C. SF Reconnaissance Team.

D. SF Special Project Unit.

14.8 Cultural references

Main article: United States Army Special Forces in popular culture

Books, movies...

- 1965: *The Green Berets*, a book by Robin Moore.[39]

- 1966: "Ballad of the Green Berets", a song performed by Vietnam veteran and Green Beret, Barry Sadler. The song was written by Sadler and Robin Moore.

- 1968: *The Green Berets*, a film based on Moore's book, produced, directed, and starring John Wayne, who plays a key role in it as "Colonel Kirby".

- *Tales of the Green Beret*, a comic strip and American comic book written by Robin Moore with artwork by Joe Kubert.

- *Rambo* films: 1982, 1985, 1988, 2008: In this series of films, the central character, John Rambo, is a former Green Beret and Vietnam War veteran.

- 1965: *Outpost of Freedom*, by Medal of Honor Recipient Captain Roger H. C. Donlon (as told to Warren Rogers) 1965, McGraw-Hill

- 1975: *Parthian Shot* by former Green Beret, Loyd Little. ISBN 978-0670540631, OCLC 1119712; Winner of the 1976 Hemingway Foundation/PEN Award.[40]

- 2008: *White Passage: Red Sun*, by former Green Beret, Matt Rowe. ISBN 978-1-4389-2771-8, 2008, Authorhouse.

- 2009; 'Horse Soldiers: The Extraordinary Story of a Band of U.S. soldiers Who Rode to Victory in Afghanistan' by Doug Stanton

14.9 See also

- 1st Special Forces Operational Detachment-Delta (Delta Force)

- Central Intelligence Agency's Special Activities Division

- Defense Intelligence Agency

- Military Assistance Command, Vietnam – Studies and Observations Group

- Operation Jedburgh

- Devil's Brigade

- Alamo Scouts

- United States Army Counterintelligence (CI, or USAI)

- Phoenix Project

14.10   References

[1] Stanton, Doug (24 June 2009). "The Quiet Professionals: The Untold Story of U.S. Special Forces in Afghanistan". *Huffington Post*.

[2] "Most Popular E-mail Newsletter". *USA Today*. 9 November 2011.

[3] Joint Chiefs of Staff (17 December 2003). "Joint Publication 3-05: Doctrine for Joint Special Operations" (PDF). Retrieved 27 April 2008.

[4] Waller, Douglas C. (1994). "The Commandos: The Inside Story of America's Secret Soldiers". Dell Publishing.

[5] "FM 3-05: Army Special Operations Forces" (PDF). U.S. Department of the Army. September 2006.

[6] "FM 3-05.102 Army Special Forces Intelligence" (PDF). July 2001.

[7] Joint Chiefs of Staff (1993). "Joint Publication 3-05.5: Special Operations Targeting and Mission Planning Procedures" (PDF). Retrieved 13 November 2007.

[8] Waller, Douglas (3 February 2003). "The CIA Secret Army". *Time* (subscription required)

[9] SOG: The Secret Wars of America's Commandos in Vietnam by John L. Plaster

[10] Haney, Eric L. (2002). Inside Delta Force. New York: Delacorte Press

[11] Efran, Shawn (producer), "Army Officer Recalls Hunt For Bin Laden", 60 Minutes, CBS News, 5 October 2008.

[12] Maurer, Kevin (June 4, 2013). *Gentlemen Bastards: On the Ground In Afghanistan With America's Elite Special Forces*. New York: Berkely Trade. p. 15.

[13] Scarborough, Rowan (Jan 23, 2013). "Africa's Fast-Reaction Force Ready To Go From Colorado". *Washington Times*. Retrieved 2014-05-17.

[14] General Hugh Shelton - Without Hesitation. Hughshelton.com. Retrieved on 2014-05-24.

[15] "U.S. Army Special Forces Command (Airborne) History". U S ARMY SPECIAL OPERATIONS COMMAND. Retrieved 03/02/2013. Check date values in: |access-date= (help)

[16] Department of the Army (COL Russell W. Volckmann), FM 31-21, Organization and Conduct of Guerrilla Warfare (Washington, DC: GPO, October 1951)

[17] Officer Efficiency Report, Bank, Aaron, 11 May 1952, Aaron Bank Service Record, National Military Personnel Records Center, St. Louis, Missouri

[18] "U.S. Army Special Forces Command (Airborne) History". U.S. ARMY SPECIAL OPERATIONS COMMAND. Retrieved 03/02/2013. Check date values in: |access-date= (help)

[19] "United States Army Special Forces Command".

[20] "Structure". *Fort Campbell*. United States Army. Archived from the original on 22 March 2007. Retrieved 8 March 2007.

[21] USASOC. 'Special Forces – Shooters and thinkers'. *WWW.ARMY.MIL The official homepage of the United States army* (26 October 2009). Retrieved on 5 January 2010

[22] Special Forces Operational Detachment Alpha (SFOD A)

[23] "Qualifications & Benefits". goarmy.com. Retrieved 2014-07-14.

[24] Special Forces Officer | GoArmy.com

[25] U.S. Army Recruiting Command's Warrant Officer Recruiting Information Site

[26] Special Forces Weapons Sergeant | GoArmy.com

[27] Special Forces Engineer Sergeant | GoArmy.com

[28] Special Forces Medical Sergeant | GoArmy.com

[29] Special Forces Communications Sergeant | GoArmy.com

[30] Special Forces Candidate | GoArmy.com

[31] "History: Special Forces Green Beret". *Special Forces Search Engine*. Retrieved 8 March 2007.

[32] Simpson III, Robert B.; Rheault (1983). "Inside the Green Berets:he First Thirty Years, a History of the U.S. Army Special Forces". Presidio Press: 31–32

[33] Brown (2001 chapter=Green Beret chapter). *Historical Dictionary of the United States Army* (illustrated ed.). Greenwood Publishing Group,. p. 220 isbn=9780313293221. ISBN 9780313293221 |first1= missing |last1= in Editors list (help); Check date values in: |date= (help)

[34] Mil staff. "A Short History of the Use of Berets in the U.S. Army". *Army Black Beret*. www.army.mil. Retrieved April 2013 External link in |publisher= (help)

[35] Gamarekian, Barbara (22 November 1988). "Washington Talk: John F. Kennedy, 1917–1963; Hundreds Are in Capital For 25th Remembrance". *New York Times*. p. 2.

[36] Special Forces Tab, The Institute of heraldry, last accessed 24 June 2014

[37] U.S. Army Regulation 600–8–22: Personnel-General: Military Awards, Official Department of the Army Publications and Forms, dated 24 June 2013, last accessed 23 June 2014 (page 117-118)

[38] U.S. Army Pamphlet 670-1: Uniform and Insignia, Guide to the Wear and Appearance of Army Uniforms and Insignia, Official Department of the Army Publications and Forms, dated 31 March 2014, last accessed 23 June 2014 (pages 6, 201, 244–245, 252, 256, 258–260)

[39] Moore, Robin (2002). *The Green Berets*. St. Martin's Paperbacks. ISBN 978-0-312-98492-2.

[40] PEN/Hemingway Award for Debut Fiction: All Winners

14.11 External links

- Special Forces Command website

- Special Forces Recruiting at the Special Operations Recruiting Battalion website

- United States Army John F. Kennedy Special Warfare Center and School

- Official website of the Special Forces Association

- United States Special Operations Command

- United States Army Special Forces Overview

- Special Forces Medic talks about coming home from Iraq and Afghanistan

Chapter 15

United States Naval Special Warfare Command

The **United States Naval Special Warfare Command** (**NAVSPECWARCOM**), also known as **NAVSOC** or **NSWC**,[2] was commissioned on April 16, 1987 at Naval Amphibious Base Coronado in San Diego, California. As the Naval component of United States Special Operations Command; Naval Special Warfare Command provides vision, leadership, doctrinal guidance, resources and oversight to ensure component maritime special operations forces are ready to meet the operational requirements of combatant commanders.[3]

15.1 Background

Today's Naval Special Warfare operators can trace their origins to the Scouts and Raiders, Naval Combat Demolition Units, Office of Strategic Services Operational Swimmers, Underwater Demolition Teams, and Motor Torpedo Boat Squadrons of World War II.[4] In the Vietnam era, the Navy drew most of its SEALs from the Underwater Demolition Teams; from the early 1960s up until 1983 the SEAL Teams and UDTs coexisted. Navy SEALs typically traced their origin to the Scouts and Raiders while the Underwater Demolition Teams traced theirs to the Navy Combat Demolition Units (the Navy drew its UDTs from NCDUs). However, in 1983 the Underwater Demolition Teams were merged with the SEAL Teams. This, in turn, merged their ancestry. While none of those early organizations have survived to present, their pioneering efforts in unconventional warfare are mirrored in the missions and professionalism of the present Naval Special Warfare warriors.

To meet the need for a beach reconnaissance force, selected Army and Marine Corps personnel assembled at Amphibious Training Base Little Creek, Virginia, on 15 August 1942 to begin Amphibious Scouts and Raiders (Joint) training. The Scouts and Raiders mission was to identify and reconnoiter the objective beach, maintain a position on the designated beach prior to a landing and guide the assault waves to the landing beach.

An extensive history of Naval Special Warfare, written by men who actually served in the various units, is available at the National Navy UDT-SEAL Museum website, with a matchless collection of artifacts from that era on display at the facility.[5]

15.1.1 World War II

By the time the United States became involved in World War II, Adolf Hitler and the Axis forces had control over a large portion of Europe, Asia and North Africa. If the Allied forces were to stand a chance, there would have to be several full-scale landings. The U.S. Navy decided that to do the job right required sending in their own. They needed men to reconnoiter the landing beaches, take note of obstacles and defenses and ultimately guide the landing forces in. Later, during the war, the Army Engineers passed down demolition jobs to the U.S. Navy. They were to clear any obstacles and/or defenses in the near shore area, beginning a tradition that continues today. [6]

Scouts & Raiders

See also: Observer Group

The Navy Scouts and Raiders were created before the Navy Combat Demolition Units (NCDUs). The Scouts and Raiders were first formed in September 1942, nine months after the attack on Pearl Harbor, from the Observer Group, a joint Marine Corps-Army-Navy unit. The Observer Group was the first unit trained in amphibious reconnaissance.[7] They trained in inflatable boat insertions from submarines around the Chesapeake Bay and at the Amphibious Training Base (ATB) Little Creek in Virginia and in Fort Pierce, Florida. They were training for an intense clandestine mission in North Africa.[8]

With US Marines limited to the Pacific Theatre of Operations, the Observer Group was disbanded, with the Marine Corps counterpart forming the Amphib Recon Company; the Army/Navy unit formed the **Scouts and Raiders** with the Army later leaving. The U.S. Navy began the Scouts and Raiders to provide reconnaissance and raiding missions to support amphibious landings. The unit could conduct raids and sabotage missions from a pair of men to platoon sized operations.[9]

The unit continued its deployment to North Africa as planned,[8] where they earned eight Navy Crosses. Robert Halperin, a former NFL football player and future Olympic medalist, received a Presidential Citation and the Navy Cross for his work during the amphibious landings in French Morocco.[10] This was just the first of many war-time missions for the versatile Scouts and Raiders.[11]

First group   The first group included Phil H. Bucklew, the "Father of Naval Special Warfare," after whom the Naval Special Warfare Center building is named. Commissioned in October 1942, this group saw combat in November 1942 during Operation Torch, the first allied landings in Europe, on the North African coast. Scouts and Raiders also supported landings in Sicily, Salerno, Anzio, Normandy, and southern France.[4]

Second group   A second group of Scouts and Raiders, code-named Special Service Unit No. 1, was established on 7 July 1943, as a joint and combined operations force. The first mission, in September 1943, was at Finschafen on New Guinea. Later operations were at Gasmata, Arawe, Cape Gloucester, and the East and South coast of New Britain, all without any loss of personnel. Conflicts arose over operational matters, and all non-Navy personnel were reassigned. The unit, renamed 7th Amphibious Scouts, received a new mission, to go ashore with the assault boats, buoy channels, erect markers for the incoming craft, handle casualties, take offshore soundings, blow up beach obstacles and maintain voice communications linking the troops ashore, incoming boats and nearby ships. The 7th Amphibious Scouts conducted operations in the Pacific for the duration of the conflict, participating in more than 40 landings.

Scout landings were done at night during the new moon. The men were brought to a lagoon by submarine, and came ashore with rubber paddle boats. (Goodyear invented inflatable rubber boats just for this purpose) They would bury the boats in the sand and begin recon. Their mission was to clear the area prior to the main Naval landing which would then take over the island. They stayed from 3 days to as long as 7 days engaging in covert operations and 'taking no prisoners'. They had learned martial arts (judo) and were armed with Thompson sub machine guns, sidearms and knives. The entire Navy Scouts program was strictly volunteer, since it was considered too dangerous to order men to do this job. When the island was secured, they would transmit code to the sub, which would pick them up the next night. A typical loss would be 12 men going in and 3-5 coming back alive. Sometimes only 1 would come back.[12]

Third group   The third Scout and Raiders organization deployed to fight with the Sino-American Cooperative Organization (SACO) in China. Admiral Ernest J. King ordered that 120 officers and 900 enlisted sailors be trained for "Amphibious Raider" at the Scout and Raider school at Fort Pierce, Florida in order to support this mission. They formed the core of what was envisioned as a "guerrilla amphibious organization of Americans and Chinese operating from coastal waters, lakes and rivers employing small steamboats and sampans." Elements of the third Scouts and Raiders saw active service conducting surveys of the upper Yangtze River in the spring of 1945 and, disguised as coolies, conducting a detailed three-month survey of the Chinese coast from Shanghai to Kitchioh Wan, near Hong Kong. The majority of the force remained garrisoned at Camp Knox in Calcutta, India.[13]

15.1.2 Naval Combat Demolition Units

In September 1942, 17 Navy salvage personnel arrived at ATB Little Creek, Virginia for a one-week concentrated course on demolitions, explosive cable cutting and commando raiding techniques. The units were organised in a six-man team of an officer, a petty officer and four seamen using a seven-man LCRS inflatable boat to carry their explosives and gear.[14]

On 10 November 1942, this first combat demolition unit succeeded in cutting a cable and net barrier across the Wadi Sebou River during Operation Torch in North Africa. Their actions enabled the USS *Dallas* (DD-199) to traverse the river and insert Army Rangers, who proceeded to capture the Port Lyautey aerodrome.

Plans for a massive cross-channel invasion of Europe had begun and intelligence indicated that the Germans were placing extensive underwater obstacles on the beaches at Normandy. On 7 May 1943, Lieutenant Commander Draper L. Kauffman, "The Father of Naval Combat Demolition," was directed to set up a school and train people to eliminate obstacles on an enemy-held beach prior to an invasion. On 6 June 1943, LCDR Kaufmann established Naval Combat Demolition Unit training at Fort Pierce. By April 1944, a total of 34 NCDUs were deployed to England in preparation for Operation OVERLORD, the amphibious landing at Normandy.

On 6 June 1944, in the face of great adversity, the NCDUs at Omaha Beach managed to blow eight complete gaps and two partial gaps in the German defenses. The NCDUs suffered 31 killed and 60 wounded, a casualty rate of 52%. Meanwhile, the NCDUs at Utah Beach met less intense enemy fire. They cleared 700 yards (640 m) of beach in two hours, another 900 yards (820 m) by the afternoon. Casualties at Utah Beach were significantly lighter with six killed and eleven wounded. During Operation OVERLORD, not a single demolitioneer was lost to improper handling of explosives.

In August 1944, NCDUs from Utah Beach participated in the landings in southern France, the last amphibious operation in the European Theater of Operations. NCDUs also operated in the Pacific theater. NCDU 2, under LTjg Frank Kaine, after whom the Naval Special Warfare Command building is named, and NCDU 3 under LTjg Lloyd Anderson, formed the nucleus of six NCDUs that served with the Seventh Amphibious Force tasked with clearing boat channels after the landings from Biak to Borneo.

15.1.3 OSS Operational Swimmers

Some of the earliest World War II predecessors of the SEALs were the Operational Swimmers of the Office of Strategic Services, or OSS.[15] Many current SEAL missions were first assigned to them. OSS specialized in special operations, dropping operatives behind enemy lines to engage in organized guerrilla warfare as well as to gather information on such things as enemy resources and troop movements. [16]

British Combined Operations veteran LCDR Wooley, of the Royal Navy, was placed in charge of the OSS Maritime Unit in June 1943. Their training started in November 1943 at Camp Pendleton, California, moved to Santa Catalina Island, California in January 1944, and finally moved to the warmer waters of The Bahamas in March 1944. Within the U.S. military, they pioneered flexible swimfins and diving masks, closed-circuit diving equipment (under the direction of Dr. Chris Lambertsen), the use of Swimmer Delivery Vehicles (a type of submersible), and combat swimming and limpet mine attacks.[15]

In May 1944, General Donovan, the head of the OSS, divided the unit into groups. He loaned Group 1, under Lieutenant Arthur Choate, Jr to Admiral Nimitz, as a way to introduce the OSS into the Pacific theater. They became part of UDT-10 in July 1944, with Lt. Commander Choate commanding the unit. Five OSS men participated in the very first UDT submarine operation with the USS *Burrfish* (SS-312) in the Caroline Islands in August 1944.

15.1.4 Beach Jumpers

Beach Jumper Unit One was formed at the Amphibious Training Base at Camp Bradford, Virginia on 16 March 1943 for deception operations to simulate large scale amphibious raids and invasions.

Main article: Beach Jumpers

15.1.5 Underwater Demolition Teams

Main article: Underwater Demolition Team
On 23 November 1943, the U.S. Marine landing and subsequent battle at Tarawa Atoll emphasized the need for hydrographic reconnaissance and underwater demolition of obstacles prior to any amphibious landing. After Tarawa, 30

Patch of the Underwater Demolition Teams

officers and 150 enlisted men were moved to the Waimānalo Amphibious Training Base to form the nucleus of a demo-lition training program. This group became Underwater Demolition Teams (UDT) ONE and TWO.

The UDTs saw their first combat on 31 January 1944, during Operation Flintlock in the Marshall Islands. FLINTLOCK became the real catalyst for the UDT training program in the Pacific Theater. In February 1944, the Naval Combat Demolition Training and Experimental Base was established at Kīhei, Maui, next to the Amphibious Base at Kamaole. Eventually, 34 UDT teams were established. Wearing swim suits, fins, and dive masks on combat operations, these "Naked Warriors" saw action across the Pacific in every major amphibious landing including: Eniwetok, Saipan, Guam, Tinian, Angaur, Ulithi, Peleliu, Leyte, Lingayen Gulf, Zambales, Iwo Jima, Okinawa, Labuan, Brunei Bay, and on 4 July 1945 at Balikpapan on Borneo, which was the last UDT demolition operation of the war.

The rapid demobilization at the conclusion of the war reduced the number of active duty UDTs to two on each coast with a complement of seven officers and 45 enlisted men each.

The Korean War began on 25 June 1950, when the North Korean army invaded South Korea. Beginning with a detachment of 11 personnel from UDT 3, UDT participation expanded to three teams with a combined strength of 300 men. As part of the Special Operations Group, or SOG, UDTs successfully conducted demolition raids on railroad tunnels and bridges along the Korean coast. On 15 September 1950, UDTs supported Operation Chromite, the amphibious landing at Incheon. UDT 1 and 3 provided personnel who went in ahead of the landing craft, scouting mud flats, marking low points in the channel, clearing fouled propellers, and searching for mines. Four UDT personnel acted as wave-guides for the Marine landing.

In October 1950, UDTs supported mine-clearing operations in Wonsan Harbor where frogmen would locate and mark mines for minesweepers. On 12 October 1950, two U.S. minesweepers hit mines and sank. UDTs rescued 25 sailors. The next day, William Giannotti conducted the first U.S. combat operation using an "aqualung" when he dove on the USS Pledge (AM-277). For the remainder of the war, UDTs conducted beach and river reconnaissance, infiltrated guerrillas behind the lines from sea, continued mine sweeping operations, and participated in Operation Fishnet, which severely damaged the North Korean's fishing capability.

15.2 Navy SEALs & SWCC

Naval Special Warfare personnel comprise less than one percent of U.S. Navy personnel. SEAL and SWCC units operate across the spectrum of conflict and in operations other than war in a controlled manner; their ability to provide real time intelligence and "eyes on target", offer decision makers immediate options in the face of rapidly changing world crises.[17]

15.2.1 SEALs

Main article: United States Navy SEALs

SEALs are Special Operations Command's force-of-choice to conduct small-unit maritime military operations which originate from, and return to a river, ocean, swamp, delta or coastline. This littoral capability is considered more important now than ever, as half the world's infrastructure and population is located within one mile (1.6 km) of an ocean or river.[18]

Responding to President John F. Kennedy's desire for the Services to develop an Unconventional Warfare (UW) capabil-ity, the U.S. Navy established SEAL Team ONE and SEAL Team TWO in January 1962. Formed entirely with personnel from Underwater Demolition Teams, the SEALs mission was to conduct counter guerrilla warfare and clandestine oper-ations in maritime and riverine environments. [19]

Navy SEALs have distinguished themselves as an individually reliable, collectively disciplined and highly skilled maritime force. Because of the dangers inherent in NSW, prospective SEALs go through what is considered by many military experts to be the toughest training in the world. The intense physical and mental conditioning it takes to become a SEAL begins at Basic Underwater Demolition/SEAL (BUD/S) training.

SEAL candidates begin BUD/S training at the Naval Special Warfare Center, NAB Coronado, California. This six-month course of instruction focuses on physical conditioning, small boat handling, diving physics, basic diving techniques, land warfare, weapons, demolitions, communications, and reconnaissance.

Navy Special Warfare Trident Insignia worn by qualified U.S. Navy SEALs.

First Phase trains, develops, and assesses SEAL candidates in physical conditioning, water competency, teamwork, and mental tenacity. Second (Diving) Phase trains, develops, and qualifies SEAL candidates as competent basic combat swimmers. During this period, physical training continues and becomes even more intensive. Emphasis is placed on long distance underwater dives with the goal of training students to become basic combat divers, using swimming and diving techniques as a means of transportation from their launch point to their combat objective. This is a skill that separates SEALs from all other Special Operations forces. Third Phase trains, develops, and qualifies SEAL candidates in basic weapons, demolition, and small unit tactics. Third Phase concentrates on teaching land navigation, small-unit tactics, patrolling techniques, rappelling, marksmanship, and military explosives. The final three and a half weeks of Third Phase are spent at NALF San Clemente Island,[20] where students apply all the techniques they have acquired during training. [21]

SDVTs

SEAL Delivery Vehicle Teams' historical roots began during WWII with the earliest human torpedos to see use: Maiale, used by Italy's Decima Flottiglia MAS, and Chariots, used by British commando frogmen. Naval Special Warfare entered the wet submersible field in the 1960s when the Coastal Systems Center in Panama City, FL developed the Mark 7, a free-flooding SDV of the type used today, and the first SDV to be used in the fleet. The Mark 8 and 9 followed in the late 1970s.

Today's Mark 8 Mod 1 provides NSW with an unprecedented capability that combines the attributes of clandestine underwater mobility and the combat swimmer. The Advanced SEAL Delivery System (ASDS) program that would have provided NSW a new (dry) submersible for long range infiltration missions was abandoned in 2009.

15.2.2   SWCC

The exclusive mission of Special Warfare Combatant-craft Crewmen operators is to expertly drive and provide large-caliber gunfire support on specialized high-tech, high-speed, and low-profile Surface Combatant Craft to secretly infiltrate and exfiltrate Navy SEALs on Special Operations missions worldwide. These missions include direct action on land, sea, coastline or rivers (such as strikes, captures, and ship take downs by Visit, Board, Search, and Seizure), special reconnaissance, coastal patrol and interdiction of suspect ships and surface craft, counter-terrorism operations, riverine

SEALs using a SEAL Delivery Vehicle

warfare, deception operations, search and rescue operations, and foreign internal defense missions. [22] Although SEALs and SWCC undergo different training programs, both are focused on special operations in maritime environments. The SWCC program includes extensive training on craft and weapons tactics, techniques, and procedures. Like SEALs, SWCC must show physical fitness, possess strong motivation, be combat focused, and maintain responsiveness in high stress situations. [23]

The SWCC designation is a relatively new Naval Special Warfare career path that is independent of the regular line Navy. Today's Special Boat Teams have their origins in the PT boats of WWII and the "Brown Water" naval force that was created in 1965 at the onset of the Vietnam War. Patrol Coastal and Patrol Torpedo ships are the ancestors of today's Cyclone class patrol ships and Mark V Special Operations Craft.

15.3 Structure

Naval Special Warfare Group 10 was established at Virginia Beach, Va. on May 25, 2011.[24]

15.4 Global War on Terror

NSW is committed to combating the global terrorist threats. In addition to being experts in special reconnaissance and direct action missions, the skill sets needed to combat terrorism; NSW is postured to fight a dispersed enemy on their territory. NSW forces can operate from forward-deployed Navy ships, submarines and aviation mobility platforms as well as overseas bases and its own overseas units.

SWCC in the Special Operations Craft-Riverine

15.4.1   War in Afghanistan

In response to the attacks on America 11 Sep 2001, Naval Special Warfare forces put operators on the ground in Afghanistan in October. The first military flag officer to set foot in Afghanistan was a Navy SEAL, Rear Admiral Albert Calland, in charge of Special Operations Command Central (SOCCENT), which was responsible for all special operations for Central Command.[25] Additionally, a Navy SEAL captain commanded Combined Joint Special Operations Task Force (CJSOTF) South. Commonly referred to as Task Force K-Bar, the task force included Navy, Army, Air Force and Coalition Special Operations forces. During Operation Enduring Freedom, NSW forces carried out more than 75 special reconnaissance and direct action missions, destroying more than 500,000 pounds of explosives and weapons; positively identifying enemy personnel and conducting Leadership Interdiction Operations in the search for terrorists trying to escape by seagoing vessels.

Operation Red Wings, a counter insurgent mission in Kunar Province, Afghanistan, involved four Navy SEALs and took place on 28 June 2005. The SEALs were on a mission to try to find a key Taliban leader. However, goat herders stumbled

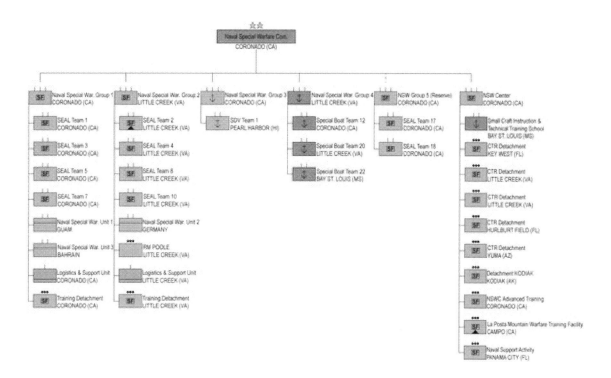

Naval Special Warfare Command Structure & Units

upon their hiding place and alerted local Taliban fighters, and they were subsequently surrounded by Taliban forces. The four SEALs requested back up after the Taliban had surrounded them. In the attempt to rescue the four SEALs on the ground a Boeing CH-47 Chinook containing members of SEAL delivery team one and several Army "Nightstalker" pilots was shot down. This is the biggest single loss of life for Naval Special Warfare forces since World War II. A firefight ensued, killing three SEALs. The fourth, Marcus Luttrell, was protected by local villagers and later rescued by the U.S. military. The team leader, SEAL Lieutenant Michael P. Murphy, was posthumously awarded the Medal of Honor.

SEAL Senior Chief Petty Officer Dan Healy was awarded the Bronze Star with Combat "V" for Valor, Purple Heart, and Afghanistan Campaign Medal, posthumously.

15.4.2   Iraq War

Naval Special Warfare has played a significant role in Operation Iraqi Freedom, employing the largest number of SEALs and SWCC in its history. NSW forces were instrumental in numerous special reconnaissance and direct action missions including the securing of the southern oil infrastructures of the Al Faw peninsula and the off-shore gas and oil terminals; the clearing of the Khawr Abd Allah and Khawr Az Zubayr waterways that enabled humanitarian aid to be delivered to the vital port city of Umm Qasr; reconnaissance of the Shatt al-Arab waterway; capture of high-value targets, raids on suspected chemical, biological and radiological sites; and the first POW rescue since WWII. Additionally, NSW is also fighting the war on terrorism in other global hot spots including the Philippines and the Horn of Africa. [26]

SEAL Petty Officer Second Class Michael A. Monsoor was posthumously awarded the Medal of Honor for actions in Ramadi, Iraq.

15.5   See also

- United States Navy SEALs

- List of Navy SEALs

- United States Navy SWCC

- United States Naval Special Warfare Development Group

- Naval Special Warfare Group 3

- Naval Special Warfare Center

- Underwater Demolition Team

15.6 References

Much of this text in this article was taken from Official U.S. Navy SWCC web site which as a work of the U.S. Government is presumed to be a public domain resource.

Notes

[1] SOCOM Public Affairs (2014). *SOCOM Fact Book 2014* (PDF). SOCOM Public Affairs.

[2] "United States Naval Special Warfare Command". U.S. Navy. Retrieved 2012-09-04.

[3] "Naval Special Warfare". U.S. Navy. Retrieved 2012-09-04.

[4] https://navysealmuseum.com/about-navy-seals/seal-history-the-naval-special-warfare-story/seal-history-origins-of-naval-special-warf

[5] https://navysealmuseum.com/about-navy-seals/seal-history-the-naval-special-warfare-story/

[6] {https://navysealmuseum.com/about-navy-seals/seal-history-the-naval-special-warfare-story/seal-history-origins-of-naval-special-war

[7] Shinn, lstLt Leo B. (April 1945). "Amphibious Reconnaissance". *Marine Corps Gazette* **29** *(4)*.

[8] Bruce F. Meyers, Swift, Silent, and Deadly: Marine Amphibious Reconnaissance in the Pacific, 1942–1945, (Annapolis, MD: Naval Institute Press, 2004).

[9] pp.168-177 *Brutsman, Bud, & Dockery, Kevin* Scouts and Raiders *in* Navy SEALs: The Early Years *Berkley Publishing 2007*

[10] Kenan Heise (9 May 1985). "Robert Halperin, 77, War Hero, Executive". *Chicago Tribune*. Retrieved 11 July 2011.

[11] "Scouts & Raiders history". Retrieved 2 January 2008.

[12] Lawrence Taylor, USN Scout

[13]

[14] p.34 Brutsman, Bud & Dockery, Kevin *Navy SEALs: A History of the Early Years* Berkley Publishing 2001

[15] Butler FK (2004). "Closed-circuit oxygen diving in the U.S. Navy". *Undersea Hyperb Med* **31** (1): 3–20. PMID 15233156. Retrieved 19 March 2009.

[16] "OSS History". Retrieved 2 January 2008.

[17] "NAVSOC mission". U.S. Navy. Retrieved 21 January 2008.

[18] "Navy SEAL History". NavySEALs.com (private web community). Retrieved 21 January 2008.

[19] "Official U.S. Navy SEAL Information Website, Into". Retrieved 21 January 2008.

[20] "Naval Auxiliary Landing Field, San Clemente Island". *Naval Base Coronado*. United States Navy. Retrieved 18 November 2008.

[21] "BUD/S (Basic Underwater Demolition / SEAL) – Naval Special Warfare Center". *Official U.S. Navy SEAL Information Website*. United States Navy. Retrieved 21 January 2008.

[22] "Navy SWCC – The Navy's Elite Boat Warriors". NavySEALs.com. Retrieved 2 January 2008.

[23] "Introduction to SWCC and Naval Special Warfare". *Official U.S. Navy SWCC Information.* United States Navy. Retrieved 2 January 2008.

[24] Communication, Mass. "Naval Special Warfare Welcomes Group 10 to Force". Navy.mil. Retrieved 7 April 2013.

[25] "NSWarrior - Military Forum". MilitaryLTD.com. Retrieved 2012-09-04.

[26] "NAVSOC History". Retrieved 2 January 2008.

Bibliography

- Naval Special Warfare website

- Naval Special Warfare, History page

- Official U.S. Navy Seal Information Website

- Official U.S. Navy SWCC Information Website

- Luttrell, Marcus. (2007). *Lone Survivor: The Eyewitness Account of Operation Redwing and the Lost Heroes of SEAL Team 10,* New York: Hachette Book Group USA. (ISBN 0-316-06759-8)

- Cunningham, Chet. (2005). *The Frogmen of World War II: An Oral History of the U.S. Navy's Underwater Demolition Teams,* New York: Pocket Books. (ISBN 0-7434-8216-6)

15.7   External links

- U.S. Naval Special Warfare Command – official site.

- NavySeals.com

- ShadowSpear.com Special Operations

Chapter 16

Air Force Special Operations Command

United States Air Force Special Operations Command (**AFSOC**) is the special operations component of the United States Air Force and the U.S. Air Force component command to the United States Special Operations Command (USSO-COM), a unified combatant command located at MacDill Air Force Base, Florida. AFSOC provides Air Force Special Operations Forces (SOF) for worldwide deployment and assignment to regional unified combatant commands.

AFSOC was initially established on 10 February 1983 as Twenty-Third Air Force (23 AF), a subordinate numbered air force of the Military Airlift Command (MAC), with 23 AF headquarters established at Hurlburt Field, Florida.

On 22 May 1990, 23 AF was redesignated as AFSOC and became a separate major command (MAJCOM) responsible for all USAF special operations forces (SOF), aircraft and personnel in the Regular Air Force, and the operational "gaining command" for all USAF SOF, aircraft and personnel in the Air Force Reserve (AFRES)...AFRES subsequently being redesignated the Air Force Reserve Command (AFRC) in 1997...and the Air National Guard (ANG).

16.1   Predecessor special operations

16.1.1   World War II

- 1st Air Commando Group: Late 1943 – November 1945

- Operation Carpetbagger: Early 1944 – July 1945

16.1.2   Korean War

- Air Resupply and Communications Service: 23 February 1951 – 12 October 1956

- Combined Command Reconnaissance Activities, Korea: December 1951 – December 1953

- B Flight, 6167th Operations Squadron: 1 April 1952 – 31 December 1953

- 6004th Air Intelligence Service Squadron: c. March 1951 – 1955

- 6006th Air Intelligence Service Squadron: c. 1953 – 1955

- 22nd Crash Rescue Boat Squadron: c. July 1952 – 1954

- 581st Air Supply and Communications Wing: July 1951 – September 1955

- 582nd Air Supply and Communications Wing

- 580th Air Supply and Communications Wing

16.1.3   Early Cold War era

- 129th Air Resupply Group: April 1955 – c. 1975

- 130th Air Resupply Group: October 1955 – c. 1960

- 135th Air Resupply Group: August 1955 – c. 1971

- 143rd Special Operations Group: November 1955 – 1975

- 1045th Observation, Evaluation, and Training Group: 23 February 1951 – 1 January 1954[3]

16.1.4   Vietnam War era

- Jungle Jim

- Farm Gate

- Operation Waterpump

- Raven Forward Air Controllers

- Project 404

- Palace Dog

- 56th Air Commando Wing

16.1.5   Late Cold War era

- 4400th Combat Crew Training Group

- 1st Special Operations Wing

- 23rd Air Force

16.2   Lineage

- Established as **Twenty-Third Air Force** on 10 February 1983

  Activated on 1 March 1983

- Redesignated **Air Force Special Operations Command**, with the status of a major command, on 22 May 1990

16.2.1   Assignments

- Tactical Air Command, April 1961 – 9 February 1983

- Military Airlift Command, 10 February 1983 – 22 May 1990

16.2.2   Stations

- Scott AFB, Illinois, 1 March 1983

- Hurlburt Field, Florida, 1 August 1987 – **present**

16.2.3   Components

- Air Forces Special Operations (later, 623d Air and Space Operations Center): 13 Dec 2005 – 1 Jan 2008

- Twenty-Third Air Force (Air Forces Special Operations Forces): 1 Jan 2008 – 4 April 2013

- **AFSOC Operations Center**: 4 April 2013 – **present**[4]

- 2d Air Division, 1 March 1983 – 1 February 1987

- Aerospace Rescue and Recovery Service, 1 March 1983 – 1 August 1989

- **1st Special Operations Wing (later, 16th Special Operations Wing; 1st Special Operations Wing)**, 1 February 1987 – **present**

- **24th Special Operations Wing**, 12 June 2012 – **present**

- **27th Special Operations Wing**, 1 Oct 2007 – **present**

- 41st Rescue and Weather Reconnaissance Wing, 1 October 1983 – 1 August 1989

- **352d Special Operations Wing, lineage from 39th Aerospace Rescue & Recovery Wing (later, 39th Special Operations Wing; 352d Special Operations Group)**, 1 October 1983 – **present**

- **353d Special Operations Group, lineage from 353d Special Operations Wing (later, 353d Special Operations Group), 6 April 1989** – present

- 375th Aeromedical Airlift Wing: 1 January 1984 – 1 February 1990

- 720th Special Tactics Group: 1 October 1987 – 12 June 2012

- 724th Special Tactics Group: 29 Apr 2011 – 12 June 2012

- 1550th Aircrew Training and Test Wing (later, 1550th Combat Crew Training Wing): 1 October 1983 – 21 May 1990

- USAF Special Operations School, 1 February 1987 – 22 May 1990

- Air Force Special Operations Training Center, 8 October 2008 – 11 February 2013

- **Air Force Special Operations Air Warfare Center**, 11 February 2013 – **present** [5]

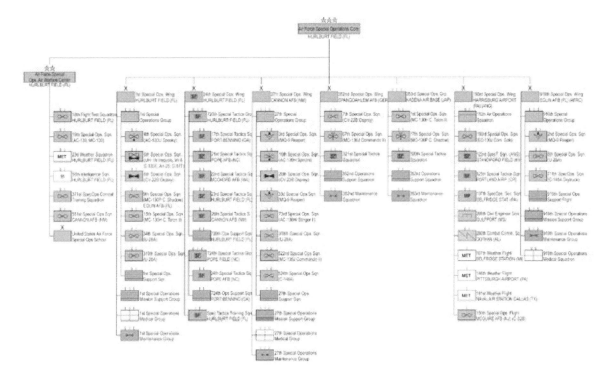

Air Force Special Operations Command OrBat

Several aircraft of the 1st Special Operations Wing belonging to the 6th Special Operations Squadron

16.3   Units

- AFSOC Operations Center,[4] Hurlburt Field, Florida

    23d Weather Squadron

- 1st Special Operations Wing, Hurlburt Field, Florida

    1st Special Operations Support Squadron

4th Special Operations Squadron, AC-130U Spooky

8th Special Operations Squadron, CV-22B Osprey

9th Special Operations Squadron (GSU at Eglin AFB, Florida, MC-130P Combat Shadow

11th Intelligence Squadron

Det 1, 11th Intelligence Squadron, Fort Bragg, North Carolina

15th Special Operations Squadron, MC-130H Combat Talon II

23d Special Operations Weather Squadron[6]

34th Special Operations Squadron, U-28A

319th Special Operations Squadron, U-28A[7]

- 24th Special Operations Wing, Hurlburt Field, Florida

  - 720th Special Tactics Group, Hurlburt Field, Florida

    17th Special Tactics Squadron, Fort Benning, Georgia
    21st Special Tactics Squadron, Pope Field, North Carolina
    22d Special Tactics Squadron, Joint Base Lewis-McChord, Washington
    23d Special Tactics Squadron, Hurlburt Field, Florida
    26th Special Tactics Squadron, Cannon AFB, New Mexico
    720th Operations Support Squadron

  - 724th Special Tactics Group, Pope Field (former Pope AFB), North Carolina

    24th Special Tactics Squadron
    724th Operations Support Squadron
    724th Intelligence Squadron
    724th Special Tactics Training Squadron, Hurlburt Field, Florida

- 27th Special Operations Wing, Cannon AFB, New Mexico

  3d Special Operations Squadron, MQ-1 Predator

  16th Special Operations Squadron, AC-130H Spectre

  20th Special Operations Squadron, CV-22B Osprey

  27th Special Operations Support Squadron

  33d Special Operations Squadron, MQ-9 Reaper

  43d Intelligence Squadron

  56th Special Operations Intelligence Squadron

  73d Special Operations Squadron, AC-130W Stinger II

  318th Special Operations Squadron, U-28A, C-145A Skytruck

  522d Special Operations Squadron, MC-130J Commando II

  524th Special Operations Squadron C-146A

- 352d Special Operations Wing, RAF Mildenhall, United Kingdom (AFSOC support to USEUCOM, SOCEUR and USAFE)

  7th Special Operations Squadron, CV-22B Osprey

  67th Special Operations Squadron, MC-130J Commando II

  321st Special Tactics Squadron

- 353d Special Operations Group, Kadena Air Base, Japan (AFSOC support to USPACOM, SOCPAC and PACAF)

      1st Special Operations Squadron MC-130H Combat Talon II

      17th Special Operations Squadron MC-130N/P Combat Shadow

      320th Special Tactics Squadron

- Air Force Special Operations Air Warfare Center, Hurlburt Field, Florida[8]

      6th Special Operations Squadron, UH-1N Iroquois, Mi-8, C-130E Hercules, An-26, C-47T

      18th Flight Test Squadron

          Det 1, 18th Flight Test Squadron – GSU at Edwards AFB, California

      19th Special Operations Squadron, AC-130, MC-130

      371st Special Operations Combat Training Squadron

      551st Special Operations Squadron, Cannon AFB, New Mexico

      United States Air Force Special Operations School, Hurlburt Field, Florida

16.3.1 Air National Guard units

- 193d Special Operations Wing, Pennsylvania Air National Guard, Harrisburg Air National Guard Base, Pennsylvania[9]

      193d Special Operations Squadron, EC-130J Commando Solo

      150th Special Operations Flight, New Jersey Air National Guard, McGuire AFB, New Jersey; C-32B[10]

- AFSOC-gained ANG units aligned under AMC-gained or ACC-gained ANG wings[11]

      123d Special Tactics Squadron, Kentucky Air National Guard, Louisville ANGB, Kentucky

      125th Special Tactics Squadron, Oregon Air National Guard, Portland ANGB, Oregon

      137th Special Operations Security Forces Squadron, Michigan Air National Guard, Selfridge ANGB, Michigan

      280th Combat Communications Squadron, Alabama Air National Guard, Dothan Regional Airport ANGD, Alabama

      209th Special Operations Civil Engineer Squadron, Mississippi Air National Guard, Gulfport Combat Readiness Training Center, Mississippi

      107th Weather Flight, Michigan Air National Guard, Selfridge ANGB, Michigan

      146th Weather Flight, Pennsylvania Air National Guard, Pittsburgh IAP Air Reserve Station, Pennsylvania

      181st Weather Flight, Texas Air National Guard, NAS Fort Worth JRB/Carswell Field, Texas

16.3.2 Air Force Reserve Command units

- 919th Special Operations Wing, Eglin AFB Auxiliary Field #3 / Duke Field, Florida

      2d Special Operations Squadron (GSU at Hurlburt Field, Florida), MQ-9 Reaper

      5th Special Operations Squadron, U-28

      711th Special Operations Squadron, C-145A Skytruck

16.3.3 Personnel and resources

AFSOC has approximately 15,000 active-duty, Air Force Reserve, Air National Guard and civilian personnel.[12]

The commander of AFSOC is Lieutenant General Bradley A. Heithold. Major General O.G. Mannon is Vice Commander, and Chief Master Sergeant Bill Turner is the Command Chief Master Sergeant, Air Force Special Operations Command.

The command's SOF units are composed of highly trained, rapidly deployable Airmen who are equipped with specialized aircraft. These forces conduct global special operations missions ranging from precision application of firepower, to infiltration, aviation foreign internal defense, exfiltration, resupply and refueling of SOF operational elements. The command's Special Tactics Squadrons are led by Special Tactics Officers (STOs). Special Tactics Squadrons combine Combat Controllers, TACP, Special Operations Weather Technicians, Pararescuemen and combat rescue officers to form versatile SOF teams. AFSOC's unique capabilities include airborne radio and television broadcast for psychological operations, as well as combat aviation advisors to provide other governments military expertise for their internal development.

Special Tactics is the US Air Force special operations ground force. Similar in ability and employment to Marine Special Operations Command (MARSOC), Army Special Forces and Navy SEALs, Air Force Special Tactics personnel are typically the first to enter combat and often find themselves deep behind enemy lines in demanding, austere conditions, usually with little or no support. Due to the rigors of the career field, Special Tactics' year-long training is one of the most demanding in the military, with attrition rates between 80 to 90 percent. In an attempt to reduce the high attrition, Special Tactics is very selective when choosing their officers. Special Tactics Officers (STO) undergo a highly competitive process to gain entry into the Special Tactics career field, ensuring only the most promising and capable leaders are selected. STO leadership and role modeling during the difficult training reduces the attrition rate for enlisted trainees.

STO selection is a two-phase process. Beginning with Phase One, a board of veteran STOs reviews application packages consisting of letters of recommendation, fitness test scores, and narratives written by the applicants describing their career aspirations and reasons for applying. Based on Phase One performance, approximately 8 to 10 applicants are invited to the next phase. Phase Two is a weeklong battery of evaluations, ranging from physical fitness and leadership to emotional intelligence and personality indicators. At the end of Phase Two, typically 2 to 4 applicants are selected to begin the year-plus Special Tactics training pipeline.

16.3.4 Aircraft

Current

AFSOC operates the following aircraft as part of its regular inventory:[13]

- AC-130H/U/W Spectre/Spooky/Stinger II
- CV-22B Osprey
- C-32 (Boeing 757)
- EC-130J Commando Solo
- MC-130E Combat Talon I / MC-130H Combat Talon II / MC-130J Commando II / MC-130P Combat Shadow
- C-145A Skytruck
- C-146A Wolfhound
- U-28A
- MQ-1 Predator
- MQ-9 Reaper
- RQ-11 Raven
- Scan Eagle

- Wasp III

Additionally, AFSOC units possess and operate a small number of the following aircraft for special training mission and Aviation Foreign Internal Defense missions:

- An-26 Curl

- C-47T Sky Train

- C-212 Aviocar

- CN-235-100

- Mi-17 Hip

- UH-1H and UH-1N Huey

Future

New MC-130J aircraft based on the Lockheed Martin KC-130J Super Hercules tanker variant will be acquired.[14]

16.4   History

16.4.1   Twenty-Third Air Force

In December 1982, the Air Force transferred responsibility for Air Force special operations from Tactical Air Command (TAC) to Military Airlift Command (MAC). Consequently, in March 1983, MAC activated Twenty-Third Air Force (23 AF) at Scott Air Force Base, Illinois. This new numbered air force's responsibilities included worldwide missions of special operations, combat rescue, weather reconnaissance and aerial sampling, security support for intercontinental ballistic missile sites, training of USAF helicopter and HC-130 crewmen, pararescue training, and medical evacuation.

Operation Urgent Fury

In October 1983, 23 AF participated in the successful rescue of Americans from the island nation of Grenada. During the seven day operation, centered at Point Salines Airport, 23 AF furnished MC-130s, AC-130s, aircrews, maintenance, and support personnel. An EC-130 from the 193rd Special Operations Wing of the Air National Guard (ANG), played a significant psy-war role. An MC-130 pilot from the 8th Special Operations Squadron won the MacKay Trophy for his actions in leading the air drop on the Point Salines Airport.

US Special Operations Command

In May 1986, the Goldwater-Nichols Department of Defense Reorganization Act led to the formation of the United States Special Operations Command. Senators William Cohen and Sam Nunn introduced the Senate bill, and the following month Congressman Dan Daniel introduced a like measure in the House of Representatives. The key provisions of the legislation formed the basis to amend the 1986 Defense Authorizations Bill. This bill, signed into law in October 1986, in part directed the formation of a unified command responsible for special operations. In April 1987 the DoD established the United States Special Operations Command (USSOCOM) at MacDill Air Force Base, Florida, and Army GEN James J. Lindsay assumed command. Four months later, 23 AF moved to Hurlburt Field, Florida.

In August 1989, Gen Duane H. Cassidy, MAC Commander in Chief, divested 23rd AF of its non-special operations units. Thus, 23 AF served a dual role—still reporting to MAC, but also functioning as the air component to USSOCOM.

Operation Just Cause

From late December 1989 to early January 1990, 23 AF participated in the invasion of the Republic of Panama during Operation Just Cause. Special operations aircraft included both active duty and reserve AC-130 Spectre gunships, EC-130 Volant Solo psychological operations aircraft from the Air National Guard, HC-130P/N Combat Shadow tankers, MC-130E Combat Talons, and MH-53J Pave Low and MH-60G Pave Hawk helicopters. Special tactics Combat Controllers and Pararescuemen provided important support to combat units during this operation.

Spectre gunship crews of the 1st SOW earned the Mackay Trophy and Tunner Award for their efforts, a 919th SOG Spectre crew earned the President's Award, and a 1st SOW Combat Talon crew ferried the captured Panamanian President, Manuel Noriega, to prison in the United States. Likewise, the efforts of the 1st SOW maintenance people earned them the Daedalian Award.

On 22 May 1990, General Larry D. Welch, Air Force Chief of Staff, redesignated Twenty-Third Air Force as **Air Force Special Operations Command** (AFSOC). This new major command consisted of three wings: the 1st, 39th and 353rd Special Operations Wings as well as the 1720th Special Tactics Group (STG), the U.S. Air Force Special Operations School, and the Special Missions Operational Test and Evaluation Center.

Currently, after major redesignations and reorganizations, AFSOC direct reporting units include the 16th SOW, the 352nd Special Operations Group, the 353rd Special Operations Group, the 720th Special Tactics Group (STG), the USAF Special Operations School and the 18th Flight Test Squadron (FLTS). During the early 1990s a major reorganization occurred within AFSOC. The 1720th STG became the 720th STG in March 1992; the transfer of ownership of Hurlburt Field from Air Mobility Command (AMC, and formerly MAC) to AFSOC in October 1992, followed by the merger of the 834th Air Base Wing (ABW) into the 1st SOW which assumed host unit responsibilities. A year later the 1st SOW became the 16th SOW in a move to preserve Air Force heritage.

Meanwhile, the Special Missions Operational Test and Evaluation Center (SMOTEC), which explored heavy lift frontiers in special operations capabilities, while pursuing better equipment and tactics development, was also reorganized. In April 1994, the Air Force, in an effort to standardize these types of organizations, redesignated SMOTEC as the 18th Flight Test Squadron.

Gulf War

From early August 1990 to late February 1991, AFSOC participated in Operation Desert Shield and Operation Desert Storm, the protection of Saudi Arabia and liberation of Kuwait. Special tactics personnel operated throughout the theater on multiple combat control and combat rescue missions. Special operations forces performed direct action missions, combat search and rescue, infiltration, exfiltration, air base ground defense, air interdiction, special reconnaissance, close air support, psychological operations, and helicopter air refuelings. Pave Low crews led the helicopter assault on radars to blind Iraq at the onset of hostilities, and they also accomplished the deepest rescue for which they received the Mackay Trophy.

Combat Talons dropped the largest conventional bombs of the war and, along with Combat Shadows, dropped the most psy-war leaflets. The AC-130s provided valuable fire support and armed reconnaissance, but they also suffered the single greatest combat loss of coalition air forces with the shooting down of Spirit 03. All fourteen crew members aboard were lost.

16.4.2   AFSOC

Post-Gulf War

In December 1992, AFSOC special tactics and intelligence personnel supported Operation Restore Hope in Somalia. In late 1994, AFSOC units spearheaded Operation Uphold Democracy in Haiti, and in 1995 Operation Deliberate Force in the Balkans.

Operation Enduring Freedom

Then-MSgt Bart Decker from the 23rd STS, on horseback in the Balkh valley, during the initial days of the U.S. invasion of Afghanistan in 2001.

The terrorist attacks on the World Trade Center in New York City, and the Pentagon, Washington D.C., on 11 September 2001 pushed the United States special operations forces to the forefront of the war against terrorism. By the end of September 2001, AFSOC deployed forces to southwest Asia for Operation Enduring Freedom to help destroy the al Qaeda terrorist organization and remove the Taliban regime in Afghanistan. AFSOC airpower delivered special tactics forces to the battle ground and they in turn focused U.S. airpower and allowed Afghanistan's Northern Alliance ground forces to dispatch the Taliban and al Qaeda from Afghanistan. AFSOC personnel also deployed to the Philippines to help aid that country's efforts against terrorism.

Operation Iraqi Freedom

In March 2003, AFSOC again deployed forces to southwest Asia this time in support of what would become Operation Iraqi Freedom – the removal of Saddam Hussein and his Baathist government. The command's personnel and aircraft teamed with SOF and conventional forces to quickly bring down Saddam Hussein's government by May 2003. AFSOC forces have continued to conduct operations since then, in support of the new Iraqi government against insurgents and terrorists.

16.5 Commanders

AFSOC has had nine commanders since its inception in 1990.

16.6 Contingency operations

A PJ from the 23rd STS searching for survivors of the 2010 Haiti earthquake in Port-au-Prince

Operation Unified Response, earthquake relief, Haiti

16.7 Gallery

- AFSOC's first CV-22—Sunset, Hurlburt Field, Florida
- Combat Controllers practice seizing an airfield
- AFSOC Special Operations Weathermen
- MC-130Ps punching flares

16.8 See also

- V-22 Osprey
- Air Resupply And Communications Service

16.9   Notes

[1] SOCOM Public Affairs (2014). *SOCOM Fact Book 2014* (PDF). SOCOM Public Affairs.

[2] SOCOM Public Affairs (2013). *SOCOM Fact Book 2013* (PDF). SOCOM Public Affairs.

[3] Haas, *Apollo's Warriors: U.S. Special Operations During the Cold War*

[4] 23rd AF deactivates. Afsoc.af.mil. Retrieved on 2013-07-21.

[5] AFSOC stands up Air Warfare Center. Afsoc.af.mil. Retrieved on 2013-07-21.

[6] http://www.afhra.af.mil/factsheets/factsheet.asp?id=15052

[7] AirForce-magazine.com: *The SOF Makeover* (Air Force Special Operations Command's aircraft and review), by Marc V. Schanz, June 2010, Vol. 93, No. 6.

[8] http://www2.afsoc.af.mil/news/story.asp?id=123336024

[9] http://www.afsoc.af.mil/AboutUs/FactSheets/Display/tabid/140/Article/162540/air-force-special-operations-command.aspx

[10] http://www.afsoc.af.mil/AboutUs/FactSheets/Display/tabid/140/Article/162540/air-force-special-operations-command.aspx

[11] http://www.afsoc.af.mil/AboutUs/FactSheets/Display/tabid/140/Article/162540/air-force-special-operations-command.aspx

[12] U.S. Seeks Faster Deployment; Smaller, More Flexible Special-Operations Teams Would Tackle Emerging Threats Under New Plan 7 May 2012

[13] USAF Special Operations Command Official Site.

[14] FlightGlobal.com: *Lockheed Martin C-130J selected for new special operations role*, by Stephen Trimble, Washington DC, 18 Jun 2008; accessed: 20 Feb 2012

[15] http://www.afsoc.af.mil/library/afsocheritage/index.asp

16.10   Further reading

- Chinnery, Philip D. *Any Time, Any Place: Fifty Years of the USAF Air Commando and Special Operations Forces, 1944–1994*. Annapolis, Md: Naval Institute Press, 1994. ISBN 1557500371

- Haas, Michael E. *Apollo's Warriors: U.S. Air Force Special Operations During the Cold War*. 2002, University Press of the Pacific, Honolulu. ISBN 9781410200099.

- Hebert, Adam J. "The Air Commandos". *Air Force Magazine*, March 2005 (vol. 88, no. 3).

- Marquis, Susan L. *Unconventional Warfare: Rebuilding U.S. Special Operations Forces*. Washington, D.C.: Brookings Institution, 1997. ISBN 0815754760

- Pushies, Fred J. *Deadly Blue Battle Stories of the U.S. Air Force Special Operations Command*. New York: American Management Assoc, 2009. <http://www.books24x7.com/marc.asp?bookid=32471>. ISBN 9780814413616

- Sine, William F. *Guardian Angel: Life and Death Adventures with Pararescue, the World's Most Powerful Commando Rescue Force*. Havertown, Pa: Casemate, 2012. ISBN 9781612001227

16.11   External links

- Air Force Special Operations Command Home Page—Official AFSOC public site
- AFSOC Factsheet, public site
- United States Air Force—Official website
- ShadowSpear Special Operations: AFSOC

Chapter 17

United States Marine Corps Forces Special Operations Command

United States Marine Corps Forces Special Operations Command (**MARSOC**) is a component command of the United States Special Operations Command that comprises the Marine Corps' contribution to SOCOM. Its core capabilities are direct action, special reconnaissance and foreign internal defense. MARSOC has also been directed to conduct counter-terrorism, and information operations.[2]

17.1   History and Lineage

Marine Raiders conduct combat operations in eastern Afghanistan.

153

Its creation was announced on 23 November 2005 by US Defense Secretary Donald Rumsfeld, following a meeting between him, the USSOCOM commander General Bryan D. Brown, and the Marine Corps Commandant General Michael Hagee on 28 October 2005. MARSOC was officially activated on 24 February 2006 with ceremonies at Camp Lejeune, North Carolina.

The potential participation of the Marine Corps in SOCOM has been controversial since SOCOM was formed in 1986. At the time, Marine Corps leaders felt that their Force Reconnaissance units were best kept in the Marine Corps' MAGTF command structure, and that the detachment of an "elite" Marine Special Operations unit from the Marine Corps would be to the detriment of the Marine Corps as a whole. A re-evaluation following the September 11 attacks and the War on Terrorism, along with new policy established by Secretary Rumsfeld and then-Commandant Gen. James L. Jones at The Pentagon, caused the Marine Corps to work towards integration with SOCOM. The establishment of MARSOC represented the most significant step towards that goal, and followed the establishment of MCSOCOM Detachment One (DET1), a small Marine Corps detachment formed as a pilot program to test Marine Corps integration into SOCOM. It was made up of mostly Force Recon Marines from 1st and 2nd Force Reconnaissance Companies along with other hand picked support men and served with Navy SEALs under Naval Special Warfare Group One. Detachment 1 conducted a multitude of special operations in Iraq alongside their Special Operations brothers of the sister services. SOCOM conducted a study of the unit's deployment, which clearly indicated success and strong performance. Detachment 1 was disbanded in 2006 soon after the creation of MARSOC.

The first Marine Special Operations Company was stood up in June 2006, shortly after the creation of MARSOC and were sent to Afghanistan. It was deployed supporting the Global War on Terrorism in December 2013 alongside the 26th Marine Expeditionary Unit (Special Operations Capable) where they conducted various special operations missions, ranging from Direct action (military), reconnaissance and other mission sets.[3]

The first Marine Special Operations Individual Training Course began at Camp Lejeune on 6 October 2008.[4] MARSOC's stated end-goal is 850 CSOs.[5]

17.2   Organization

MARSOC is composed of about 2500 Marines[6] and Sailors, and is currently commanded by Major General Joseph L. Osterman. MARSOC's organization was finalized in 2007. The base unit of MARSOC is the fourteen-man Marine Special Operations Team (MSOT), commanded by a captain (O-3) as Team Commander, assisted by a master sergeant (E-8) as Team Chief. Each team has two identical squads, or Tactical Elements, each led by a gunnery sergeant (E-7) as Element Leader. MARSOC is based at Camp Lejeune, North Carolina and is split into three subordinate commands:

17.3   Special Operations Combat Service Specialist

Special Operations Combat Service Specialists (SOCS-Ss) are Combat Service Support Marines who serve one standard tour with MARSOC in their primary MOS, such as Motor Transport or Logistics. Their training includes core skills for joint and interagency work as well as enhanced SOF combat skills training to enable their successful integration and survivability in special operations environments.[13]

17.4   Special Operations Capabilities Specialist

Special Operations Capabilities Specialists (SOCS) are Combat Support Marines that are able to join MARSOC based upon their MOS skill. They receive advanced special operations forces training and certification. SOCSs are operational and tactical force multipliers and frequently deploy alongside Critical Skills Operators (CSOs). SOCS billet fields include Intelligence, Communications, Explosive Ordnance Disposal, Dog Handlers, and Fire-Control Specialists. Special Operations Capabilities Specialist are awarded the AMOS of 8071, and return to the operating forces after an extended tour of service with MARSOC.[13]

A Marine Raider glides towards his target during HALO operations.

17.4.1 Prerequisites

All Marines are screened to ensure that the Marines joining MARSOC meet the established prerequisites for duty within the command.

- Have a minimum GT score of 105.[14]

- Have a minimum PFT of 225.

- Be able to pass the MARSOC swim assessment.

- Meet the MARSOC medical screening criteria.

- Be eligible to obtain and maintain a secret clearance.

- Be willing, upon selection, to make a lateral move to the critical skills operator MOS.

17.4.2 Screening

Selection of the right personnel begins with a rigorous screening process designed to identify the right Marines for the right billet within MARSOC. Operational billets are open only to males. Screening takes place in 3 stages: record screening, physical screening, and a psychological and medical evaluation.

17.4.3   Special Operations Training Course

The Special Operations Training Course (STC) is six weeks of unhindered, realistic, challenging basic and intermediate Special Operations Forces (SOF) war fighting skills training. During STC the Special Operations Capabilities Specialists will also attend Survival, Evasion, Resistance and Escape (SERE) training along with a MARSOF Level 1 Course specific to their MOS: Explosive Ordnance Disposal (6 weeks), Communications (12 weeks), Intelligence (4–6 weeks), Joint Terminal Attack Controller (4 weeks), Multi-Purpose Canine (10 weeks).[13]

17.5   Critical Skills Operators

Main article: United States Marine Corps Critical Skills Operator

Critical Skills Operators are the primary special operations Marines within MARSOC. They are trained to execute a variety of missions. Specialized training also provides capabilities in language fluency necessary for crossing cultural barriers, allowing CSOs to connect with the local forces as well as civilians.[15] Marines designated CSOs are awarded MOS 0372. Critical Skills Operators (CSOs) are assigned to Marine Special Operations Teams (MSOT), Companies (MSOC) and Battalions (MSOBs).[16]

17.6   Raider Legacy

On August 6 of 2014, MARSOC claimed and officially bestowed the prestigious Marine Raider moniker upon their subordinate combat units (Marine Special Operations Regiment) in commemoration of the fabled and elite amphibious light infantry unit that operated during World War II.[17]

17.7   See also

- Organization of the United States Marine Corps

- United States Special Operations Command

- United States Naval Special Warfare Command

- United States Army Special Operations Command

- Air Force Special Operations Command

- Special Operations

- MCSOCOM Detachment One

- Marine Raiders

- 2007 Shinwar shooting

17.8   References

This article incorporates public domain material from websites or documents of the United States Marine Corps.

Notes

[1] SOCOM Public Affairs (2014). *SOCOM Fact Book 2014* (PDF). SOCOM Public Affairs.

[2] Hejlik, Major General Dennis J; Gilmore, Major Cliff W; Ingram, Sergeant Major Matthew P (August 2006). "Special Operations Marines and the Road Ahead". *Marine Corps Gazette* (Marine Corps Association). ISSN 0025-3170. Cite uses deprecated parameter |coauthors= (help)

[3] MARSOC, Part 1: Devil Dogs of SOCOM. Sadefensejournal.com (2012-02-10). Retrieved on 2014-05-24.

[4] Armistead, Michael Warren (20 October 2008). "First US MARSOF Individual Training Course has begun" (Press release). United States Marine Corps. Retrieved 15 November 2008.

[5] Kyle McNally. "ITC 2-11 Graduation". Marines.mil.

[6] U.S. Seeks Faster Deployment; Smaller, More Flexible Special-Operations Teams Would Tackle Emerging Threats Under New Plan May 7, 2012

[7] http://www.marinecorpstimes.com/story/military/2015/06/11/marsoc-units-raiders-name-10-month-delay/71072932/

[8] Stahlman, Josephh (28 August 2007). "MSOAG Marines get LIT". United States Marine Corps. Archived from the original on 15 June 2008. Retrieved 20 November 2008.

[9] "Questions & Responses Page". *U.S Marine Corps Forces Special Operations Command*. United States Marine Corps. 30 October 2007. Retrieved 28 May 2008.

[10] "Marine Special Operations Support Group". *U.S. Marine Corps Forces Special Operations Command*. United States Marine Corps. 15 November 2008.

[11] http://www.marsoc.marines.mil/Units/MarineRaiderSupportGroup.aspx

[12] Maurer, Kevin (26 October 2008). "Marine Leader: Unit A Good Fit". *Fayetteville Observer*. Associated Press.

[13] Join Us - MARSOC Recruiting. Marsoc.com. Retrieved on 2014-05-24.

[14] MARSOC.com

[15]

[16] Critical Skills Operator Training & Selection. Americanspecialops.com. Retrieved on 2014-05-24.

[17] Lamothe, Dan (6 Aug 2014). "Marine Corps to adopt iconic Raiders name for its Special Operations troops". *Washington Post* (WashingtonPost.com). Retrieved 29 August 2014.

Web

- U.S. Marine Corps Forces Special Operations Command official website

- 2013 SOCOM Factbook

- ShadowSpear Special Operations: MARSOC

- MARSOC Prerequisites and Recruitment Phases

Marine Raiders conduct CQB training.

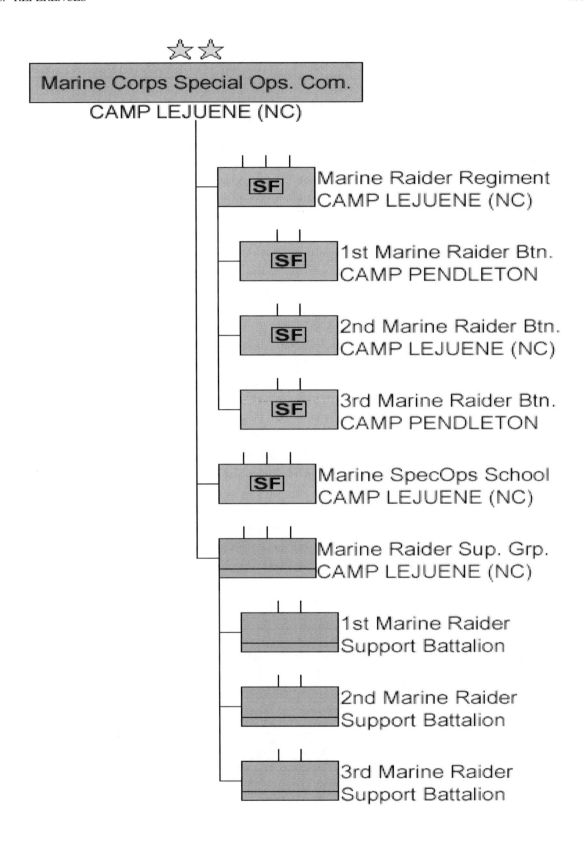

Chapter 18

United States Navy SEALs

The United States Navy's **Se**a, **A**ir and **L**and Teams, commonly known as the **Navy SEALs**, are the U.S. Navy's principal special operations force and a part of the Naval Special Warfare Command and United States Special Operations Command.[3] One of the SEALs' primary functions is to conduct small-unit maritime military operations which originate from, and return to a river, ocean, swamp, delta, or coastline. SEALs can negotiate shallow water areas such as the Persian Gulf coastline, where large ships and submarines are limited due to depth.[4] The Navy SEALs are trained to operate in all environments (Sea, Air, and Land) for which they are named. SEALs are also prepared to operate in a variety of climates, such as desert, arctic, and jungle.

All SEALs are male members of the United States Navy.[4][5][6][7] The CIA's highly secretive Special Activities Division (SAD) and more specifically its elite Special Operations Group (SOG) recruits operators from the SEAL Teams.[8] Joint Navy SEALs and CIA operations go back to the MACV-SOG during the Vietnam War.[9] This cooperation still exists today and is seen in the wars in Iraq and Afghanistan.[10][11]

18.1 History

18.1.1 Origins

The modern day U.S. Navy SEALs can trace their roots to World War II.[4] The United States Navy recognized the need for the covert reconnaissance of landing beaches and coastal defenses. As a result, the Amphibious Scout and Raider School was established in 1942 at Fort Pierce, Florida.[7] The Scouts and Raiders were formed in September of that year, just nine months after the attack on Pearl Harbor, from the Observer Group, a joint U.S. Army-Marine-Navy unit

18.1.2 Scouts and Raiders

Recognizing the need for a beach reconnaissance force, a select group of Army and Navy personnel assembled at Amphibious Training Base Little Creek, Virginia on August 15, 1942 to begin Amphibious Scouts and Raiders (joint) training. The Scouts and Raiders mission was to identify and reconnoiter the objective beach, maintain a position on the designated beach prior to a landing, and guide the assault waves to the landing beach.[4]

The first group included Phil H. Bucklew, the "Father of Naval Special Warfare," after whom the Naval Special Warfare Center building is named. Commissioned in October 1942, this group saw combat in November 1942 during Operation Torch on the North African coast. Scouts and Raiders also supported landings in Sicily, Salerno, Anzio, Normandy, and southern France.[12]

A second group of Scouts and Raiders, code-named Special Service Unit No. 1, was established on 7 July 1943, as a joint and combined operations force. The first mission, in September 1943, was at Finschafen on New Guinea. Later operations were at Gasmata, Arawe, Cape Gloucester, and the East and South coast of New Britain, all without any loss of personnel. Conflicts arose over operational matters, and all non-Navy personnel were reassigned. The unit, renamed 7th Amphibious Scouts, received a new mission, to go ashore with the assault boats, buoy channels, erect markers for the incoming craft, handle casualties, take offshore soundings, clear beach obstacles and maintain voice communications linking the troops ashore, incoming boats and nearby ships. The 7th Amphibious Scouts conducted operations in the Pacific for the duration of the conflict, participating in more than 40 landings.[4]

The third and final Scouts and Raiders organization operated in China. Scouts and Raiders were deployed to fight with the Sino-American Cooperative Organization, or SACO. To help bolster the work of SACO, Admiral Ernest J. King ordered that 120 officers and 900 men be trained for "Amphibious Raider" at the Scout and Raider school at Fort Pierce, Florida. They formed the core of what was envisioned as a "guerrilla amphibious organization of Americans and Chinese operating from coastal waters, lakes and rivers employing small steamboats and sampans." While most Amphibious Raider forces remained at Camp Knox in Calcutta, three of the groups saw active service. They conducted a survey of the upper Yangtze River in the spring of 1945 and, disguised as coolies, conducted a detailed three-month survey of the Chinese coast from Shanghai to Kitchioh Wan, near Hong Kong.[4]

18.1.3   Naval Combat Demolition Units

In September 1942, 17 Navy salvage personnel arrived at ATB Little Creek, VA for a week long course in demolitions, explosive cable cutting and commando raiding techniques. On November 10, 1942, the first combat demolition unit successfully cut cable and net barriers across the Wadi Sebou River during Operation Torch in North Africa. This enabled the USS *Dallas* (DD-199) to traverse the water and insert U.S. Rangers who captured the Port Lyautey airdrome.[4]

On 7 May 1943, Lieutenant Commander Draper L. Kauffman, "The Father of Naval Combat Demolition," was directed to set up a school and train people to eliminate obstacles on an enemy-held beach prior to an invasion. On 6 June 1943, LCDR Kauffman established Naval Combat Demolition Unit training at Fort Pierce.[7] Most of Kauffman's volunteers came from the navy's engineering and construction battalions. Training commenced with a gruelling week designed to filter out under-performing candidates. By April 1944, a total of 34 NCDUs were deployed to England in preparation for Operation Overlord, the amphibious landing at Normandy.[4] On 6 June 1944, in the face of great adversity, the NCDUs at Omaha Beach managed to blow eight complete gaps and two partial gaps in the German defenses. The NCDUs suffered 31 killed and 60 wounded, a casualty rate of 52%. Meanwhile, the NCDUs at Utah Beach met less intense enemy fire. They cleared 700 yards (640 metres) of beach in two hours, another 900 yards (820 metres) by the afternoon.

Casualties at Utah Beach were significantly lighter with six killed and eleven wounded. During Operation Overlord, not a single demolitioneer was lost to improper handling of explosives. In August 1944, NCDUs from Utah Beach participated in the landings in southern France, the last amphibious operation in the European Theater of Operations.[7] NCDUs also operated in the Pacific theater. NCDU 2, under LTjg Frank Kaine, after whom the Naval Special Warfare Command building is named, and NCDU 3 under LTjg Lloyd Anderson, formed the nucleus of six NCDUs that served with the Seventh Amphibious Force tasked with clearing boat channels after the landings from Biak to Borneo.

18.1.4   OSS Operational Swimmers

Some of the earliest World War II predecessors of the SEALs were the Operational Swimmers of the Office of Strategic Services, or OSS.[11] Many current SEAL missions were first assigned to them. OSS specialized in special operations, dropping operatives behind enemy lines to engage in organized guerrilla warfare as well as to gather information on such things as enemy resources and troop movements.[13] British Combined Operations veteran LCDR Wooley, of the Royal Navy, was placed in charge of the OSS Maritime Unit in June 1943. Their training started in November 1943 at Camp Pendleton, California, moved to Santa Catalina Island, California in January 1944, and finally moved to the warmer waters of The Bahamas in March 1944. Within the U.S. military, they pioneered flexible swimfins and diving masks, closed-circuit diving equipment (under the direction of Dr. Christian J. Lambertsen),[13][14] the use of Swimmer Delivery Vehicles (a type of submersible), and combat swimming and limpet mine attacks.[11] In May 1944, Colonel "Wild Bill" Donovan, the head of the OSS, divided the unit into groups. He loaned Group 1, under Lieutenant Choate, to Admiral Nimitz, as a way to introduce the OSS into the Pacific theater. They became part of UDT-10 in July 1944. Five OSS men participated in the very first UDT submarine operation with the USS *Burrfish* in the Caroline Islands in August 1944.

18.1.5   Underwater Demolition Teams (UDT)

UDT members using the casting technique from a speeding boat

On 23 November 1943, the U.S. Marine landing on Tarawa Atoll emphasized the need for hydrographic reconnaissance and underwater demolition of obstacles prior to any amphibious landing. The islands in this area have unpredictable tide changes and shallow reefs preventing the naval transport vessels from progressing. The first wave crossed the reef in Amtracs, but the second in Higgins boats were not as successful. They got stuck on a reef due to low tide. The Marines were forced to unload and wade to shore. This proved to be a daunting task and many Marines were killed or drowned before reaching the beach. Without support from the second wave the Marines in Amtracs were slaughtered on the beach. This was a valuable lesson that the Navy did not want to be repeated. After the Tarawa landing, Rear Admiral Richmond K. Turner directed the formation of nine Underwater Demolition Teams. Thirty officers and 150 enlisted men were moved to the Waimānalo Amphibious Training Base to form the nucleus of a demolition training program. This group became Underwater Demolition Teams (UDT) ONE and TWO.[4]

The UDTs saw their first combat on 31 January 1944, during Operation Flintlock in the Marshall Islands. Flintlock became the real catalyst for the UDT training program in the Pacific Theater. In February 1944, the Naval Combat Demolition Training and Experimental Base was established at Kīhei, Maui, next to the Amphibious Base at Kamaole. Eventually, 34 UDT teams were established. Wearing swim suits, fins, and dive masks on combat operations, these "Naked Warriors" saw action across the Pacific in every major amphibious landing including: Eniwetok, Saipan, Guam, Tinian, Angaur, Ulithi, Peleliu, Leyte, Lingayen Gulf, Zambales, Iwo Jima, Okinawa, Labuan, Brunei Bay, and on 4 July 1945 at Balikpapan on Borneo, which was the last UDT demolition operation of the war. The rapid demobilization at the conclusion of the war reduced the number of active duty UDTs to two on each coast with a complement of seven officers and 45 enlisted men each.[7]

18.1.6 Korean War

The Korean War began on 25 June 1950, when the North Korean army invaded South Korea. Beginning with a detachment of 11 personnel from UDT 3, UDT participation expanded to three teams with a combined strength of 300 men. During the "Forgotten War" the UDTs fought heroically, beginning to employ demolition expertise gained from WWII and use it for an offensive role. Continuing to use water as cover and concealment as well as an insertion method, the Korean Era UDTs targeted bridges, tunnels, fishing nets and other maritime and coastal targets. They also developed a close working relationship with the Republic of Korea naval special forces which continues today.[4]

The UDTs refined and developed their commando tactics during the Korean War, through their focused efforts on demolitions and mine disposal. The UDTs also accompanied South Korean commandos on raids in the North to demolish train tunnels. This was frowned upon by higher-ranking officials because they believed it was a non-traditional use of Naval forces. Due to the nature of the war the UDTs maintained a low operational profile. Some of the missions include transporting spies into North Korea and the destruction of North Korean fishing nets used to supply the North Korean Army.[4]

As part of the Special Operations Group, or SOG, UDTs successfully conducted demolition raids on railroad tunnels and bridges along the Korean coast. The UDTs specialized in a somewhat new mission: Night coastal demolition raids against railroad tunnels and bridges. The UDT men were given the task because, in the words of UDT Lieutenant Ted Fielding, "We were ready to do what nobody else could do, and what nobody else wanted to do." (Ted Fielding was awarded the Silver Star during Korea, and was later promoted to the rank of Captain).[15] On 15 September 1950, UDTs supported Operation Chromite, the amphibious landing at Incheon. UDT 1 and 3 provided personnel who went in ahead of the landing craft, scouting mud flats, marking low points in the channel, clearing fouled propellers, and searching for mines. Four UDT personnel acted as wave-guides for the Marine landing. In October 1950, UDTs supported mine-clearing operations in Wonsan Harbor where frogmen would locate and mark mines for minesweepers. On 12 October 1950, two U.S. minesweepers hit mines and sank. UDTs rescued 25 sailors. The next day, William Giannotti conducted the first U.S. combat operation using an "aqualung" when he dove on the USS *Pledge* (AM-277). For the remainder of the war, UDTs conducted beach and river reconnaissance, infiltrated guerrillas behind the lines from sea, continued mine sweeping operations, and participated in Operation Fishnet, which devastated the North Korean's fishing capability.[4]

18.1.7 Birth of Navy SEALs and Vietnam

Main article: Vietnam War

President John F. Kennedy, aware of the situation in Southeast Asia, recognized the need for unconventional warfare and special operations as a measure against guerrilla warfare. In a speech, to Congress, on 25 May 1961, Kennedy spoke of his deep respect for the United States Army Special Forces. While his announcement of the government's plan to put a man on the moon drew most of the attention, in the same speech he announced his intention to spend over $100 million to strengthen U.S. special operations forces and expand American capabilities in unconventional warfare. Some people erroneously credit President Kennedy with creating the Navy SEALs. His announcement was actually only a formal acknowledgement of a process that had been under way since Korea.[16]

The Navy needed to determine its role within the special operations arena. In March 1961, Admiral Arleigh Burke, the Chief of Naval Operations, recommended the establishment of guerrilla and counter-guerrilla units. These units would be able to operate from sea, air or land. This was the beginning of the Navy SEALs. All SEALs came from the Navy's Underwater Demolition Teams, who had already gained extensive experience in commando warfare in Korea; however, the Underwater Demolition Teams were still necessary to the Navy's amphibious force.[17][18]

The first two teams were formed in January 1962[19] and stationed on both US coasts: Team One at Naval Amphibious Base Coronado, in San Diego, California and Team Two at Naval Amphibious Base Little Creek, in Virginia Beach, Virginia. Formed entirely with personnel from UDTs, the SEALs mission was to conduct counter guerilla warfare and clandestine operations in maritime and riverine environments.[7] Men of the newly formed SEAL Teams were trained in such unconventional areas as hand-to-hand combat, high-altitude parachuting, demolitions, and foreign languages. The SEALs attended Underwater Demolition Team replacement training and they spent some time training in UDTs. Upon making it to a SEAL team, they would undergo a SEAL Basic Indoctrination (SBI) training class at Camp Kerry in the

Members of SEAL Delivery Vehicle Team Two in a Dry Deck Shelter of the submerged USS Philadelphia

Cuyamaca Mountains. After SBI training class, they would enter a platoon and conduct platoon training.

According to founding SEAL team member Roy Boehm, the SEALs' first missions were directed against communist Cuba. These consisted of deploying from submarines and carrying out beach reconnaissance in prelude to a proposed US amphibious invasion of the island. On at least one occasion Boehm and another SEAL smuggled a CIA agent ashore to take pictures of Soviet nuclear missiles being unloaded on the dockside.[20]

The Pacific Command recognized Vietnam as a potential hot spot for unconventional forces. At the beginning of 1962, the UDTs started hydrographic surveys and along with other branches of the US Military, the Military Assistance Command Vietnam (MACV) was formed. In March 1962, SEALs were deployed to South Vietnam as advisors for the purpose of training Army of the Republic of Vietnam commandos in the same methods they were trained themselves.

The Central Intelligence Agency began using SEALs in covert operations in early 1963. The SEALs were involved in the CIA sponsored Phoenix Program where it targeted key North Vietnamese Army personnel and Vietcong sympathizers for capture and assassination.

The SEALs were initially deployed in and around Da Nang, training the South Vietnamese in combat diving, demolitions, and guerrilla/anti-guerrilla tactics. As the war continued, the SEALs found themselves positioned in the Rung Sat Special Zone where they were to disrupt the enemy supply and troop movements and in the Mekong Delta to fulfill riverine operations, fighting on the inland waterways.

Combat with the Viet Cong was direct. Unlike the conventional warfare methods of firing artillery into a coordinate location, the SEALs operated close to their targets. Into the late 1960s, the SEALs were successful in a new style of warfare, effective in anti-guerrilla and guerrilla actions. SEALs brought a personal war to the enemy in a previously safe area. The Viet Cong referred to them as "the men with green faces," due to the camouflage face paint the SEALs wore during combat missions.[21]

In February 1966, a small SEAL Team One detachment arrived in Vietnam to conduct direct actions missions. Operating from Nha Be, in the Rung Sat Special Zone, this detachment signaled the beginning of a SEAL presence that would eventually include 8 SEAL platoons in country on a continuing basis. SEALs also served as advisors for Provincial

SEALs on patrol in the Mekong Delta

Reconnaissance Units and the Lein Doc Nguio Nhia, the Vietnamese SEALs. The last SEAL platoon departed Vietnam on Dec 7, 1971. The last SEAL advisor left in March 1973.[7]

SEALs continued to make forays into North Vietnam and Laos, and covertly into Cambodia, controlled by the Studies and Observations Group. The SEALs from Team Two started a unique deployment of SEAL team members working alone with South Vietnamese Commandos (ARVN). In 1967, a SEAL unit named Detachment Bravo (Det Bravo) was formed to operate these mixed US and ARVN units, which were called South Vietnamese Provincial Reconnaissance Units (PRUs).

At the beginning of 1968, the North Vietnamese and the Viet Cong orchestrated a major offensive against South Vietnam: the "Tet Offensive". The North hoped it would prove to be America's Dien Bien Phu, attempting to break the American public's desire to continue the war. As propaganda, the Tet Offensive was successful in adding to the American protest of the Vietnam war. However, North Vietnam suffered tremendous casualties, and from a purely military standpoint, the Tet Offensive was a major disaster for the Communists.[22]

By 1970, President Richard Nixon initiated a Plan of Vietnamization, which would remove the US from the Vietnam War and return the responsibility of defense back to the South Vietnamese. Conventional forces were being withdrawn; the last SEAL advisor, left Vietnam in March 1973 and Vietnam fell to the communists in 1975. The SEALs were among the highest decorated units for their size in the war, receiving 2 Navy Crosses, 42 Silver stars, 402 Bronze Stars, 2 Legions of Merit, 352 Commendation Medals, 3 Presidential Unit Citations[23][24] and 3 Medals of Honor. By the end of the war, 48 SEALs had been killed in Vietnam, but estimates of their kill count are as high as 2,000. The Navy SEAL Museum in Fort Pierce, FL displays a list of the 48 SEALs who lost their lives in combat during the Vietnam War.[25]

18.1.8 Grenada

Main article: Invasion of Grenada

Both SEAL Team 4 and SEAL Team 6, the predecessor to DEVGRU, participated in the US invasion of Grenada. The SEALs' two primary missions were the extraction of Grenada's Governor-General and the capture of Grenada's only radio tower. Neither mission was well briefed or sufficiently supported with timely intelligence and the SEALs ran into trouble from the very beginning. One of their two transport planes missed its drop zone, and four SEALs drowned in a rain squall while making an airborne insertion with their boats off the island's coast. Their bodies were never recovered.

After regrouping from their initial insertion the SEALs split into two teams and proceeded to their objectives. After digging in at the Governor's mansion, the SEALs realized they had forgotten to load their cryptographic satellite phone. As Grenadian and Cuban troops surrounded the team, the SEALs' only radio ran out of battery power, and they used the mansion's land line telephone to call in AC-130 gunship fire support. The SEALs were pinned down in the mansion overnight and were relieved and extracted by a group of Marines the following morning.

The team sent to the radio station also ran into communication problems. As soon as the SEALs reached the radio facility they found themselves unable to raise their command post. After beating back several waves of Grenadian and Cuban troops supported by BTR-60 armoured personnel carriers, the SEALs decided that their position at the radio tower was untenable. They destroyed the station and fought their way to the water where they hid from patrolling enemy forces. After the enemy had given up their search the SEALs, some wounded, swam into the open sea where they were extracted several hours later after being spotted by a reconnaissance plane.

18.1.9   Iran-Iraq War

Main article: Operation Prime Chance

During the closing stages of the Iran–Iraq War the United States Navy began conducting operations in the Persian Gulf to protect US-flagged ships from attack by Iranian naval forces. A secret plan was put in place and dubbed Operation Prime Chance. Navy SEAL Teams 1 and 2 along with several Special Boat Units and EOD techs were deployed on mobile command barges and transported by helicopters from the Army's 160th Special Operations Aviation Regiment. Over the course of the operation SEALs conducted VBSS (Visit, Board, Search, and Seizure) missions to counter Iranian mine laying boats. The only loss of life occurred during the take down of the *Iran Ajr*. Evidence gathered on the *Iran Ajr* by the SEALs later allowed the US Navy to trace the mines that struck the USS *Samuel B. Roberts* (FFG-58). This chain of events lead to Operation Praying Mantis, the largest US Naval surface engagement since the Second World War.

During Operation Desert Shield and Storm, Navy SEALs trained Kuwaiti Special Forces. They set up naval special operations groups in Kuwait, working with the Kuwaiti Navy in exile. Using these new diving, swimming, and combat skills, these commandos took part in combat operations such as the liberation of the capital city.

18.1.10   Panama

Main article: United States invasion of Panama

The United States Navy contributed extensive special operations assets to the invasion of Panama, code named Operation Just Cause. This included SEAL Teams 2 and 4, Naval Special Warfare Unit 8, and Special Boat Unit 26, all falling under Naval Special Warfare Group 2; and the separate Naval Special Warfare Development Group (DEVGRU). DEVGRU fell under Task Force Blue, while Naval Special Warfare Group 2 composed the entirety of Task Force White. Task Force White was tasked with three principal objectives: the destruction of Panamanian Defense Forces (PDF) naval assets in Balboa Harbor and the destruction of Manuel Noriega's private jet at Paitilla Airport (collectively known as Operation Nifty Package), as well as isolating PDF forces on Flamenco Island.

The strike on Balboa Harbor by Task Unit Whiskey is notably marked in SEAL history as the first publicly acknowledged combat swimmer mission since the Second World War. Prior to the commencement of the invasion four Navy SEALs, Lt Edward S. Coughlin, EN-3 Timothy K. Eppley, ET-1 Randy L. Beausoleil, and PH-2 Chris Dye, swam underwater into the harbor on Draeger LAR-V rebreathers and attached C4 explosives to and destroyed Noriega's personal gunboat the *Presidente Porras*.

Task Unit Papa was tasked with the seizure of Paitilla airfield and the destruction of Noriega's plane there. Several SEALs were concerned about the nature of the mission assigned to them being that airfield seizure was usually the domain of

Members of SEAL Team 4 immediately before the start of Operation Just Cause

the Army Rangers. Despite these misgivings and a loss of operational surprise, the SEALs of TU Papa proceeded with their mission. Almost immediately upon landing, the 48 SEALs came under withering fire from the PDF stationed at the airfield. Although Noriega's plane was eventually destroyed, the SEALs suffered four dead and thirteen wounded. Killed were Lt. John Connors, Chief Petty Officer Donald McFaul, Torpedoman's Mate 2nd Class Issac Rodriguez, and Boatswain's Mate 1st Class Chris Tilghman.

18.1.11   Gulf War

Main article: Gulf War

In August 1990, SEALs were the first western forces to deploy to the Persian Gulf as part of Operation Desert Shield. They infiltrated the capital city of Kuwait within hours of the invasion and gathered intelligence and developed plans to rescue US embassy staff should they become hostages. SEALs were also the first to capture Iraqi Prisoners of War when they assaulted nine Kuwaiti Oil platforms on 19 January 1991. On 23 February 1991, a six-man SEAL team led by Lieutenant Tom Dietz, launched a mission to trick the Iraqi military into thinking an amphibious assault on Kuwait by coalition forces was imminent by setting off explosives and placing marking buoys 500 meters off the Kuwaiti coast. The mission was a success and Iraqi forces were diverted east away from the true coalition offensive.[26]

18.1.12   Somali Intervention

In August 1993 a four-man DEVGRU SEAL sniper team was deployed to Mogadishu to work alongside Delta Force as part of Task Force Ranger in the search for Somali warlord Mohammed Farrah Aidid. They took part in several operations in support of the CIA and Army culminating in the 3 October 'Battle of Mogadishu' where they were part of the ground convoy raiding the Olympic Hotel. All four SEALs would be later awarded the Silver Star in recognition of their bravery whilst Navy SEAL Howard E. Wasdin would be awarded a Purple Heart after continuing to fight despite being wounded three times during the battle. [27]

18.1.13   Afghanistan

Main article: War in Afghanistan (2001–present)

Invasion

Navy SEALs STG2 Matthew Axelson (right) with Lt. Michael Murphy in Afghanistan

In the immediate aftermath of the 11 September attacks, Navy SEALs quickly dispatched to Camp Doha, and those already aboard US Naval vessels in the Persian Gulf and surrounding waters began conducting VBSS operations against ships suspected of having ties to or even carrying al Qaeda operatives. SEAL Teams 3 and 8 also began rotating into Oman from the United States and staging on the island of Masirah for operations in Afghanistan. One of the SEALs' immediate concerns was their lack of suitable vehicles to conduct special reconnaissance (SR) missions in the rough, landlocked terrain of Afghanistan. After borrowing and retrofitting Humvees from the Army Rangers also staging on Masirah, the SEALs inserted into Afghanistan to conduct the SR of what would become Camp Rhino, as part of Operation Enduring Freedom (OEF). These early stages of OEF were commanded by a fellow SEAL, Rear Admiral Albert Calland.

The SR mission in the region of Camp Rhino lasted for four days, after which two United States Air Force Combat Control

Teams made a nighttime HALO jump to assist the SEALs in guiding in Marines from the 15th Marine Expeditionary Unit who seized control of the area and established a Forward operating base. While at Camp Rhino, the CIA passed on intelligence from a Predator drone operating in the Paktia province that Taliban Mullah Khirullah Said Wali Khairkhwa was spotted leaving a building by vehicle convoy. SEALs and Danish Jægerkorpset commandos boarded Air Force Pave Low helicopters and seized Khairkhwa on the road less than two hours later. The SEALs continued to perform reconnaissance operations for the Marines until leaving after having spent 45 days on the ground.

Task Force K-Bar SEALs at one of the entrances to the Zhawar Kili cave complex

Subsequent SEAL operations during the invasion of Afghanistan were conducted within Task Force K-Bar, a joint special operations unit of Army Special Forces, United States Air Force Special Tactics Teams, and special operations forces from Norway, Germany, Australia, New Zealand, Canada, and Denmark, under the command of Navy SEAL Captain Robert Harward. Task Force K-Bar conducted combat operations in the massive cave complexes at Zhawar Kili, the city of Kandahar and surrounding territory, the town of Prata Ghar and hundreds of miles of rough terrain in southern and eastern Afghanistan. Over the course of six months Task Force K-Bar killed or captured over 200 Taliban and al Qaeda fighters, and destroyed tens of thousands of pounds of weapons and ordnance.

Navy SEALs participated extensively in Operation Anaconda. During insertion, AB1 Neil Roberts was thrown from his helicopter when it took fire from entrenched al Qaeda fighters. Roberts was subsequently killed after engaging and fighting dozens of enemies for almost an hour. Several SEALs were wounded in a rescue attempt and their Air Force Combat Controller, Technical Sergeant John Chapman, was killed. Attempts to rescue the stranded SEAL also led to the deaths of several US Army Rangers and an Air Force Pararescueman acting as a Quick Reaction Force.

SEALs were present at the Battle of Qala-i-Jangi alongside their counterparts from the British Special Boat Service. Chief Petty Officer Stephen Bass was awarded the Navy Cross for his actions during the battle.

Lieutenant Michael P. Murphy was posthumously awarded the Medal of Honor after his four-man counterinsurgency

Task Force K-Bar SEALs searching munitions found in the Zhawar Kili cave complex

team was almost wiped out during Operation Red Wings in June 2005. After the four man team lost Danny P. Dietz, he put himself in open view to call in the QRF. He soon after died from injuries sustained. Matthew G. Axelson also died on this operation. The QRF never reached the scene, it was struck by an RPG killing 8 Navy SEALs and 8 Army Night Stalkers. Marcus Luttrell was the only survivor from this operation.

In December 2012, the unit rescued a US doctor who had been kidnapped a few days earlier. However, during the operation the unit suffered a fatality, Petty Officer 1st Class Nicolas D. Checque.[28]

In May 2013, Rear Adm. Sean Pybus, commander of Navy Special Warfare stated that the unit would cut in half the number of SEAL platoons in Afghanistan by the end of 2013. Rear Adm. Sean Pybus also added that the unit is already "undergoing a transition back to its maritime roots" by placing more emphasis on sea-based missions after being involved in mostly landlocked missions since 2001.[29]

18.1.14   Iraq War

Main article: Iraq War

Al Faw and Iraqi oil infrastructure

Several days before the beginning of the invasion of Iraq two SDV teams were launched from Mark V Special Operations Craft in the Persian Gulf. Their objectives were the hydrographic reconnaissance of the Al Basrah (MABOT) and Khawr

US military security personnel on the Al Basrah Oil Terminal after its capture

Al Amaya (KAAOT) Oil Terminals. After swimming under the terminals and securing their Mark 8 mod 1s the SDV SEALs spent several hours taking pictures and surveying Iraqi activity on both platforms before returning to their boats. SEALs' later secured several oil infrastructures on the Al Faw peninsula and the offshore oil terminals, they helped clear the Khawr Abd Allah and Khawr Az Zubyar waterways which enabled humanitarian supplies to be delivered to the port of Umm Qasr.[26]

Mukarayin Dam

Coalition military planners were concerned that retreating Iraqi forces would destroy the Mukatayin hydroelectric dam northeast of Baghdad in an attempt to slow advancing US troops. In addition to restricting the maneuver of Coalition forces, the destruction of the dam would deny critical power needs to the surrounding area as well as cause massive flooding and loss of Iraqi civilian life. A mixed team of SEALs from SEAL Team Five and Polish GROM was called in to seize the dam. This force was flown several hours by US Air Force MH-53 Pave Lows to the dam. The SEALs employed DPVs into blocking positions to defend against counter-attack and roving bands of Iranian bandits that had been crossing the border and raiding Iraqi towns. As in Al Faw the SEALs found their DPVs to be ineffective and this marked the last time they would employ them in Iraq.

The SEALs and GROM on foot fast-roped out of their helicopters and immediately stormed the dam. The minimal Iraqi security forces on site surrendered, and with the exception of a GROM soldier who broke an ankle during the insertion, no casualties were sustained in the operation. After several hours of searching the dam for remaining hostile forces or any explosives, the SEALs secured the dam and were later relieved by advancing elements of the US Army.

Michael Monsoor, 2nd Navy SEAL who was killed in Iraq. This photo was taken during an extraction after a firefight and the smoke was used to conceal their movements from the enemy.

18.1.15 *Maersk Alabama* hijacking

Main article: Maersk Alabama hijacking

On 12 April 2009, in response to a hostage taking incident off of the coast of Somalia by Somalian pirates, three Navy SEALs from DEVGRU simultaneously engaged and killed the three pirates who were closely holding the hostage, Captain Richard Phillips, of the freighter ship, the *Maersk Alabama*. The pirates and their hostage were being towed in a lifeboat approximately 100 yards behind the *USS Bainbridge (DDG-96)* when each of the pirates were killed by a different DEVGRU sniper with a single shot to the head.[30]

18.1.16 Death of Osama bin Laden

Main article: Death of Osama bin Laden

In the early morning of May 1, 2011 local time, a team of 40 Navy SEALs from Seal Team 6 along with a Belgian Malinois Military Working Dog (Cairo), supported by Special Activities Division officers on the ground, killed Osama bin Laden in Abbottabad, Pakistan about 35 miles (56 km) from Islamabad in a CIA operation.[31][32] The Navy SEALs were part of the Naval Special Warfare Development Group (DEVGRU), previously called "SEAL Team 6".[33] President Barack Obama later confirmed the death of bin Laden, but did not directly mention the involvement of DEVGRU, saying only that a "small team" of Americans undertook the operation to bring down bin Laden.[31] The unprecedented media coverage raised the public profile of the SEAL community, particularly the counter-terrorism specialists commonly known as SEAL Team 6. The Walt Disney Company tried unsuccessfully to trademark the name "SEAL Team 6" the day after the raid.[34] The official name of the military operation was Operation NEPTUNE SPEAR. The model of the compound used in the *60 Minutes* documentary was donated by CBS to the Navy SEAL Museum.[35]

18.1.17   Wardak Province helicopter crash

Main article: 2011 Chinook shootdown in Afghanistan

On 6 August 2011, seventeen Navy SEALs were killed when their CH-47 Chinook helicopter was shot down by an RPG fired by Taliban militants. The SEALs were en route to support U.S. Army Rangers who were taking fire while attempting to capture a senior Taliban leader in the Tangi Valley. Fifteen of the SEALs belonged to the Naval Special Warfare Development Group.[36][37][38] Two others were SEALs assigned to a West Coast-based Naval Special Warfare unit.[36][39] A total of 30 Americans and eight Afghans were killed in the crash, making it the single largest loss of American lives in the Global War on Terrorism.

18.1.18   Morning Glory oil tanker

On March 16, 2014, US Navy SEALs took control of *MV Morning Glory*, a tanker full of oil loaded from a rebel-held port in Libya. The raid by Navy SEALs took place in international waters off the coast of Cyprus.[40]

18.2   Selection and training

U.S. Navy SEALs conducting training with SCAR rifles.

Main article: United States Navy SEAL selection and training

Before getting accepted into Basic Underwater Demolition/SEAL training, a prospective candidate must pass a certain

Students conduct CQB drills during SEAL Qualification Training.

number of both mental and physical requirements.[41] These tests include: Pre-enlistment medical screening, ASVAB, AFQT, C-SORT, and PST. Then, the candidate must get a SEAL contract by passing the SEAL Physical Screening Test: 500 yard swim in 12:30, 50 push ups in 2 minutes, 50 sit-ups in 2 minutes, 10 consecutive pull-ups in 2 minutes, and a 1.5 mile run in 10:30. If the candidate receives a passing score, he may then be admitted into training to become a Navy SEAL.[42] SEAL training is extremely rigorous, with the dropout rate sometimes over 80 percent.[43] The average candidate spends over a year in a series of formal training environments before being awarded the Special Warfare Operator Naval Rating and the Navy Enlisted Classification (NEC) 5326 Combatant Swimmer (SEAL) or, in the case of commissioned naval officers, the designation Naval Special Warfare (SEAL) Officer.

Navy SEAL training pipeline:

- 8-week Naval Special Warfare Prep School

- 24-week Basic Underwater Demolition/SEAL (BUD/S) Training

- 3-week Parachute Jump School

- 26-week SEAL Qualification Training (SQT)

Upon graduation from SQT, trainees receive the coveted Navy SEAL Trident, designating them as Navy SEALs. They are subsequently assigned to a SEAL Team or SEAL Delivery Vehicle (SDV) Team and begin 18-months of predeployment training before they are considered deployable. This training consists of:[44][45]

- 6-month Professional Development - Individual Specialty Training (ProDev)

- 6-month Unit Level Training (ULT)

- 6-month Squadron Integration Training (SIT)[46]

Those Enlisted SEALs with a medical rating will first attend the Special Operation Combat Medic Course for 6 months in Fort Bragg North Carolina[47] before joining a team in order to become a SEAL medic. Those pursuing Officer positions first attend the Junior Officer Training Course to learn about operations planning and how to perform team briefings. In total it can take over 2.5 years to completely train a Navy SEAL for his first deployment.[44][45]

18.2.1 Women

In August 2015, it was reported that the "Navy is planning to open its elite SEAL teams to women who can pass the grueling training regimen." [48] "Adm. Jon Greenert said he and the head of Naval Special Warfare Command, Rear Adm. Brian Losey, believe that if women can pass the legendary six-month Basic Underwater Demolition/SEAL training, they should be allowed to serve."[48] In August 2015, "[f]inal approval [for admission of women] is still pending." [48] On 3 December 2015, it was announced that there are now "no exceptions" to all military roles in the US, and women can become Navy SEALs.[49]

18.3 Navy SEAL teams and structures

Two members of SEAL Delivery Team 2 conduct lockout training with the USS Hawaii in 2007.

SEALs from SEAL Delivery Vehicle Team Two fast-rope to the deck of the USS Toledo *(2005)*

18.3.1   Naval Special Warfare Groups

Naval Special Warfare Command is organized into the following configuration:

- Naval Special Warfare Group 1: SEAL Teams 1, 3, 5, 7

- Naval Special Warfare Group 2: SEAL Teams 2, 4, 8, 10

- Naval Special Warfare Group 3: SEAL Delivery Vehicle Team 1

- Naval Special Warfare Group 4: Special Boat Teams 12, 20, 22

- Naval Special Warfare Group 11: SEAL Teams 17, 18 (formerly *Operational Support Teams* 1, 2)[50]

The total number of Navy SEALs assigned to Naval Special Warfare Command is approximately 2,000 out of a total staffing of 6,500. About half of the SEAL contingent are based at Little Creek Naval Amphibious Base and Dam Neck Annex in Virginia Beach, Virginia. The other half of the SEAL contingent is based at Naval Amphibious Base Coronado, California.

18.3.2   SEAL Teams

SEAL Teams are organized into two groups: Naval Special Warfare Group One (West Coast), and Naval Special Warfare Group Two (East Coast), which come under the command of Naval Special Warfare Command, stationed at NAB Coronado, California. As of 2006, there are eight confirmed Navy SEAL Teams. The original SEAL Teams in the Vietnam War were separated between West Coast (Team ONE) and East Coast (Team TWO) SEALs. The current SEAL Team deployments include Teams 1, 2, 3, 4, 5, 7, 8, and 10. The most recent to come into being are SEAL Team 7 and SEAL Team 10, which were formed in March and April 2002 respectively.[51][52]

The Teams deploy as Naval Special Warfare Squadrons or Special Operations Task Forces and can deploy anywhere in the world. Squadrons will normally be deployed and fall under a Joint Task Force (JTF) or a Combined Joint Special Operations Task Force (CJSOTF) as a Special Operations Task Force (SOTF).

Each SEAL Team is commanded by a Navy Commander (O-5), and has a number of operational SEAL platoons and a headquarters element.

A SEAL Team has a Staff Headquarters element and three 40-man Troops. Each Troop consist of a Headquarters element consisting of a Troop Commander, typically a Lieutenant Commander (O-4), a Troop Senior Enlisted (E-8), a Targeting/Operations Officer (O-2/3) and a Targeting/Operations Leading/Chief Petty Officer (E-6/7). Under the HQ element are two SEAL platoons of 16–20 men (two officers, 14–16 enlisted SEALs, and sometimes assigned non-NSW support personnel); a company-sized Combat Service Support (CSS) and/or Combat Support (CS) consisting of staff N-codes (the Army and Marine Corps use S-codes); N1 Administrative support, N2 Intelligence, N3 Operations, N4 Logistics, N5 Plans and Targeting, N6 Communications, N7 Training, and N8 Air/Medical.

Each Troop can be task organized for operational purposes into four squads, of eight 4–5 man fire teams. The size of each SEAL "Team" with Troops and support staff is approximately 300 personnel. The typical SEAL platoon has an OIC (Officer in Charge, usually a Lieutenant (O-3)), an AOIC (Assistant Officer in Charge, usually a Lieutenant (junior grade), O-2), a platoon chief (E-7), an Operations NCO/LPO (Leading Petty Officer, E-6) and other operators (E-4 to E-6). The core leadership in the Troop and Platoon are the Commander/OIC and the Senior Enlisted NCO (Senior Chief/Chief).

Troop core skills consist of: Sniper, Breacher, Communicator, Maritime/Engineering, Close Air Support, Corpsman, Point-man/Navigator, Primary Driver/Navigator (Rural/Urban/Protective Security), Heavy Weapons Operator, Sensitive Site Exploitation, Air Operations Master, Lead Climber, Lead Diver/Navigator, Interrogator, Explosive Ordnance Disposal, Technical Surveillance, and Advanced Special Operations.

Naval Amphibious Base Little Creek, a naval base in Virginia Beach, Virginia, is home to SEAL Teams 2, 4, 8, and 10. Naval Amphibious Base Coronado, a naval base in Coronado, California, is home to SEAL Teams 1, 3, 5, and 7. There is also a SEAL Delivery Vehicle (SDV) unit, SDVT-1, located in Pearl Harbor, Hawaii. SDVT-2 was based in Virginia; it was disestablished and merged into SDVT-1. SDV Teams are SEAL teams with an added underwater delivery capability. An SDV platoon consists of 12–15 SEALs. Declassified locations:

18.3.3   Special warfare ratings

The Special Warfare Operator rating (SO) and Special Warfare Boat Operator rating (SB), were established in 2006.[53] Special Warfare Operators (SEALs) and Special Warfare Boat Operators (SWCCs), are no longer required to maintain the original rating they qualified in upon joining the navy [54][55]

The following ratings are specific to Navy SEALs[56][57][58]

(*see: Template:US enlisted ranks*)

18.4   United States Navy Parachute Team "Leap Frogs"

The primary mission of the Navy Parachute Team (NPT) is to support Naval Special Warfare recruiting by gaining access and exposure to appropriate candidates through aerial parachuting demonstrations.[59] The U.S. Navy Parachute Team is a fifteen-man team composed of U.S. Navy SEALs. Each member comes to the team for a three-year tour from one of the two Naval Special Warfare Groups located on the east and west coasts. On completion of the tour, members return to operational units.[60] The parachute team began in 1969 when Navy SEALs and Frogmen volunteered to perform at weekend air shows. The Team initially consisted of five jumpers: LCDR Olson, PHC Gagliardi, SK2 "Herky" Hertenstein, PR1 Al Schmiz and PH2 "Chip" Maury. Schmiz and Maury were members of the original "Chuting Stars."[61] When LCDR Olson was transferred to California, PHC Gene "Gag" Gagliardi (D 546) of UDT ELEVEN introduced him to the local jumping elite with the San Diego Skydivers, one of the nation's first sports parachuting clubs. He convinced the Commander Naval Operations Support Group, PACIFIC to create a small demonstration team consisting of a cadre of highly qualified freefall jumpers. Its activities were to be conducted on a "not to interfere" basis with other military duties and at no cost to the government, other than utilizing normally scheduled aircraft. This group eventually adopted the "Leap Frogs" name.[61]

The team was officially commissioned as the U.S. Navy Parachute Team in 1974 by the Chief of Naval Operations and assigned the mission of demonstrating Navy excellence throughout the United States. The East Coast-based "Chuting Stars" were disbanded in the 1980s with the "Leap Frogs" taking on all official parachute demonstrations within the Navy.

A typical Leap Frogs performance consists of six jumpers leaping out of an aircraft at an altitude of 6,000 feet. After freefalling sometimes using smoke or streamers, the Leap Frogs fly their canopies together to build canopy-relative work formations. After performances, the Leap Frogs make themselves available to the public to answer questions about the Navy and the Naval Special Warfare community, as well as to sign autographs.

18.5   Influence on foreign units

From its predecessors the Underwater Demolition Teams to its current form, the SEALs have influenced the training and formation of several foreign units. In 1955 the Underwater Demolition Teams provided funding and training for the Republic of Korea Naval Special Warfare Flotilla, who are also known as UDT/SEALs. The Philippine Naval Special Warfare Group is also patterned off of the training and implementation of the US Navy SEALs and the UDTs. Upon the creation of the Indian MARCOS in 1987, three officers were sent to undergo a hard training schedule with the SEALs that would help them further shape their unit's capabilities. Due to their reputation as being one of America's premier special operations forces, SEALs (particularly operators from DEVGRU) will often do exchanges with allied SOFs.[62][63][64]

18.6   National Navy UDT-SEAL Museum and memorial

Main article: National Navy UDT-SEAL Museum

The National Navy UDT-SEAL Museum, in Fort Pierce, Florida, was founded in 1985[65] and was recognized as a National Museum by an act of Congress.[66] The museum is dedicated to preserving the history of the Navy SEALs and their predecessors. The SEAL Museum stands on the training site of the first Navy frogmen. There through World War II, thousands of service members were trained as members of Naval Combat Demolition Units and Underwater Demolition Teams. The Museum houses rare historic artifacts from the founding of the UDT to present day, including weapons, vehicles, equipment, and most recently added, the *Alabama Maersk* lifeboat aboard which Somali pirates held Captain Richard Phillips hostage.

18.7   In popular culture

Main article: United States Navy SEALs in popular culture

The well-known fictional representations of the U.S. Navy SEALs in the mass media include the private investigator Thomas Magnum in the 1980–1988 TV series Magnum, P.I., who is depicted as a former Navy SEAL from the late 1960s to the late 1970s, and various characters in Tom Clancy novels (e.g., *Rainbow Six* and *Without Remorse*) and the G.I. Joe universe. SEALs have been portrayed in films such as *Navy SEALs* (1990), *Act of Valor* (2012), *Lone Survivor* (2013) and *American Sniper* (2014). SEALs have also been portrayed in popular video game franchises such as the *Call of Duty* series, the *Medal of Honor: Warfighter* video game, and the *Counter-Strike* series.

18.8   See also

- List of Navy SEALs

- Red Cell

- SEAL Delivery Vehicle

- Underwater Demolition Team

- United States Naval Special Warfare Development Group

- Naval Special Warfare Command

- Death of Osama bin Laden

- Special Activities Division

18.9 References

[1] [sealswcc.comhttp://www.public.navy.mil/nsw/Pages/Mission.aspx "Naval Special Warfare Mission"]. United States Navy. Retrieved 2015-03-12. more than 2,500 active-duty Special Warfare Operators, 700 Special Warfare Boat Operators (SWCC)

[2] Wentz, Gene; B. Abell Jurus (1993). *Men In Green Faces*. St. Martin's Paperbacks. ISBN 978-0-312-95052-1.

[3] Perry, Anthony (27 July 1990). "SEALs Surface to Blow Holes in Navy Nerd Image". *Los Angeles Times*. Retrieved 28 December 2010.

[4] "Navy SEAL History". navyseals.com. Retrieved 16 May 2014.

[5] US Navy. SEAL requirements "SEAL Requirements" Check |url= value (help). navyseals.com. Retrieved 1 July 2011.

[6] Jill Laster. "Program letting Coasties train as SEALs on hold". Navy Times.

[7] "Navy SEAL History". sealswcc.com. Retrieved 20 April 2014.

[8] Waller, Douglas (3 February 2003). "The CIA Secret Army". TIME (Time Inc). http://www.time.com/time/magazine/article/0,9171,1004145,00.html

[9] *SOG: The Secret Wars of America's Commandos in Vietnam* by John L. Plaster

[10] Haney, Eric L. (2002). *Inside Delta Force*. New York: Delacorte Press.

[11] Efran, Shawn (producer), "Army Officer Recalls Hunt for Bin Laden", *60 Minutes*, CBS News, 5 October 2008.

[12] SEAL History: Origins of Naval Special Warfare-WWII | National Navy UDT-SEAL Museum. Navysealmuseum.com. Retrieved on 2014-05-24.

[13] Vann RD (2004). "Lambertsen and O2: beginnings of operational physiology". *Undersea Hyperb Med* 31 (1): 21–31. PMID 15233157. Retrieved 14 January 2012.

[14] Butler FK (2004). "Closed-circuit oxygen diving in the U.S. Navy". *Undersea Hyperb Med* 31 (1): 3–20. PMID 15233156. Retrieved 14 January 2012.

[15] SEAL History: Underwater Demolition Teams in the Korean War | National Navy UDT-SEAL Museum. Navysealmuseum.com. Retrieved on 2014-05-24.

[16] Genesis of the U.S. Navy's SEa, Air, Land (SEAL) Teams | National Navy UDT-SEAL Museum. Navysealmuseum.com. Retrieved on 2014-05-24.

[17] "Navy SEAL History". SOFREP Inc. Retrieved 12 May 2013.

[18] Watson, James (1997). *Walking Point: The Experience of a Founding Member of the Elite Navy SEALs*. New York, New York: William Morrow & Co. ISBN 0-688-14302-4.

[19] US Navy Videos. Navy.mil. Retrieved on 2014-05-24.

[20] First SEAL: Amazon.co.uk: Ray Boehm, Charles Sasser: Books. Amazon.co.uk. Retrieved on 2014-05-24.

[21] Point Man by Chief James Watson & Kevin Dockery, 1993, ISBN 0-380-71986-X

[22] Edwin E. Moïse. "The Vietnam Wars, Section 8: The Tet Offensive and its Aftermath". Clemson University. Retrieved 1 July 2011.

[23] "President Cites Seal Team", *The New York Times* (ProQuest), 12 November 1968, p. 21

[24] "Washington For the Record", *The New York Times* (ProQuest), 19 June 1970, p. 4

[25] Couch, Dick (2008). *The Sheriff of Ramadi*. Annapolis, MD: Naval Institute Press. ISBN 1-59114-138-9.

[26] Cawthorne, Nigel, *The Mammoth Book of Inside the Elite Forces*, Robinson, 2008 ISBN 1-84529-821-7 ISBN 978-1-84529-821-0

[27] Seal Team Six: The incredible story of an elite sniper - and the special operations unit that killed Osama Bin Laden: Amazon.co.uk: Howard E. Wasdin, Stephen Templin: Books. Amazon.co.uk. Retrieved on 2014-05-24.

[28] Shumaker, Lisa (11 December 2012). "Navy identifies SEAL killed in hostage rescue in Afghanistan". *Yahoo News*. Archived from the original on 18 December 2012. Retrieved 27 July 2015.

[29] SEALs to Undergo 'Evolution in Reverse' as They Return to Maritime Operations - Blog. Nationaldefensemagazine.org. Retrieved on 2014-05-24.

[30] "U.S. warship near boat carrying pirates — CNN.com". CNN. 9 April 2009. Retrieved 4 May 2011.

[31] "The raid on Osama bin Laden's compound". *CBS News*. 2 May 2011.

[32] "Osama bin Laden killed in CIA operation". The Washington Post. May 8, 2011. Retrieved May 19, 2011

[33] Flock, Elizabeth (2 May 2011). "Navy SEALs who killed Osama bin Laden are from the elite 'Team 6'". *The Washington Post*. Retrieved 2 May 2011.

[34] Winter, Jana (25 May 2011). "Mickey Mouse Surrenders to Navy SEALs in Trademark Battle". Fox News. Retrieved 8 June 2011.

[35] Model of Osama bin Laden Abbottabad Compound | National Navy UDT-SEAL Museum. Navysealmuseum.com. Retrieved on 2014-05-24.

[36] "DOD Identifies Service Members Killed In CH-47 Crash". U.S. Department of Defense Office of the Assistant Secretary of Defense (Public Affairs). August 11, 2011. Retrieved September 20, 2012.

[37] SEAL Team 6 members among 38 killed in Afghanistan. *Los Angeles Times* 6 August 2011.

[38] Helicopter Crash in Afghanistan Reportedly Kills Members of SEAL Team 6. *Fox News*, 6 August 2011.

[39] Pentagon releases names of Chinook crash victims , CNN News blog, 12 August 2011. Retrieved 14 August 2011.

[40] "Navy Seals board rogue Libya oil tanker Morning Glory". *BBC News*. 17 March 2014. Retrieved 6 October 2014.

[41] Command, Navy SEAL + SWCC Scout Team, Naval Special Warfare. "Navy SEAL Enlisted General Requirements - SEAL-SWCC.COM | Official website U.S. Navy SEALs". Retrieved 2015-09-28.

[42] "Enlisted SEAL Requirements | Navy SEALs". Retrieved 2015-09-28.

[43] SEAL+SWCC. "Content". sealswcc.com. Retrieved 30 May 2015.

[44] Navy.com. "Navy SEALs".

[45] sealswcc.com. "Navy SEALs Training Stages Overview".

[46] Navy SEAL Platoon Training | Navy SEALs Information & Resources. Information.usnavyseals.com (2009-09-04). Retrieved on 2014-05-24.

[47] "Special Operations Combat Medic Course". Retrieved 6 October 2014.

[48] Larter, David; Myers, Meghann (19 August 2015). "Navy SEALs set to open to women, top admiral says". *http://www.navytimes.com*. Navy Times. Retrieved 16 October 2015. External link in |website= (help)

[49] Crockett, Emily (3 December 2015). ""No exceptions": Women can now serve in all military combat roles". *Vox*. Retrieved 5 December 2015.

[50] Communication, Mass. "Naval Special Warfare Reserve Command Renamed". Navy.mil. Retrieved 1 October 2011.

[51] Dunia emas: US Navy SEALs. Duniakemilauemas.blogspot.com. Retrieved on 2014-05-24.

[52] SEAL Team 7 Holds Change of Command. Navy.mil. Retrieved on 2014-05-24.

[53] Navy Special Warfare Operator Rating (SEAL). Navycs.com. Retrieved on 2014-05-24.

[54] NSW Community Establishes New SO and SB Ratings. Navy.mil. Retrieved on 2014-05-24.

[55] SEALs and SWCCs drop source ratings [Archive] - SOCNET: The Special Operations Community Network. SOCNET. Retrieved on 2014-05-24.

[56] Job Title. (PDF) . Retrieved on 2014-05-24.

[57] http://www.trident.edu/Media/Default/NavyRoadMaps/SOCNAV-SO_082713.pdf

[58] "Welcome To Governors State" (PDF). Retrieved 6 October 2014.

[59] Navy Parachute Team handbook PDF

[60] "Official U.S. Navy Parachute Team Web Site – Leap Frogs". Leapfrogs.navy.mil. Retrieved 1 October 2011.

[61] SEAL History: The Leap Frogs-Origins of the Navy SEAL Parachuting Exhibition Team | National Navy UDT-SEAL Museum. Navysealmuseum.com. Retrieved on 2014-05-24.

[62] Couch, Dick (October 1, 2008). *Sheriff of Ramadi*. Annapolis: Naval Institute Press. p. 54.

[63] Kyle, Chris (October 15, 2013). *American Sniper*. New York: HarperCollins.

[64] Falconer, Duncan (July 1, 2001). *First Into Action: A Dramatic Personal Account of Life in the SBS*. London: Little, Brown Book Group.

[65] The Origin of the UDT-SEAL Museum | National Navy UDT-SEAL Museum. Navysealmuseum.com. Retrieved on 2014-05-24.

[66] "Ft. Pierce Museum Now the Official National Museum of Navy SEALs and Their Predecessors". NavySEALs.com. Retrieved 1 October 2011.

18.10   Bibliography

- Besel, Jennifer M. *The Navy SEALs*. Mankato, Minn: Capstone Press, 2011. ISBN 1-4296-5380-9 OCLC 649079630

- Bosiljevac, T.L. *SEALs: UDT/SEAL Operations in Vietnam*. Ballantine Books, 1990. ISBN 0-8041-0722-X. OCLC 23228772

- Bosiljevac, T.L. *SEAL Team Roll-Back*. New York: Avon Books, 1999. ISBN 0-380-78714-8. OCLC 41020614

- Bahmanyar, Mir. *US Navy SEALs*. Oxford: Osprey Publishing, 2005. ISBN 1-84176-807-3. OCLC 62176513

- Bahmanyar, Mir with Chris Osman. *SEALs: The US Navy's Elite Fighting Force*. Osprey Publishing, 2008. ISBN 1-84603-226-1. OCLC 191922842

- Couch, Dick. *May the Seals: Their untold history* (2014)

- Couch, Dick. *The Sheriff of Ramadi: Navy SEALs and the Winning of al-Anbar*. U.S. Naval Institute Press, 2008. ISBN 1-59114-138-9. OCLC 1591141389

- Couch, Dick. *The Warrior Elite: The Forging of SEAL Class 228.* New York: Three Rivers Press, 2003. ISBN 1-4000-4695-5. OCLC 802957824

- Couch, Dick. *The Finishing School: Earning the Navy SEAL Trident.* New York: Three Rivers Press, 2004. ISBN 0-609-81046-4. OCLC 60563833

- Couch, Dick. *Down Range: Navy SEALs in the War on Terrorism.* New York: Three Rivers Press, 2005. ISBN 1-4000-8101-7. OCLC 71199069

- Cummings, Dennis J. *The Men Behind the Trident: SEAL Team One in Viet Nam.* New York: Bantam Books, 1998. ISBN 0-553-57928-2 OCLC 39494815

- Denver, Rorke, and Ellis Henican. *Damn Few: Making the Modern SEAL Warrior.* New York: Hyperion, 2013. ISBN 1-4013-1280-2 OCLC 795757181

- Dockery, Kevin. *Navy SEALs: A History of the Early Years.* New York: Berkley Books, 2001. ISBN 0-425-17825-0 OCLC 0425178250

- Dockery, Kevin. *Navy SEALs: A History Part II: The Vietnam Years.* New York: Berkley Books, 2002. ISBN 0-425-18348-3 OCLC 48449554

- Dockery, Kevin. *Navy SEALs: A History Part III: Post-Vietnam to the Present.* New York: Berkley Books, 2003. ISBN 0-425-19034-X OCLC 51818673

- Dockery, Kevin. *Weapons of the Navy SEALs.* New York: Berkley Books, 2004. ISBN 0-425-19834-0 OCLC 56347561

- Donald, Mark L., and Scott Mactavish. *Battle Ready: Memoir of a SEAL Warrior Medic.* New York: St. Martin's Press, 2013. ISBN 1-250-00976-6 OCLC 759914152

- Fawcett, Bill. *Hunters and Shooters: An Oral History of the U.S. Navy SEALs in Vietnam.* New York: W. Morrow and Co., 1995. ISBN 0-688-12664-2 OCLC 31520013

- Freid-Perenchio, Stephanie, and Jennifer Walton. *SEAL: The Unspoken Sacrifice.* [Ketchum, ID]: SFP Studio, 2009. ISBN 0-615-30322-6 OCLC 525383689

- Greitens, Eric. *The Heart and the Fist: The Education of a Humanitarian, the Making of a Navy SEAL.* Boston: Houghton Mifflin Harcourt, 2011. ISBN 0-547-42485-X OCLC 646308409

- Halberstadt, Hans. *US Navy SEALs in Action.* Osceola, WI: Motorbooks International, 1995. ISBN 0-87938-993-1 OCLC 32275764

- Jansing, Chris (29 January 2010). "A typical SEAL? Think 007, not Rambo". NBC Field Notes (NBC News). Retrieved 29 January 2010.

- Kelly, Orr. *Never Fight Fair!: Navy SEALs' Stories of Combat and Adventure.* Novato, CA: Presidio Press, 1995. ISBN 0-89141-519-X OCLC 30894438

- Luttrell, Marcus. *Lone Survivor: The Eyewitness Account of Operation Redwing and the Lost Heroes of SEAL Team 10.* Little, Brown and Company, 2009. ISBN 0-316-04469-5. OCLC 319610219

- Luttrell, Marcus., and James D. Hornfischer. *Service: A Navy SEAL at War.* New York, NY: Little, Brown and Co., 2012. ISBN 0-316-18536-1 OCLC 756584153

- Mann, Don, and Ralph Pezzullo. *Inside SEAL Team Six: My Life and Missions with America's Elite Warriors.* New York, NY: Little, Brown & Co., 2011. ISBN 0-316-20431-5 OCLC 729343843

- McEwen, Scott, and Richard Miniter. *Eyes on Target: Inside Stories from the Brotherhood of the U.S. Navy SEALs.* New York: Center Street, 2014. ISBN 1-4555-7569-0 OCLC 828891431

- Neville, Leigh. *Takur Ghar: The SEALs and Rangers on Roberts Ridge, Afghanistan 2002.* Oxford, UK: Osprey Pub., 2013. ISBN 1-78096-198-7 OCLC 798058824

- Owen, Mark, and Kevin Maurer. *No Easy Day: The Autobiography of s Navy SEAL: the Firsthand Account of the Mission That Killed Osama Bin Laden.* New York, NY: Dutton, 2012. ISBN 0-525-95372-8 OCLC 808121503

- Padden, Ian. *U.S. Navy SEALs.* Toronto: Bantam Books, 1985. ISBN 0-553-24954-1 OCLC 12264420

- Pfarrer, Chuck. *SEAL Target Geronimo: The Inside Story of the Mission to Kill Osama Bin Laden.* New York: St. Martin's Press, 2011. ISBN 1-250-00635-X OCLC 733234790

- Pfarrer, Chuck. *Warrior Soul: The Memoir of a Navy SEAL.* New York: Random House, 2004. ISBN 1-4000-6036-2 OCLC 52165997

- Redman, Jason, and John R. Bruning. *The Trident: The Forging and Reforging of a Navy SEAL Leader.* New York: William Morrow, 2013. ISBN 0-06-220832-2 OCLC 827260093

- Robinson, Patrick. *Honor and Betrayal: The Untold Story of the Navy SEALs Who Captured the "Butcher of Fallujah"- and the Shameful Ordeal They Later Endured.* Cambridge, Massachusetts: Da Capo Press, 2013. ISBN 0-306-82308-X OCLC 861508106

- Sasser, Charles W. *Encyclopedia of the Navy SEALs.* New York: Facts on File, 2002. ISBN 0-8160-4569-0. OCLC 48383497

- Wasdin, Howard E., and Stephen Templin. *SEAL Team Six: Memoirs of an Elite Navy SEAL Sniper.* New York: St. Martin's Press, 2011. ISBN 0-312-69945-X OCLC 681499659

18.11 External links

- US Navy SEAL & SWCC—official website

- United States Navy Parachute Team—official website

- "Navy Fact File: Navy SEALs". San Diego: United States Navy. April 2002. Archived from the original on 3 March 2005. Retrieved 25 June 2006.

- Peterson, Lt. Cmdr Erick (June 2009). "The Strategic Utility of U.S. Navy SEALs". *Master thesis (dtic.mil).* NAVAL POSTGRADUATE SCHOO. Retrieved 17 January 2012.

- SEAL The Unspoken Sacrifice exhibit at the Pritzker Military Museum & Library

- McCoy, Shane T. (August 2004). "Testing Newton's Law", *All Hands Magazine*, p. 33.

- Obringer, Lee Ann. "How the Navy SEALs Work". How Stuff Works. Retrieved 14 June 2006.

- Navy SEALs 50 – Commemorating the 50th Anniversary of the Establishment of the U.S. Navy SEALs

- Ethos of the Navy SEALs

- A Veteran of SEAL Team Six Describes His Training

SEAL Team 5 conducts an exercise in a Combat Rubber Raiding Craft in 2000

Navy SEALs training with MP5 submachine guns.

A member of the U.S. Navy Parachute Demonstration Team, the "Leap Frogs," returns to earth after a successful jump

US Navy SEALs and Polish naval warfare team members practicing boarding skills near Gdansk, Poland, 2009.

18.12   Text and image sources, contributors, and licenses

18.12.1   Text

- **United States special operations forces** *Source:* https://en.wikipedia.org/wiki/United_States_special_operations_forces?oldid=697573897 *Contributors:* Mav, Slrubenstein, Gabbe, IZAK, Haakon, Angela, Jiang, Hadal, Unyounyo, Fabiform, JamesMLane, DocWatson42, Halda, Lupin, David Esrati, Niteowlneils, Grant65, Golbez, Joseph Dwayne, Utcursh, Necrothesp, Efriedman, Bbpen, Ukexpat, Canterbury Tail, N328KF, Vsmith, Seafort, Prospero, Officiallyover, Espoo, Knucmo2, Autopilots, Brianboru, Jigen III, Ricky81682, Lord Pistachio, Gulfstorm75, L33th4x0rguy, Axeman89, Falcorian, Mhazard9, Dangman4ever, Ddye, Graham87, A Train, Kane5187, The wub, SchuminWeb, Vidkun, Coolhawks88, Noclador, RazorICE, TDogg310, Alex43223, Scott Lawson, CLW, Black Falcon, K.Nevelsteen, Chase me ladies, I'm the Cavalry, 6a4fe8aa039615ebd9ddb83d6acf9a1dc1b684f7, Tommythegun, Mercenary2k, Streltzer, JDspeeder1, Nick-D, SmackBot, Looper5920, EvilCouch, Delldot, Mauls, Pretendo, Hmains, ERcheck, Parableman, Can't sleep, clown will eat me, NoIdeaNick, Шизомби, Ohconfucius, Swatjester, Jefe619, Nkcs, Joffeloff, Publicus, Tonster, MrDolomite, Dl2000, Yosy, Patrickwooldridge, Rob1bureau, Sakurambo, CmdrObot, Sllu22, Harej bot, James5, Cydebot, ST47, Capmaster, Bushido Brown, DumbBOT, Aldis90, Sselbor, Bobblehead, Signaleer, OdeSSa, Luna Santin, QuiteUnusual, SummerPhD, Res2216firestar, Ioeth, Paul1776, RM Gillespie, Tekuli, Mark Rizo, Magioladitis, Appraiser, Puddhe, Buckshot06, Cgingold, ShadowSpear, BilCat, Smokizzy, Johnny542, Novis-M, Ndunruh, Gregfitzy, Hamburmk, DMCer, Andy Marchbanks, Ripberger, Indubitably, EricSerge, Mnomrs, Skyski, Ng.j, LeaveSleaves, Buffs, Black6, Bahamut0013, Wavehunter, Sephiroth storm, Paulghspro, Cclavette, Shink X, Arundhati lejeune, Outdawg, Spencer1157, Drmies, Cirt, Niteshift36, Carriearchdale, RekonDog, Ajahewitt, MatthewVanitas, Addbot, LCoolo, Yobot, Mackin90, Evans1982, Webmgr, Osgood11, AnomieBOT, Subcontinent, Assuredly, Materialscientist, Citation bot, GB fan, EverettMcGill, Sionus, Wiiwiiwiiwii1, Srich32977, Riotrocket8676, Quillake, FFlixx7481, Tobby72, BlackHawk101, Der rikkk, Iqinn, Bobmack89x, Ricramirez2, RedBot, Himynameissudip, Reaper Eternal, Diannaa, Awong1133, Beyond My Ken, EmausBot, WikitanvirBot, Akjar13, RenamedUser01302013, TreacherousWays, Navysealscouts, Wikipelli, K6ka, Access Denied, Donner60, Thewolfchild, Aohara22, ClueBot NG, PattonWarKing, Compfreak7, Dainomite, NeptuneSpeared, Mercenary115, Snow Blizzard, NorthCoastReader, Achowat, Cyberbot II, F111ECM, 86steveD, SNAAAAKE!!, David Penn101, Diniquo, Icemanwcs, Dainophone, Jmm313, FrB.TG, Timdlee, El Felberino, Lugnuthemvar, Coveops, SyriaWarLato, Andy Dusk, Jonathon12 and Anonymous: 368

- **Special forces** *Source:* https://en.wikipedia.org/wiki/Special_forces?oldid=697199250 *Contributors:* The Epopt, Wesley, Uriyan, The Anome, AlexWasFirst, Wheat, Roadrunner, Zoe, Mintguy, Olivier, Stevertigo, Edward, Lir, GABaker, Wapcaplet, TUF-KAT, Jniemenmaa, Aarchiba, Александър, Julesd, Michael Shields, Cimon Avaro, Jiang, Evercat, BillBell, David Latapie, Lou Sander, Rvolz, Zoicon5, DJ Clayworth, Pedant17, Nv8200pa, Thue, Hajor, NightCrawler, CVA, PBS, Chris 73, Romanm, Modulatum, Sam Spade, Neckro, SoLando, Zaui, Mattflaschen, GreatWhiteNortherner, Foxcub, Julianp, DocWatson42, Gtrmp, Axeman, Mintleaf~enwiki, Nichalp, Varlaam, Golbez, Joseph Dwayne, Jasper Chua, GeneralPatton, Antandrus, Wareware, Benw, MisfitToys, Mark5677, Mzajac, Balcer, Sam Hocevar, Huaiwei, Klemen Kocjancic, Avatar, Canterbury Tail, Rob cowie, NrDg, Pmsyyz, Seafort, Abelson, SpookyMulder, Bender235, Kross, Tronno, Cmdrjameson, Franey, Maurreen, La goutte de pluie, Kelsomallette, Numerousfalx, Sam Korn, Espoo, Sherurcij, Andrew Gray, Darrelljon, Logologist, T-1000, Mac Davis, Snowolf, Max rspct, SidP, Jrleighton, BLueFiSH.as, Elchup4cabra, Woohookitty, LOL, TomTheHand, Pol098, Apokrif, Torqueing, GraemeLeggett, Behun, Graham87, Descendall, BD2412, Jclemens, Ketiltrout, Rjwilmsi, WehrWolf, Nightscream, Kinu, CoStar, Nigosh, Fish and karate, Ground Zero, JdforresterBot, Bubbleboys, Redwolf24, Jay-W, DemonicTruism, Mmx1, Chwyatt, Wasted Time R, YurikBot, Noclador, Wavelength, Arado, Hede2000, Walbanger, Bhny, Curuinor, Stephenb, Ksyrie, Dagamezmasta, Wiki alf, Pagrashtak, Spot87, Welsh, SigPig, Liebermann~enwiki, CecilWard, Marshall, Julienlecomte, NpaK13, Mkill, EEMIV, Stevefis, BoonDock, CLW, Scott Adler, Chipmunkchewer, Ktoto, Modify, Mercenary2k, GraemeL, Ladysway1985, LeonardoRob0t, Emigrant123, DearPrudence, Domingo chavez, Nick-D, SmackBot, Looper5920, EvilCouch, Shorty114, Ominae, Deon Steyn, Ariedartin, KocjoBot~enwiki, Jagged 85, Mauls, Portillo, Ohnoitsjamie, Hmains, ERcheck, Carryit, Bluebot, Mixmatch, Jprg1966, Snori, Mgeorg~enwiki, Moshe Constantine Hassan Al-Silverburg, Famspear, Cplakidas, OrphanBot, Onorem, OneEuropeanHeart, Hippo43, MilitaryTarget, Daniel.o.jenkins, Kellyprice, ALR, Thejerm, Angela26, Robomaeyhem, Swatjester, Ergative rlt, Joffeloff, Ckatz, CyrilB, Mr Stephen, Julthep, Mushmush123, Publicus, RyJones, Darz Mol~enwiki, Krait, ScreaminEagle, Raymond1964, OnBeyondZebrax, Iridescent, Aeternus, Octane, Yosy, Yendor1958, Tawkerbot2, JForget, VMAAXT, Ledboots, Estéban, Orca1 9904, Coldwinter1281, Korinwoodo, Hydraton31, Gogo Dodo, Bellerophon5685, Ctatkinson, Evogol, Doug Weller, DumbBOT, King konger, Malleus Fatuorum, Wandalstouring, Sendbinti, Peer-LAN, Warrior-Mentor, Archangel1, Hcobb, Signaleer, Dsw, Heroeswithmetaphors, Eikichi 00, Mwithers, Sensemaker, AntiVandalBot, Howard61313, Modernist, Lfstevens, Tashtastic, Dybdal~enwiki, Canadian-Bacon, DagosNavy, Avaya1, Parsecboy, VoABot II, JNW, GrabacrOfnirRazgriz, Buckshot06, Bzero, Froid, Indon, ClovisPt, BilCat, Nat, LorenzoB, MCG, Ghostscg, Gavin Wilson, Yhinz17, MartinBot, WhyTanFox, Roastytoast, R'n'B, CommonsDelinker, KTo288, EdBever, Nev1, Trusilver, Maurice Carbonaro, Elkost, New Hampshirite, Akinchen, Mrg3105, RoboMaxCyberSem, Comp25, IDFSF, Imacphee, SJP, Olegwiki, Andy Farrell, Scote95, Remember the dot, Xyl 54, Treisijs, Ripberger, Meyerj, Shubu fubu, HJ32, Koonter, Philip Trueman, Mohykan9, Technopat, EggyNL, Dormskirk, Cowie1337, Leafyplant, Ng.j, BotKung, StillTrill, ODA233, Buffs, Wh1sky-M1ke, Cowlinator, Kernel Saunters, Matthew Yeager, Gilsinan, Zatoichi1564, Oxymoron83, Mesoso2, Kumioko, Spitfire19, ZH Evers, Martin H., Varunkrish89, Bombaw, Outdawg, Denisarona, ClueBot, Hutcher, Airbornecal, EoGuy, Uncle Milty, Foofbun, Dxbmanu, Niteshift36, Callinus, Smidsy999, Whiterussian1974, TomPointTwo, Sexy me 12, Jim Sweeney, Addbot, Emotology, Mortense, SuperSmashBros.Brawl777, Okhota, MartinezMD, Elmondo21st, Zarcadia, Download, Green Squares, Tide rolls, Lightbot, Matekm, Yobot, Mach101, Legobot II, Phinicky, Mo7amedsalim, Aturus~enwiki, AnomieBOT, Georgejdorner, Jim1138, Tavrian, Citation bot, Inbodyspazz, Belvucker2, Tylerwade123, Impacter444, SFBubba, Jbruin152, Capricorn42, CaliSEAL, Millahnna, Srich32977, Sanshouhammer, Jeff4ya, Pigby, Anotherclown, Mark Schierbecker, HoyaProff, AustralianRupert, Jonorza, DITWIN GRIM, MH6M, Highfield1730, FrescoBot, Paine Ellsworth, Originalwana, Tobby72, Flurgblorg, Zenithpress, Dger, TawsifSalam, Haeinous, Hchc2009, AstaBOTh15, Bobmack89x, Pinethicket, Elockid, Majestic27, MJ94, My very best wishes, SF1SHER07, CertainMiracle, Lotje, Callanecc, The Catholic Knight, Товарищ, Wikimastername, Tbhotch, RjwilmsiBot, IshmaelMarcos, NameIsRon, Camp northern lights, 933064corvair, Beyond My Ken, Salvio giuliano, Jtsb87, Surlyduff50, GoingBatty, Solarra, TreacherousWays, Wikipelli, LightAj, USASF, Bitthalns, Michael Essmeyer, Kapiteni, Anir1uph, Chemicalinterest, Bear32ie, Slovolyub, Δ, ProfessorJane, KazekageTR, Quantumor, SuperJewishBrain, Noodleki, Furbissima, JohnWitherspoon, MakmoudHassan, HarvardDoctor, PapouMenager, CharlieEchoTango, ClueBot NG, Nateho, Johannesvonshladen, Loginnigol, Corusant, Intforce, MerlIwBot, Helpful Pixie Bot, Gob Lofa, Lowercase sigmabot, BG19bot, Murry1975, TrinityGate, Sergeispb-10, Compfreak7, BeNeLux Is The Best, Hngrbfevdwc, Dainomite, Nautilusvideo, Wodrow, Trần Ái Quốc, R1990u, Klilidiplomus, Tomh903, Stonewaters, Cyberbot II,

Pissant, FrankWilliams, Dreadstar, Derek R Bullamore, Weregerbil, Last Avenue, Het, ALR, Antheii, ComputerWhizIA, DCB4W, Ohconfucius, Redlegsfan21, Evets70, Synthe, Greyman, Esrever, Swatjester, Rklawton, AmeriCan, Ergative rlt, Hotspur23, LWF, Nkcs, Neovu79, Joffeloff, Mgiganteus1, BigFatPaulie, Ocatecir, IronGargoyle, Nobunaga24, Stwalkerster, Muadd, Grandpafootsoldier, PRRfan, Wtg87, Tonster, E71, MoltenBoron, Chart123, DouglasCalvert, MARK S., Dpaymas, CzarB, LeyteWolfer, Aeternus, Sanandros, Amakuru, Yosy, Phoenixrod, Túrelio, Pjbflynn, Tawkerbot2, Gebrah, Randroide, Lahiru k, Ehistory, Serbitar, HDCase, Thud495, Rob1bureau, Wafulz, Estéban, OldSoldier, ShelfSkewed, Jordan2, James5, Orca1 9904, J-boogie, Nilfanion, Cydebot, Wikien2009, Warmachine021, RelentlessRecusant, Jimduchek, Bellerophon5685, Adamtw, Signin11, Psuliin, Añoranza, BetacommandBot, Thijs!bot, Unicyclopedia, Jmg38, N5iln, RobotEater, Mojo Hand, Beaverdam100, Deathbunny, Bossesjoe, Z10x, Archangel1, Signaleer, Dsw, Heroeswithmetaphors, DaRk StRiDeR, USMA, OdeSSa, AntiVandalBot, Cultural Freedom, Fru1tbat, Marokwitz, DarkAudit, Aceee, TimVickers, Zchris87v, Spartaz, Tashtastic, Dreaded Walrus, MikeLynch, Hydezeppelin, MER-C, ElComandanteChe, Lan Di, Jarrodm, RumoriousBIG~enwiki, Dwhit8, Doom777, ThrawN, Parsecboy, VoABot II, Pratj, Jacce, Swpb, GrabacrOfnirRazgriz, Buckshot06, Soulbot, Michele Konrad, Ed!, Andypayne, Fabrictramp, Fallschirmjäger, ShadowSpear, Mike Searson, The velociraptor, FlieGerFaUstMe262, Kronnang Dunn, CommonsDelinker, AlexiusHoratius, Delmet, ChDV, Headcase2k6, Tgeairn, J.delanoy, Rgoodermote, Uncle Dick, FordGT90Concept, -CentraSpike-, Johnny542, Novis-M, Ndunruh, Stymphal, Benreser, Bushy33, Dehbach, Halmstad, Specter01010, Nojamus, NJguy281, Eaglestorm, Mien Marine, Chaos5023, HJ32, Dreddmoto, Scurry928, Mickwsmith, Philip Trueman, JuneGloom07, Revmqo, Smash05, Bmili, Jimbo88~enwiki, Retiono Virginian, Imasleepviking, SGT141, Davwillev, Alborz Fallah, Tmaull, RandomXYZb, Black6, Aaron mcd, Superlunk, Schnellundleicht, Cor87, Laval, AlleborgoBot, PGWG, Atlantabravz, Redart2, Blatopilot1, Blackshod, BonesBrigade, Robbor, Krawi, Rcsrodolfo, Caltas, Thehornet, Sephiroth storm, PsychoFerd, Gilsinan, Jonsimon, Bentogoa, Flyer22 Reborn, Tiptoety, Crashtech, BIGShorts, Spartan198, ZH Evers, Jbgreen, Shovonma17, Hamiltondaniel, MarkMLl, Jackf314, Outdawg, Mcase07, Spencer1157, Stevecalloway, ClueBot, The Thing That Should Not Be, Mkodama, AussieRain, AmishSexy, Jonybond, A professional dancing weasel, Rebelheartous, Gerdaaegesdotter, The Flying Bunny, Thefischer, Dr. B. R. Lang, Excirial, Eeekster, Niteshift36, Cathal mansfield, Lertsky, Coinmanj, Jonjames1986, Eustress, Ewsraven, La Pianista, Morgan quieres huevos, Johnnybgood3293, Floul1, DumZiBoT, ApocalypseNow115, Lex0nyc, Jlmiller858, TheUbergamer, Thornberrylc, Ziphead, Kwjbot, Darealmccoy, TomPointTwo, Addbot, Baron Von Wiki, Landon1980, SpartanSWAT10, Ronhjones, Dumbfood, Mikec62001, Kman543210, Wakkapooo, Reedmalloy, Download, Shizz4553, Holyhendy, Chzz, LinkFA-Bot, Milk's Favorite Bot, Kngspook, ScottFreeRJH, Lightbot, OlEnglish, Zorrobot, Droobie6, Bcreamer, OlderGhost, Luckas-bot, Yobot, Ptbotgourou, Senator Palpatine, Evans1982, Jnivekk, Charlie Tango Bravo, THEN WHO WAS PHONE?, Ironmanlogan, AnomieBOT, Octillion88, Citation bot, Adie111, Lqstuart, SFBubba, Xqbot, Swimmer0118, Tubulartoad, 4twenty42o, Tragino, TheLoneWarrior, Qo.0p, Tyrol5, Paulkappelle, Ghser99, Riotrocket8676, Plumtree100, Mathonius, SCARECROW, HoyaProff, Ugotbplus, Shadowjams, MH6M, Bxsullivan, Dtlwarrior, Captain Cheeks, FrescoBot, LucienBOT, Tobby72, Lumoy, Vepres, Girace, Airborne84, HamburgerRadio, Citation bot 1, Bobmack89x, Pinethicket, Degen Earthfast, Jozefa12, RedBot, Impala2009, Marbito11, SaadMuhammad, NsMARSOC, Ionisiso, Hankleyhog, TobeBot, Valdemarasl, Lotje, Overagainst, Grammarxxx, The Catholic Knight, TangoSixZero, Aoidh, Zink Dawg, Reaper Eternal, Tbhotch, Sideways713, Pierpao, Shadyaftrmathgunit, Rjwilmsi-Bot, TjBot, Icemamba, NerdyScienceDude, LcawteHuggle, EmausBot, Az29, Sumnderd2, Ssclimber92, Mach1988, Tommy2010, Mmeijeri, Lucas Thoms, ZéroBot, Illegitimate Barrister, Fæ, Shuipzv3, N512ma, Speedbird536, GrayFox1991, Demonkoryu, Nick 0405, Wayne Slam, Jay-Sebastos, Bluegreen1011, Donner60, Armtdog, Thewolfchild, Jakeno911, Coyote Squid, UltimateThinker, JanetteDoe, Kstrohma, Afranelli, Mjbmrbot, Gmt2001, ClueBot NG, Takgu, Jack Greenmaven, Goalloverhere, Wedittor, Ocalafla, Widr, Paolau.kalani, Patton-WarKing, Helpful Pixie Bot, Sambo212, Regulov, Chris0834, Hambone155, McChizzle, The Mark of the Beast, PTJoshua, Blued2013, Holliswood, Ltjct8295, Pritishp333, Dainomite, Outlawsbf, NeptuneSpeared, PlasmaTime, USCG MSRT, Sulfurboy, Pratyya Ghosh, Cyberbot II, ForwardObserver85, Ngoquangduong, V.cross99, Tornadoisme, EuroCarGT, Dexbot, SFK363, Irunwiki, Svbesouw, Fat Grumpy Cat, Alexander9595, Charliemaia, Militarystuff123, AusRaven, Tekogi, Thornberrylc12, SOTGMichael, Doublekill10, Redshang053, Jmm313, Doughtar, Quenhitran, UnbiasedVictory, Trident1983, GraniteSand, Gdgolder, OJOM, JamesBourne1002, Monkbot, Armynut15, IrishSpook, Lugnuthemvar, Gutson217, GWA88, BenedickSFODD, ChamithN, JT2958, Swimbuddy888888, Citadel48, Bestfromstirling, LoneEditor, Star72, S6235178654, BOPEfollower, RockApe27, SyriaWarLato, KasparBot, Nyxnax, Pdez1788, Nezi1111 and Anonymous: 996

- **Intelligence Support Activity** *Source:* https://en.wikipedia.org/wiki/Intelligence_Support_Activity?oldid=691240474 *Contributors:* Cjrother, DocWatson42, Halda, Skywolf, Klemen Kocjancic, Kdammers, Bender235, Stesmo, Rackham, Polarscribe, Hohum, Woohookitty, Apokrif, Kgrr, Tabletop, Mandarax, Artoro, Thiseye, Nikkimaria, SmackBot, John Lunney, Chris the speller, Bluebot, Ck lostsword, Ohconfucius, Will Beback, Phinn, Ergative rlt, Cmh, Mbisgaier, Kevin W., DouglasCalvert, CzarB, Rob1bureau, CmdrObot, Hildenja, Estéban, AndrewHowse, Cydebot, Wikien2009, SithiR, Thijs!bot, OrenBochman, Nick Number, Alphachimpbot, ShortShadow, Spartaz, Paul1776, Lan Di, GrabacrOfnirRazgriz, Buckshot06, Papalatiolais, Ekki01, CommonsDelinker, Consciousnessbliss, SaviorSix, VAcharon, Johnny542, Novis-M, Tagus, DMCer, Drmargi, Manikmann, Enigmaman, Black6, Hughey, DGGenuine, Veronicabeebe, Outdawg, TubularWorld, Spearhead30, Mild Bill Hiccup, Niceguyedc, Buffalosoldier92, Frozen4322, SchreiberBike, TomPointTwo, Addbot, Kman543210, Kngspook, The Bushranger, Yobot, Bunnyhop11, Evans1982, Charlie Tango Bravo, AnomieBOT, Eumolpo, RightCowLeftCoast, FrescoBot, D'ohBot, Pinethicket, SeoMac, Peash, ZéroBot, Ksu6500, Chazz3d, Bcaulf, Thewolfchild, ClueBot NG, Helpful Pixie Bot, Chris0834, Dainomite, Virtuallyironic, Hitonem, JaniceDolittle, Redsquirrel118, Jack100001, Cerabot~enwiki, Redcell254, David Penn101, Zatchbell549, TACIT RAINBOW, Mattyi13, GRAN EAGLE, Sciophobiaranger, JT2958, 11B3XTVF7, Abnsoldier and Anonymous: 113

- **SEAL Team Six** *Source:* https://en.wikipedia.org/wiki/SEAL_Team_Six?oldid=697706714 *Contributors:* KAMiKAZOW, Jpatokal, Darrell Greenwood, Jengod, WhisperToMe, Cjrother, Scott Sanchez, Bjørn, Dale Arnett, Axeman, Halda, Cool Hand Luke, Marcika, Neuro, Niteowlneils, Hazzamon, Comatose51, Gadfium, OverlordQ, ShakataGaNai, Bbpen, Klemen Kocjancic, Zro, Mike Rosoft, Rich Farmbrough, Vsmith, Night Gyr, Bender235, Ylee, FrankTownend, KSlayer, TomStar81, Stesmo, Keron Cyst, Larryv, Anthony Appleyard, LtNOWIS, Free Bear, Geo Swan, Lord Pistachio, Malo, Grenavitar, Mattbrundage, Wavehawk, Dan100, Zntrip, Woohookitty, Pol098, Apokrif, M412k, Mb1000, RichardWeiss, Kbdank71, Rjwilmsi, Nightscream, Linuxbeak, Sgkay, FlaBot, Mongol, RussBot, Dblandford, Sanjosanjo, Briaboru, Austinmayor, Ytcracker, Nutiketaiel, JLClark, DAJF, Mikeblas, TDogg310, EEMIV, MN, DeadEyeArrow, Thendcomes, Georgewilliamherbert, Bdell555, Petri Krohn, Rwh86, Garion96, Hoorah25, Dmax, SmackBot, Cdogsimmons, WookieInHeat, Cla68, KelvinMo, Kintetsubuffalo, Onebravemonkey, Flamarande, SmartGuy Old, Tennekis, Chris the speller, Jprg1966, Mjm13186, Oni Ookami Alfador, Dual Freq, Hongooi, Jcb10, OrphanBot, Wen D House, Deathsythe, Badboyjamie, Derek R Bullamore, Ultraexactzz, Ohconfucius, Evets70, Greyman, Rklawton, John, Ergative rlt, Gobonobo, Neovu79, Martinvincent, Mgiganteus1, Ocatecir, IronGargoyle, Cowbert, JHunterJ, InedibleHulk, Jrt989, MrDolomite, Dl2000, Kevin W., DouglasCalvert, Iridescent, JHP, Sanandros, Courcelles, Eastlaw, Kendroche, Rob1bureau, Dycedarg, J-boogie, Cydebot, RelentlessRecusant, CurtisJohnson, Monkeybait, JCO312, Aldis90, Paragon12321, Seaphoto, Georgert, Spar-

Scottie theNerd, Ortzinator, Mrtorrent, Davptb, Xyzzy n, Mistress Selina Kyle, Rory737, Tanis118, Ohconfucius, Synthe, SashatoBot, Esrever, Swatjester, Wavy G, SEWalk, AmeriCan, Kuru, Ergative rlt, MayerG, Gobonobo, JohnI, Gnevin, Ktinga, Nobunaga24, Stwalkerster, Darz Mol~enwiki, Neddyseagoon, Virus-X, Coaxial, Tonster, MrDolomite, MARK S., CzarB, Dubrules, Dp462090, CaptWillard, Dlohcierekim, HDCase, Rob1bureau, Ateamfog, CmdrObot, Patchouli, Estéban, Toms2866, James5, Neelix, LCpl, J-boogie, CPT Spaz, Cydebot, Khatru2, Kevin23, Adolphus79, Signin11, Dynaflow, Zer0faults, Aldis90, CalculatinAvatar, Añoranza, Thijs!bot, Epbr123, Ishdarian, Memty Bot, Hcberkowitz, Warrior-Mentor, Bobblehead, Woody, Dfrg.msc, Signaleer, Heroeswithmetaphors, Mwithers, Dcfowler1, Green Hill, Tigga, Meinsla, .K, Mct05, Tstrobaugh, Vituperex, Magioladitis, Parsecboy, VoABot II, Kahran042, JNW, Fish Cop, Buckshot06, Ed!, Tajik24, Froid, Fallschirmjäger, D.Kurdistani, Ikilled007, Yhinz17, FlieGerFaUstMe262, CommonsDelinker, KTo288, Bjordan5, ChDV, Apple8069, Uncle Dick, Novis-M, Notreallydavid, Gurchzilla, Mrg3105, RoboMaxCyberSem, Comp25, Lygophile, Brian Pearson, Shoessss, Serenthia, Iolusnaught, AzureCitizen, Upthera23, DMCer, Andy Marchbanks, Airbornelawyer, Thecuer, VolkovBot, Meyerj, Chaos5023, HJ32, Philip Trueman, Sarenne, Broadbot, Ng.j, Jackfork, SGT141, StillTrill, Ferdinand1, Doug, Wh1sky-M1ke, Falcon8765, ChristianLAX, Aaron mcd, Schnellundleicht, This.machinery, Logan, C0N6R355, Prisonbreak12345, GirasoleDE, Blackshod, WereSpielChequers, BonesBrigade, Neutralhomer, Smilesfozwood, Gnom, Craig.mcneil, KathrynLybarger, WacoJacko, Retireduser1111, Anchor Link Bot, Shovonma17, Outdawg, DSArmageddon, ImageRemovalBot, Cuprum17, ClueBot, Ropata, Waukegan, Trfasulo, Max Mayr, Mild Bill Hiccup, Thinkbui, Jonybond, Foofbun, Gerdaaegesdotter, Ridger11, Dr. B. R. Lang, Jusdafax, PixelBot, FKrizanac, Abrech, Vital Forces, Boylann2, StienForAllTid, Iohannes Animosus, Throwsfreak, Thingg, Aitias, EpicDream86, Emt1299d, BarretB, XLinkBot, Dark Mage, WikHead, SilvonenBot, Sooofisticated0499, TomPointTwo, MystBot, Mntntm1, Addbot, Hurricanetracker, Emtguy289, Delta27, Okhota, Ronhjones, KorinoChikara, Kman543210, CanadianLinuxUser, Reedmalloy, Shizz4553, Cardshark2k4, Kngspook, Dylfre47, HerculeBot, Luckas-bot, Yobot, Amirobot, Evans1982, Charlie Tango Bravo, AnomieBOT, Jim1138, Thomas.merrill, Materialscientist, Citation bot, EverettMcGill, B. Fairbairn, LilHelpa, SFBubba, Boscaswell, 4twenty42o, Inferno, Lord of Penguins, Srich32977, Ian.de.mallie, Pfagan92, J04n, Mcndjxlefnd, Mark Schierbecker, TonyHagale, HoyaProff, Striker570, Shadowjams, ArdenHathaway, FFlixx7481, PS2801, FrescoBot, LucienBOT, Tobby72, Intifadamericana, Citation bot 1, Calmer Waters, Shanmugamp7, Utility Monster, Himynameissudip, Dinamik-bot, Hughglad, Hamilton36, Aoidh, Tlsarles, Ruger24, RjwilmsiBot, IshmaelMarcos, Wolfgangvonkrieg, Orphan Wiki, WikitanvirBot, Nothingmore Nevermore, Joe712, Mrsbehr, Alderete74, Roborobby, Dewritech, Gbsaylor, ZéroBot, Illegitimate Barrister, Lateg, H3llBot, Bxj, Realsfmaster, Brandmeister, Thewolfchild, Orange Suede Sofa, Quasimodogeniti, Coyote Squid, Arthur Water, TYelliot, CharlieEchoTango, Ebehn, Petrb, ClueBot NG, Katiker, Ocalafla, Jrgert, Widr, Marloweperel, Helpful Pixie Bot, Last Revanant, YahwehSaves, McChizzle, LittleHarryLoyd, Gunnai, Compfreak7, Militaryartist, Dainomite, Nautilusvideo, Writ Keeper, NeptuneSpeared, Oda112, BattyBot, 18exray, Bricks94, ForwarddObserver85, TheJJJunk, SNAAAAKE!!, Kevin Levin 27452, Dexbot, Collectorofinsignia, Mogism, Genghis 6, Ramos37, Alexander9595, Coldbloodedpro7, Dooleydragon, Sfcmullins, Maerwynn, Curlupndie85, Donreedjax, Mannysafe1, HashtagR6, GraniteSand, OJOM, Architect2014, Rowematthew, Sierratangoxray, Amortias, Balls0115, Depthfield, InIgnorantBliss, SyriaWarLato and Anonymous: 647

- **United States Naval Special Warfare Command** *Source:* https://en.wikipedia.org/wiki/United_States_Naval_Special_Warfare_Command? oldid=688613093 *Contributors:* Edward, Paul A, Cjrother, DocWatson42, Joseph Dwayne, Mamizou, Klemen Kocjancic, D6, Maurreen, Pschemp, Arthena, BLueFiSH.as, Falcorian, Woohookitty, Jeff3000, Kralizec!, Kbdank71, Rjwilmsi, The wub, SchuminWeb, Ground Zero, Noclador, TDogg310, Petri Krohn, SmackBot, Chris the speller, Ohconfucius, Neovu79, IronGargoyle, MrDolomite, Phuzion, MARK S., Sanandros, Courcelles, Denaar, Andkore, Cydebot, Gogo Dodo, Dcfowler1, Epeefleche, Ferritecore, Buckshot06, CommonsDelinker, Bothnia, Novis-M, Gene Hobbs, Technopat, SGT141, Bahamut0013, Lightmouse, Outdawg, ClueBot, Hutcher, Foofbun, DumZiBoT, RekonDog, Addbot, LongVo84, Sillyfolkboy, AndersBot, Yobot, Mackin90, Best O Fortuna, AnomieBOT, FreeRangeFrog, Xqbot, HoyaProff, FrescoBot, Der rikkk, Awakko, Diannaa, Harrisonmwilson, Acsian88, EmausBot, Dewritech, OHPerry, Illegitimate Barrister, JDnCoke1992, LostCause231, ClueBot NG, LDMerriam, Helpful Pixie Bot, Sonny2fresh, Dainomite, Hamish59, ChrisGualtieri, Alexander9595, Tentinator, Chris troutman, Jmm313, Lawrence5641, Hotshot2162, WPGA2345, Gitterdun123 and Anonymous: 51

- **Air Force Special Operations Command** *Source:*https://en.wikipedia.org/wiki/Air_Force_Special_Operations_Command?oldid= 697365848*Contributors:*Edward, Rlandmann, Astrotrain, DocWatson42, Joseph Dwayne, Kubieziel, Klemen Kocjancic, D6, Rich Farmbrough, Pm-syyz, Crosbiesmith, Dr Gangrene, Scriberius, BD2412, JavaWarlord, Vegaswikian, The wub, Mark Sublette, VolatileChemical, Noclador,Epolk, Los688, TDogg310, Syrthiss, Gadget850, Arthur Rubin, Jmackaerospace, SmackBot, Hmains, Bluebot, Attention whore, EagleWSO,Ohconfucius, Bwmoll3, Dl2000, DouglasCalvert, Sanandros, Octane, Courcelles, Fvasconcellos, Kemiriv, Cydebot, Capmaster, Hcobb, Dc-fowler1, Aeh4543, Buckshot06, Tedickey, Jatkins, BilCat, Jim.henderson, FLJuJitsu, LordAnubisBOT, Novis-M, Chikinsawsage, Ndunruh,Lauren.kat.johnson, Kschovan, Kyle the bot, Ng.j, Buffs, Desert thndr01, LanceBarber, Bahamut0013, Biscuittin, Flyer22 Reborn, Kumioko,Outdawg, JL-Bot, Niceguyedc, Afsocpa, Rudolph.cm, Ewsraven, EpicDream86, Addbot, Jessaveryja, Laurinavicius, Reedmalloy, ChamalN, Yobot, Evans1982, Rockwing, Turbomx42, AnomieBOT, Georgejdorner, DSisyphBot, Ronstenger, Omnipaedista, Spitfire888, Griffi-nofwales, FrescoBot, LucienBOT, VilePig, DrilBot, Tinton5, EmausBot, Sumnderd2, RenamedUser 01302013, Mmeijeri, Werieth, Demingkj,Manikind, Bill william compton, Chesipiero, SojerPL, Compfreak7, Dainomite, Riley Huntley, ChrisGualtieri, F111ECM, StealthHawk69,TeriEmbrey, Ligunny, Jmm313, Minhquangdo, Slothloveschunk69, DragonNighthawk101, LouisRobertP, Starlifter99, California Walnut andAnonymous: 99

- **United States Marine Corps Forces Special Operations Command***Source:*https://en.wikipedia.org/wiki/United_States_Marine_Corps_ Forces_Special_Operations_Command?oldid=696866405*Contributors:*Edward, Conti, Nurg, DocWatson42, Klemen Kocjancic, Rich Farmbrough, Bender235, Bobo192, Stesmo, Giraffedata, BLueFiSH.as, Drbreznjev, Strongbow, PoccilScript, Jackcall, Rjwilmsi, Vegaswikian, The wub, SchuminWeb, Mmx1, Noclador, Welsh, TDogg310, Syrthiss, DeadEyeArrow, Black Falcon, Tommythegun, GraemeL, Katieh5584, Nick-D, Aerno, SmackBot, Looper5920, GrummelJS, Cla68, Pretendo, ERcheck, Bluebot, Sadads, Igilli, Ohconfucius, Swatjester, Neovu79, Thaemcee2, Tonster, MrDolomite, MARK S., Rhetth, Tawkerbot2, JForget, J-boogie, Cydebot, Hydraton31, Mattsrevenge, Hcobb, Heroeswithmetaphors, Darklilac, Yellowdesk, PhilKnight, Buckshot06, Mike f, FlieGerFaUstMe262, Jay Litman, CommonsDelinker, RockStar31, J.delanoy, Novis-M, HJ32, Philip Trueman, CobraDragoon, Luksuh, PaladinWhite, Danblh11, Bahamut0013, Aaron mcd, Oldag07, Lucasbfrbot, Iridany, Kumioko, CsSpoolee, Outdawg, ClueBot, FieldMarine, MithraUnconquered, Drmies, State99, Jusdafax, Wkharrisjr, Mikaey, XLinkBot, RekonDog, TomPointTwo, Addbot, Xp54321, Ennui93, Debresser, Ben Ben, Luckas-bot, Shinobi-bushi, Evans1982, Charlie Tango Bravo, AdvCentral, K30, AnomieBOT, IRP, Manowar987, Materialscientist, Citation bot, Hooah-hooah, Ewhalen, HoyaProff, Griffinofwales, FrescoBot, AbdullahMo, Duderdude, Citation bot 1, Jonesey95, LiquidOcelot24, NsMARSOC, Javierito92, LawBot, Blu the Marine, IshmaelMarcos, JCRules, Don Brunett, Mach1988, Solarra, Commander edit, Illegitimate Barrister, BushidoDevilDog, UsmcMARSOC, H3llBot, Insommia, Mcshane73, ClueBot NG, Allwoundup357, MARSOC-Marine, Wolf under rain, Compfreak7, Dainomite, NeptuneSpeared, Kiltor6, ForwardObserver85, Superflyguy432, Ros Láir, FOX 52, Pablo.guardado, Fycafterpro, Jmm313, Minhquangdo, Xmanprime, Melcous, Monkbot, SantiLak, Lugnuthemvar, Danielcolbywalker, Joefitzmetz6, OldPainless, Rio197 and Anonymous: 172

- **United States Navy SEALs** *Source:* https://en.wikipedia.org/wiki/United_States_Navy_SEALs?oldid=697822815 *Contributors:* Damian Yerrick, Peter Winnberg, The Epopt, Mav, Zundark, Ed Poor, Edward, Bdesham, Lousyd, Gabbe, Prefect, Mac, Snoyes, Jiang, JidGom, Popsracer, Fuzheado, Andrewman327, Tpbradbury, Morven, Cjrother, Scott Sanchez, Pakaran, Jni, Sovbob, Bearcat, Dale Arnett, ZimZalaBim, Romanm, JosephBarillari, Delpino, SoLando, Cyrius, PBP, Clemmarshall, Smjg, DocWatson42, Cormac Canales, Philwelch, Halda, Jrquinlisk, Wwoods, Everyking, Bkonrad, FrYGuY, Mboverload, Bobblewik, Golbez, Joseph Dwayne, Btphelps, Gadfium, SoWhy, Sleep pilot, Kesac, Mpiff, Balcer, Husnock, Tin soldier, Necrothesp, Sam Hocevar, Gscshoyru, Neutrality, Joyous!, Klemen Kocjancic, Master Of Ninja, Mtnerd, Canterbury Tail, Daveirl, Alkivar, Mormegil, Neckelmann, Discospinster, Solitude, Rich Farmbrough, Guanabot, Vsmith, YUL89YYZ, Piewalker, Michael Zimmermann, Martpol, Night Gyr, Bender235, ZeroOne, Sum0, Swid, JoeSmack, Ylee, MBisanz, Kross, Shanes, Prospero, Bobo192, TomStar81, Tronno, Giraffedata, Eritain, Pschemp, MPerel, Pearle, Hooperbloob, Bfg, Jigen III, Patsw, Preuninger, Alansohn, Anthony Appleyard, LtNOWIS, Free Bear, Lord Pistachio, Luong, Mailer diablo, Avenue, Bart133, Hohum, Velella, Deathphoenix, Ianblair23, Dwbird2, Alai, Zereshk, Wavehawk, Czolgolz, Dan100, Dennis Bratland, Dismas, Zntrip, Smoth 007, CruiserBob, OwenX, Scriberius, Wnjr, Ekem, Ddye, Nick Drake, Tabletop, Dmol, Bokpasa, Stochata, BlaiseFEgan, Dysepsion, RichardWeiss, Graham87, Deltabeignet, Descendall, Teflon Don, Ketiltrout, Behemoth, Rjwilmsi, Jim Huggins, Bill37212, Rillian, Staecker, B1link82, Trlovejoy, SeanMack, The wub, Jayson Virissimo, Searayman, LAPD85, SeANMcBAY, DickClarkMises, Ucucha, SchuminWeb, AJR, JY-Ouyang, Bubbleboys, Leesamuel, NeoFreak, Wingsandsword, HVillarante, Coolhawks88, Chobot, Mmx1, Zimbabweed, Feliperijo, Srjenkins, SFjarhead, Roboto de Ajvol, Noclador, RussBot, Jtkiefer, Hede2000, Epolk, Rampagingcarrot, Ioda006, Chensiyuan, Gaius Cornelius, NawlinWiki, JD79, Doubleslash, Nathan8225, Duran, Merman, Rjensen, Ve3, Nick, Arcimpulse, TDogg310, Slearl, PonyToast, Alex43223, EEMIV, WMarsh, Cerejota, Jakubz, Plasmastik~enwiki, Elkman, CLW, Tom1234, Searchme, Crisco 1492, Richardcavell, Georgewilliamherbert, Poppy, K.Nevelsteen, TheMadBaron, Ageekgal, Mercenary2k, GraemeL, Streltzer, Terber, Nick-D, SmackBot, Looper5920, Beatdown, KnowledgeOfSelf, TracerBullet, Mrgate3, C.Fred, Sn00kie, SaxTeacher, Bwilliams, Dwanyewest, Rojomoke, Cla68, Kintetsubuffalo, Nscheffey, Yamaguchi⬚⬚, Pretendo, Gilliam, Quidam65, Ohnoitsjamie, Youremyjuliet, Skizzik, ERcheck, Manuelomar2001, Chris the speller, BullWikiWinkle, Bpauley, Jprg1966, Mjm13186, GregRM, Elagatis, PrimeHunter, Roscelese, Deli nk, Propound, Whispering, Revelations, William Allen Simpson, Rlevse, Tcpekin, DéRahier, MJBurrage, Squalla, KevM, Wine Guy, Splash22386, Stenas, Riose, Krich, Flyguy649, Cybercobra, Nakon, ShawnLee, Vindimy, Cordless Larry, Batman2005, Rory737, Salamurai, Springnuts, Primogen, Lantern-Light, Ohconfucius, Will Beback, Thehitmaker, Seeker 99, Greyman, Nishkid64, Swatjester, Doug Bell, JzG, Sjock, Euchiasmus, General Ization, Nkcs, Neovu79, Leopardjferry, Nobunaga24, A. Parrot, Werdan7, Command doh, Mr Stephen, Godfrey Daniel, Hargle, Optakeover, Darz Mol~enwiki, WildBeggar, Roundeyesamurai, MrDolomite, Working class saint, Masem, Djharrity, OnBeyondZebrax, Hayrake7, Iridescent, MARK S., Stanley666, CzarB, TheMontgomery, Picklegnome, Aeternus, IvanLanin, UncleDouggie, Scskowron, Sanandros, Octane, Courcelles, Ehistory, CuriosityCosby, Nutster, CmdrObot, Patrick Berry, Dyeslayer, Davemize, Otsego, Travitherabbi, Toms2866, Ajayfahlman, Stewsmith, Jordan2, Virose09, Ecophreek, J-boogie, Cydebot, AniMate, UncleBubba, RelentlessRecusant, Gogo Dodo, Khatru2, Hebrides, Jon Stockton, Corpx, Myscrnnm, Daniel J. Leivick, Terminator32, Christian75, Odiseo79, DumbBOT, Blackbird 4, Mafia-Capo, FastLizard4, Zer0faults, Omicronpersei8, CalculatinAvatar, Click23, Añoranza, Epbr123, Qwyrxian, Bolman Deal, Marek69, 666163, James086, Signaleer, Heroeswithmetaphors, Mactin, AntiVandalBot, Majorly, Purpleslog, Apmadoc, Jj137, Joe Schmedley, Purplenorth, Utsav80, Yellowdesk, Ok!, Tangurena, NJW494, Tashtastic, Ioeth, CombatWombat42, Avaya1, Hello32020, Albany NY, Neoman2026, Andonic, Noobeditor, East718, PhilKnight, Sophosmoros, Magioladitis, Parsecboy, Bongwarrior, VoABot II, JNW, Dboyz-x.etown, Puddhe, Buckshot06, Jim Douglas, Dinosaur puppy, Jatkins, KConWiki, Catgut, JohnnyChicago, Neilbliss, 28421u2232nfenfcenc, BilCat, SperryTS, Dcahillusa, Mcgrathrjm, Xienyao, Bigsprinta, Daveuk30, MartinBot, FlieGerFaUstMe262, Ustye, R'n'B, CommonsDelinker, AlexiusHoratius, KTo288, ChDV, Wiki Raja, J.delanoy, Gofreedom, Jbrdrumboy, J.lessard, Public Menace, Punkyhiggs, Tdadamemd, Thewolfman, Barts1a, Bothnia, Novis-M, Jeepday, Uranium grenade, Chriswiki, Comp25, Ohms law, Alex180172, Gawyb, The Watcher God, Robertgreer, Jgroub, TheChrisParker, Ledenierhomme, Bogdan~enwiki, Ibking, Blackmaster45, Bdmccray, DMCer, Varnent, MoodyGroove, Smc64130, Johnnieblue, Hammersoft, TreasuryTag, Rucha58, Jeff G., Mrcriter, Bacchus87, IIJ32, Dreddmoto, Gene Hobbs, SexyBern, Philip Trueman, Plyhmrp, Oshwah, EricSerge, Ldmerriam, Lodim3, Bdb484, A4bot, Sparkzy, Obafgkm, 18Fox, Macslacker, Martin451, Luksuh, Werideatdusk33, Jackfork, LeaveSleaves, From-cary, SGT141, Jkch13, BobWeaver112, Danblh11, Nulrich~enwiki, James Seneca, Wenli, Sarc37, Meters, SQL, Falcon8765, Bahamut0013, Nattgew, Diamondfiretail, Aaron mcd, Vitz-RS, Koalorka, Elticitl, Monty845, Stavlor, Atlantabravz, Solicitr, Czwarrior, Docclabo, 13dble, Sheetz, Yerul, RHodnett, Mikemoral, Maher-shalal-hashbaz, Swliv, Iznikarius, Krawi, Kyleisextremelyshort, Winchelsea, Yintan, Gravitan, Riving, Voldemore, Keilana, Fellr, Bentogoa, Cobatfor, Flyer22 Reborn, Radon210, Goolcap, Claudevsq, Gnfgb2, JSpung, Oxymoron83, Artoasis, Bagatelle, KoshVorlon, Lightmouse, Mesoso2, Techman224, Hobartimus, Alex.muller, PbBot, Tkmasta, Kumioko (renamed), Spartan198, ZH Evers, Frankie feyaless, Outdawg, Netstride, Stevecalloway, Navyguy, ImageRemovalBot, Martarius, ClueBot, LAX, GorillaWarfare, Hutcher, Snigbrook, Kennvido, Helenabella, FieldMarine, Gaia Octavia Agrippa, Merc5326, Niceguyedc, Blanchardb, Jim Dolbow, DEVGRU and the Teams, Auntof6, Magicfish, Dr. B. R. Lang, Excirial, Klenod, Beanerschnitzel, Mumia-w-18, Niteshift36, Vivio Testarossa, Dough007, Arjayay, Tnxman307, Eustress, SoxBot, Arimis~enwiki, Redthoreau, Zimzypoo, Ste900R, La Pianista, DarkCatalyst 08, Thingg, Lawrencema, Kevindwhite, Booyah234, Hoelzel, SoxBot III, Shawis, Vanished User 1004, XLinkBot, Gnowor, RkOrton, RekonDog, Little Mountain 5, Rasputitsa, Sidewinder008, Kwjbot, Joliver375, TomPointTwo, ZooFari, Thatguyflint, USS Noob Hunter, Chieflalala, UhOhFeeling, Addbot, Bat138, Willking1979, Colbybartlett, Roaring Siren, Landon1980, SpartanSWAT10, Blethering Scot, Darwin-rover, Aabercromby, Benchmark.stl, Matterwave, Mikec62001, CanadianLinuxUser, Leszek Jańczuk, Zeus s007, Dianadriebling, TySoltaur, Sammiiscenee, Jephray, Jared.hickel, Apukeena, Candyman777, Tide rolls, Jxl180, Apteva, Ben Ben, Legobot, Luckas-bot, Yobot, Mackin90, Fraggle81, TaBOT-zerem, Frogdaddy, Legobot II, Forged Clothing, Evans1982, Charlie Tango Bravo, BlindLogic, Nirvana888, Hartbilt, CinchBug, KamikazeBot, Citizen-of-wiki, Amusselw, TestEditBot, Naymetayken, AnomieBOT, DemocraticLuntz, Mekongdelta1, Jim1138, Royote, Piano non troppo, Chuckiesdad, Iangpacker, Kingpin13, Glenfarclas, Jeff Muscato, Citation bot, Thinkingamerican, Fagman1111, Frankenpuppy, Fagman1, Demo9237, Karaff, Jpickard5, Kelly.beamsley, Capricorn42, CaliSEAL, Ph3nom24, 4twenty42o, Sodacan, 661kts, 11boifoef, Srich32977, Millelacs, Armyjoe, Ute in DC, Anotherclown, Scubarec, Wooferpie, Spesh531, SCARECROW, HoyaProff, Ivan der Schreckliche, Sophus Bie, Gordonrox24, Infanteriesoldat, Takisstathis, FrescoBot, Tobby72, Kpuffdaddy122, Ammo303, Andre Kritzinger, Edge3, TawsifSalam, Eagle4000, Arcendet, RCPayne, Nirmos, Oakwoodacres, Shadow At Dawn, Pinethicket, Elockid, Docsman, Bejinhan, Ngyikp, A8UDI, RedBot, Stadenfan, Pbsouthwood, Turian, Merlion444, Necrojesta, Ionisiso, Altarcraft, Micro888, SF1SHER07, Prtgl93, Countscronchula, Clarkcj12, Sizzle Flambé, GreenUpGreenOut, Jonny 33rd, Suffusion of Yellow, AshBoss, Tbhotch, DARTH SIDIOUS 2, RjwilmsiBot, IshmaelMarcos, Ripchip Bot, DisturbedMTSeal, HeinzzzderMannn, Nerdy-

ScienceDude, Blademaster1975, Alison22, Rayman60, Zaqq, EmausBot, John of Reading, Howard41, Alloutlenses, Faceless Enemy, RA0808, RenamedUser01302013, Marittiell81, OHPerry, Sp33dyphil, Somebody500, Solarra, Beek91, Navysealscouts, Wikipelli, K6ka, Drudgeon, Lordregus, AvicBot, Darkman101, Ida Shaw, Illegitimate Barrister, August571, Zach1718, Kevz1140, CoreyEmerson421, H3llBot, Unreal7, MajorVariola, Ecoughlin, ChaosTheory07, Gz33, Doomsday212, Greco32, L Kensington, BuzzardHB, Nkgal, Donner60, Scoob01, Banza-ibo, Tacita620, Thewolfchild, Orange Suede Sofa, Insommia, Sven Manguard, Afranelli, DASHBotAV, Shakinglord, ClueBot NG, Dwc89, Thinktankgroup, Movses-bot, LDMerriam, Tvmark, SAJEEVJINO, Korrawit, Snotbot, Hindustanilanguage, Porkloinson, 123Hedgehog456, Widr, Supersillier, Byjinkung, Jeremy Wordsworth, Bone1234, MerllwBot, Oddbodz, Mightymights, Helpful Pixie Bot, Bravo83, FXShan-non, Strike Eagle, Karniverous, Calidum, X W T F, BG19bot, Chris0834, Rizzel3, SEALsT6, ISTB351, AvocatoBot, Billybob98, Mark Arsten, Jordonn, JRR007, Compfreak7, Rm1271, Dainomite, Joydeep, Foampositemax, Northerlywind, NeptuneSpeared, Theoneyoucall, Medo4, Shaun, Bigdaddy5431, Zackmann08, Navyeltee, USMC Lance, BobDohse, Fartman11, ForwardObserver85, Smitty1399, Titoman5, Seal827, Auprwtv, SkepticAnonymous, Kaci1851, Specijala, Tow, SEALthomas97, SirVegas, Webclient101, Mogism, Chiceidorb, Kephir, Frosty, Belairkid, Stewwie, TeriEmbrey, ThupaLink, WhiteAxe, M1921, Alexander9595, Aaaaaaay, JINXD66, Awesomgeek, Anne Delong, Mads.bahrt, JIMMYRUSELL9876, Bushdude, Ugog Nizdast, Dorrian100, Ginsuloft, Izwanikken, Quenhitran, Stratocaster27, Buck49.5, Car-petBumming, J-boogie7, Word ynopeau, Trident1983, GraniteSand, TsukiKanade, JaconaFrere, Skr15081997, 7Sidz, ZOMBIE NINJA236, Aninja6685, PsuNROTC2013, OJOM, Monkbot, Filedelinkerbot, Caroseberry, Demoniccathandler, Klarktom, ShiningEdge, Ptmoore22 2, Mballduke12, Thaydes08, Architect2014, Conan Slog, Cojac11, Swagg2495, Tuhdsk1, Bvizz84, Dj348, Jim339, Tanberetman, TranquilHope, KH-1, CSSEYS86, Quuestion, Crystallizedcarbon, Therealtred, Bestfromstirling, Anon's Around the world, Misterroblox, FlankerTangoUBF, Uslessbutton, Timedatombomb, Mememan900, Ikilledledogs, AdWipe, Alassane7, Jacob.Joyce99, Alex kus11, SyriaWarLato, Zezima5625, Nicolas Hrechko, Billybub303, Wheelers65, Rodgerc3, Benespenhorst, JGM167, CyberWarfare, NSW1962, ShoulderOfOrion44, Shanehum-mel, Dr. Andrew Wilson, Paulyd227 and Anonymous: 1663

18.12.2   Images

- **File:071031-M-3197S-023.jpg** *Source:* https://upload.wikimedia.org/wikipedia/commons/5/53/071031-M-3197S-023.jpg *License:* Public domain *Contributors:* MARSOC Website *Original artist:* MARSOC Public Affairs Office
- **File:11thSFG_Flash.png** *Source:* https://upload.wikimedia.org/wikipedia/commons/5/55/11thSFG_Flash.png *License:* CC BY 3.0 *Contributors:* jrgert *Original artist:* Jrgert
- **File:12SFG_beret_flash.svg** *Source:* https://upload.wikimedia.org/wikipedia/commons/2/22/12SFG_beret_flash.svg *License:* Public domain *Contributors:* US Army Institute Of Heraldry *Original artist:* US Army
- **File:19sfg.svg** *Source:* https://upload.wikimedia.org/wikipedia/commons/b/ba/19sfg.svg *License:* Public domain *Contributors:* Own work *Original artist:* MDragunov
- **File:19th_Special_Forces_Group_Land_Navigation_Training.jpg** *Source:* https://upload.wikimedia.org/wikipedia/commons/3/31/19th_Special_Forces_Group_Land_Navigation_Training.jpg *License:* Public domain *Contributors:* http://www.soc.mil/UNS/Photo/2011/2011/album/slides/402774.html *Original artist:* United States Army
- **File:1sfg.svg** *Source:* https://upload.wikimedia.org/wikipedia/commons/a/ab/1sfg.svg *License:* Public domain *Contributors:* US Army Institute Of Heraldry *Original artist:* US Army
- **File:20sfg.svg** *Source:* https://upload.wikimedia.org/wikipedia/commons/9/9f/20sfg.svg *License:* Public domain *Contributors:* US Army Institute Of Heraldry *Original artist:* US Army
- **File:21st_STS_JTACs_CAS_training_mission_at_Nevada_Test_and_Training_Range2.jpg** *Source:* https://upload.wikimedia.org/wikipedia/commons/5/5c/21st_STS_JTACs_CAS_training_mission_at_Nevada_Test_and_Training_Range2.jpg *License:* Public domain *Contributors:* https://secure.flickr.com/photos/47833351@N02/6211386106 http://www.nellis.af.mil/photos/mediagallery.asp?galleryID=1556&?id=$-$1&page=17&count=24 http://www.dvidshub.net/image/468893/close-air-support-training-nevada-test-and-training-range *Original artist:* Tech. Sgt. Michael R.Holzworth[1]
- **File:24th_STS_badge.jpg** *Source:* https://upload.wikimedia.org/wikipedia/commons/8/8f/24th_STS_badge.jpg *License:* Public domain *Contributors:* http://www.globalsecurity.org/military/agency/usaf/24sts.htm *Original artist:* ?
- **File:24th_Special_Operations_Wing_insignia.jpg** *Source:* https://upload.wikimedia.org/wikipedia/commons/d/de/24th_Special_Operations_Wing_insignia.jpg *License:* Public domain *Contributors:* http://www.afsoc.af.mil/library/factsheets/factsheet.asp?id=19566 *Original artist:* Unknown<a href='//www.wikidata.org/wiki/Q4233718' title='wikidata:Q4233718'><img alt='wikidata:Q4233718' src='https://upload.wikimedia.org/wikipedia/commons/thumb/f/ff/Wikidata-logo.svg/20px-Wikidata-logo.svg.png' width='20' height='11' srcset='https://upload.wikimedia.org/wikipedia/commons/thumb/f/ff/Wikidata-logo.svg/30px-Wikidata-logo.svg.png 1.5x, https://upload.wikimedia.org/wikipedia/commons/thumb/f/ff/Wikidata-logo.svg/40px-Wikidata-logo.svg.png 2x' data-file-width='1050' data-file-height='590' /></a>
- **File:3rd_Special_Forces_Group.JPG** *Source:* https://upload.wikimedia.org/wikipedia/commons/0/0c/3rd_Special_Forces_Group.JPG *License:* Public domain *Contributors:* http://www.dodmedia.osd.mil/ *Original artist:* Department of Defense
- **File:3sfg.svg** *Source:* https://upload.wikimedia.org/wikipedia/commons/d/d5/3sfg.svg *License:* Public domain *Contributors:* US Army Institute Of Heraldry *Original artist:* US Army
- **File:427th_Night_Fighter_Squadron_-_Emblem.jpg** *Source:* https://upload.wikimedia.org/wikipedia/commons/4/4b/427th_Night_Fighter_Squadron_-_Emblem.jpg *License:* Public domain *Contributors:* USAF Historical Research Agency via Mauer, Mauer, Combat Squadrons of the Air Force, World War II, 1969 *Original artist:* USAAF
- **File:427th_Night_Fighter_Squadron_P-61A-10-NO_Black_Widow_42-5628.png** *Source:* https://upload.wikimedia.org/wikipedia/commons/a/ac/427th_Night_Fighter_Squadron_P-61A-10-NO_Black_Widow_42-5628.png *License:* Public domain *Contributors:* United States ArmyAir Forces via Northrop P-61 Black Widow--The Complete History and Combat Record, Garry R. Pape, John M. Campbell and DonnaCampbell, Motorbooks International, 1991. *Original artist:* United States Army Air Forces

- **File:AlphaDASR.jpg** *Source:* https://upload.wikimedia.org/wikipedia/commons/b/b6/AlphaDASR.jpg *License:* Public domain *Contributors:* http://www.socom.mil *Original artist:* SOCOM correspondent

- **File:Ambox_important.svg** *Source:* https://upload.wikimedia.org/wikipedia/commons/b/b4/Ambox_important.svg *License:* Public domain *Contributors:* Own work, based off of Image:Ambox scales.svg *Original artist:* Dsmurat (talk · contribs)

- **File:Ambox_scales.svg** *Source:* https://upload.wikimedia.org/wikipedia/commons/5/5c/Ambox_scales.svg *License:* Public domain *Contributors:* self-made using inkscape and based off of Image:Emblem-scales.svg *Original artist:* penubag and Tkgd2007 (scales image)

- **File:Army_mil-54118-2009-10-27-091030big.jpg***Source:*https://upload.wikimedia.org/wikipedia/commons/7/71/Army_mil-54118-jpg *License:* Public domain *Contributors:* http://www.army.mil/-images/2009/10/26/54118/ *Original artist:* Spc. Joseph A. Wilson

- **File:Asiatic-Pacific_Streamer.png** *Source:* https://upload.wikimedia.org/wikipedia/commons/0/0b/Asiatic-Pacific_Streamer.png *License:* Public domain *Contributors:* http://www.tioh.hqda.pentagon.mil/Awards/service_campaign.aspx The Institute of Healrdry *Original artist:* United States Government

- **File:Barry_Goldwater.jpg** *Source:* https://upload.wikimedia.org/wikipedia/commons/9/96/Barry_Goldwater.jpg *License:* Public domain *Contributors:* Image:1-4-2007-16.jpg *Original artist:* User:Beachanchor, cropped and retouched by Kjetil_r

- **File:Battle_of_mogadishu_map_of_city.png** *Source:* https://upload.wikimedia.org/wikipedia/commons/f/f2/Battle_of_mogadishu_map_of_city.png *License:* Public domain *Contributors:* http://www.army.mil/cmh/brochures/Somalia/Somalia.htm#p9 *Original artist:* http://www.army.mil/cmh/

- **File:Bundesarchiv**wikimedia.org/wikipedia/commons/d/da/Bundesarchiv_Bild_101I-680-8283A-30A%2C_Budapest%2C_Otto_Skorzeny%2C_Adrian_v._F%C3%B6lkersam.jpg*License:*CC BY-SA3.0de*Contributors:*
This image was provided to Wikimedia Commons by theGerman Federal Archive(DeutschesBundesarchiv)as part of acooperation project. The German Federal Archive guarantees an authentic representation only using the originals(negative and/or positive),resp. the digitalization of the originals as provided by theDigital Image Archive.*Original artist:*Faupel● **File:Burnham_in_africa_close_up.jpg***Source:*https://upload.wikimedia.org/wikipedia/commons/5/51/Burnham_in_africa_close_up.jpg*License:*Public domain*Contributors:* Burnham Family Collection, Frederick Russell Burnham II (Major Burnham's grandson) and C. Atkinson,Burnham family members*Original artist* :not identified

- **File:C-212_USAF.JPEG** *Source:* https://upload.wikimedia.org/wikipedia/commons/7/7d/C-212_USAF.JPEG *License:* Public domain *Contributors:*
This Image was released by the United States Department of Defense with the ID DN-ST-94-01894 <a class='external text' href='//commons.wikimedia.org/w/index.php?title=Category:Files_created_by_the_United_States_Department_of_Defense_with_known_IDs,,&,</s-ST-94-01894#mw-category-media'>(next)</a>.This tag does not indicate the copyright status of the attached work.A normalcopyright tagis still required. SeeCommons:Licensingfor more information.
Original artist: PH2 Bruce R. Trombecky.

- **File:Carl_W_Stiner.jpg** *Source:* https://upload.wikimedia.org/wikipedia/commons/c/cf/Carl_W_Stiner.jpg *License:* Public domain *Contributors:* From [1] *Original artist:* ?

- **File:Combat_Rubber_Raiding_Craft_manned_by_SEAL-Team_5.jpg** *Source:* https://upload.wikimedia.org/wikipedia/commons/b/be/Combat_Rubber_Raiding_Craft_manned_by_SEAL-Team_5.jpg *License:* Public domain *Contributors:* DoDMedia *Original artist:* PH3 JOHN SULLIVAN, USN

- **File:Commandos_In_training.jpg** *Source:* https://upload.wikimedia.org/wikipedia/en/6/68/Commandos_In_training.jpg *License:* PD *Contributors:*
British Government Second World War photographer
Original artist:
unknown

- **File:Commons-logo.svg** *Source:* https://upload.wikimedia.org/wikipedia/en/4/4a/Commons-logo.svg *License:* ? *Contributors:* ? *Original artist:* ?

- **File:Defense.gov_News_Photo_100119-F-4177H-110.jpg** *Source:* https://upload.wikimedia.org/wikipedia/commons/0/08/Defense.gov_News_Photo_100119-F-4177H-110.jpg *License:* Public domain *Contributors:*
This Image was released by the United States Armed Forces with the ID 100119-F-4177H-110 <a class='external text' href='//commons.wikimedia.org/w/index.php?title=Category:Files_created_by_the_United_States_Armed_Forces_with_known_IDs,,&,,file from=100119-F-4177H-110#mw-category-media'>(next)</a>.This tag does not indicate the copyright status of the attached work.A normalcopyright tagis still required.SeeCommons:Licensingfor more information.
Original artist: Tech. Sgt. James L. Harper Jr., U.S. Air Force

- **File:Defense.gov_photo_essay_110220-A-7341H-045.jpg***Source:*https://upload.wikimedia.org/wikipedia/commons/f/fe/Defense.gov_essay_110220-A-7341H-045.jpg *License:* Public domain *Contributors:*
This Image was released by the United States Army with the ID110220-A-7341H-045<a class='external text' href='//commons.wikimedia.org/w/index.php?title=Category:Files_created_by_the_United_States_Army_with_known_IDs,,&,,filefrom=110220-A-7341H-045#mw-category-media'>(next)</a>.This tag does not indicate the copyright status of the attached work. A normalcopyright tagis still required. SeeCommons:Licensingfor more information.
Original artist: John D. Helms

- **File:Defense.gov_photo_essay_120602-A-WK843-082.jpg** *Source:* https://upload.wikimedia.org/wikipedia/commons/3/38/Defense.gov_photo_essay_120602-A-WK843-082.jpg *License:* Public domain *Contributors:*

  This Image was released by the United States Army with the ID 120602-A-WK843-082 <a class='external text' href='//commons.wikimedia.org/w/index.php?title=Category:Files_created_by_the_United_States_Army_with_known_IDs,,&,,filefrom=120602-A-WK843-082#mw-category-media'>(next)</a>.

  This tag does not indicate the copyright status of the attached work. A normal copyright tag is still required. See Commons:Licensing for more information.

  Original artist: Sgt. Karen Kozub

- **File:Edit-clear.svg** *Source:* https://upload.wikimedia.org/wikipedia/en/f/f2/Edit-clear.svg *License:* Public domain *Contributors:* The *Tango! Desktop Project. Original artist:*

  The people from the Tango! project. And according to the meta-data in the file, specifically: "Andreas Nilsson, and Jakub Steiner (although minimally)."

- **File:Emblem_of_the_United_States_Department_of_the_Army.svg***Source:*https://upload.wikimedia.org/wikipedia/commons/1/19/Emblem_of_the_United_States_Department_of_the_Army.svg*License:*Public domain*Contributors:*http://www.defense.gov/multimedia/web_graphics/*Original artist:*U.S. Dept. of Defense

- **File:European-African-Middle_Eastern_Campaign_Streamer.jpg***Source:*https://upload.wikimedia.org/wikipedia/commons/c/c8/Euro Eastern_Campaign_Streamer.jpg *License:* Public domain *Contributors:* http://www.tioh.hqda.pentagon.mil/Awards/EAME.aspx *Original artist:* Unied States Army

- **File:Flag_of_Argentina.svg** *Source:* https://upload.wikimedia.org/wikipedia/commons/1/1a/Flag_of_Argentina.svg *License:* Public domain *Contributors:* Here, based on: http://manuelbelgrano.gov.ar/bandera/creacion-de-la-bandera-nacional/ *Original artist:* Government of Argentina

- **File:Flag_of_Australia.svg** *Source:* https://upload.wikimedia.org/wikipedia/en/b/b9/Flag_of_Australia.svg *License:* Public domain *Contributors:* ? *Original artist:* ?

- **File:Flag_of_Bangladesh.svg** *Source:* https://upload.wikimedia.org/wikipedia/commons/f/f9/Flag_of_Bangladesh.svg *License:* Public domain *Contributors:* http://www.dcaa.com.bd/Modules/CountryProfile/BangladeshFlag.aspx *Original artist:* User:SKopp

- **File:Flag_of_Brazil.svg** *Source:* https://upload.wikimedia.org/wikipedia/en/0/05/Flag_of_Brazil.svg *License:* PD *Contributors:* ? *Original artist:* ?

- **File:Flag_of_Denmark.svg** *Source:* https://upload.wikimedia.org/wikipedia/commons/9/9c/Flag_of_Denmark.svg *License:* Public domain *Contributors:* Own work *Original artist:* User:Madden

- **File:Flag_of_East_Germany.svg** *Source:* https://upload.wikimedia.org/wikipedia/commons/a/a1/Flag_of_East_Germany.svg *License:* Public domain *Contributors:* Own work

  - *Gesetz zur Änderung des Gesetzes über das Staatswappen und die Staatsflagge der Deutschen Demokratischen Republik.* Vom 1. Oktober 1959

  - *Verordnung über Flaggen, Fahnen und Dienstwimpel der Deutschen Demokratischen Republik.* — Flaggenverordnung — Vom 3. Januar 1973

  - *Verordnung über Flaggen, Fahnen und Dienstwimpel der Deutschen Demokratischen Republik.* — Flaggenverordnung — Vom 12. Juli 1979

  Original artist:

- diese Datei: Jwnabd

- **File:Flag_of_Finland.svg** *Source:* https://upload.wikimedia.org/wikipedia/commons/b/bc/Flag_of_Finland.svg *License:* Public domain *Contributors:* http://www.finlex.fi/fi/laki/ajantasa/1978/19780380 *Original artist:* Drawn by User:SKopp

- **File:Flag_of_France.svg** *Source:* https://upload.wikimedia.org/wikipedia/en/c/c3/Flag_of_France.svg *License:* PD *Contributors:* ? *Original artist:* ?

- **File:Flag_of_Germany.svg** *Source:* https://upload.wikimedia.org/wikipedia/en/b/ba/Flag_of_Germany.svg *License:* PD *Contributors:* ? *Original artist:* ?

- **File:Flag_of_Greece.svg** *Source:* https://upload.wikimedia.org/wikipedia/commons/5/5c/Flag_of_Greece.svg *License:* Public domain *Contributors:* own code *Original artist:* (of code) cs:User:-xfi- (talk)

- **File:Flag_of_India.svg** *Source:* https://upload.wikimedia.org/wikipedia/en/4/41/Flag_of_India.svg *License:* Public domain *Contributors:* ? *Original artist:* ?

- **File:Flag_of_Indonesia.svg** *Source:* https://upload.wikimedia.org/wikipedia/commons/9/9f/Flag_of_Indonesia.svg *License:* Public domain *Contributors:* Law: s:id:Undang-Undang Republik Indonesia Nomor 24 Tahun 2009 (http://badanbahasa.kemdiknas.go.id/lamanbahasa/sites/default/files/UU_2009_24.pdf) *Original artist:* Drawn by User:SKopp, rewritten by User:Gabbe

- **File:Flag_of_Israel.svg** *Source:* https://upload.wikimedia.org/wikipedia/commons/d/d4/Flag_of_Israel.svg *License:* Public domain *Contributors:* http://www.mfa.gov.il/MFA/History/Modern%20History/Israel%20at%2050/The%20Flag%20and%20the%20Emblem *Original artist:* "The Provisional Council of State Proclamation of the Flag of the State of Israel" of 25 Tishrei 5709 (28 October 1948) provides the official specification for the design of the Israeli flag.

- **File:Flag_of_Italy.svg** *Source:* https://upload.wikimedia.org/wikipedia/en/0/03/Flag_of_Italy.svg *License:* PD *Contributors:* ? *Original artist:* ?

- **File:Folder_Hexagonal_Icon.svg** *Source:* https://upload.wikimedia.org/wikipedia/en/4/48/Folder_Hexagonal_Icon.svg *License:* Cc-by-sa-3.0 *Contributors:* ? *Original artist:* ?

- **File:Fourteenth_Air_Force_-_Emblem_(World_War_II).jpg** *Source:* https://upload.wikimedia.org/wikipedia/commons/5/51/Fourteenth_Air_Force_-_Emblem_%28World_War_II%29.jpg *License:* Public domain *Contributors:* USAAF Scan of personal patch *Original artist:* US-AAF

- **File:GEN_Bryan_Brown_official_portrait.jpg***Source:*https://upload.wikimedia.org/wikipedia/commons/c/cf/GEN_Bryan_Brown_official_portrait.jpg*License:*Public domain*Contributors:*USSOCOM History, 1987-2007*Original artist:*Unknown<a href='//www.wikidata.org/wiki/Q4233718' title='wikidata:Q4233718'><img alt='wikidata:Q4233718' src='https://upload.wikimedia.org/wikipedia/commons/thumb/f/ff/Wikidata-logo.svg/20px-Wikidata-logo.svg.png' width='20' height='11' srcset='https://upload.wikimedia.org/wikipedia/commons/thumb/f/ff/Wikidata-logo.svg/30px-Wikidata-logo.svg.png 1.5x, https://upload.wikimedia.org/wikipedia/commons/thumb/f/ff/Wikidata-logo.svg/40px-Wikidata-logo.svg.png 2x' data-file-width='1050' data-file-height='590' /></a>

- **File:GEN_James_Lindsay_1986.jpg** *Source:* https://upload.wikimedia.org/wikipedia/commons/9/96/GEN_James_Lindsay_1986.jpg *License:* Public domain *Contributors:* Defense Visual Information Center official site *Original artist:* Russell Roederer

- **File:GROM_DN-SD-04-01612.JPEG** *Source:* https://upload.wikimedia.org/wikipedia/commons/a/a2/GROM_DN-SD-04-01612.JPEG *License:* Public domain *Contributors:* ? *Original artist:* ?

- **File:GROM_with_Navy_SEALs_01.jpg** *Source:* https://upload.wikimedia.org/wikipedia/commons/8/8b/GROM_with_Navy_SEALs_01.jpg *License:* Public domain *Contributors:* gallery source image source *Original artist:* (Department of Defense photo)

- **File:GUC_Streamer.JPG** *Source:* https://upload.wikimedia.org/wikipedia/commons/a/ae/GUC_Streamer.JPG *License:* CC BY-SA 3.0 *Contributors:* Own work by the original uploader *Original artist:* EHDI5YS (talk)

- **File:Heinkel_He_111_during_the_Battle_of_Britain.jpg***Source:*https://upload.wikimedia.org/wikipedia/commons/8/82/Heinkel_He_111_during_the_Battle_of_Britain.jpg*License:*Public domain*Contributors:*This is photographMH6547from the collections of theImperial War Museums(collection no. 4700-05)*Original artist:*Unknown<a href='//www.wikidata.org/wiki/Q4233718' title='wikidata:Q4233718'><imgalt='wikidata:Q4233718' src='https://upload.wikimedia.org/wikipedia/commons/thumb/f/ff/Wikidata-logo.svg/20px-Wikidata-logo.svg.png'width='20' height='11' srcset='https://upload.wikimedia.org/wikipedia/commons/thumb/f/ff/Wikidata-logo.svg/30px-Wikidata-logo.svg.png1.5x, https://upload.wikimedia.org/wikipedia/commons/thumb/f/ff/Wikidata-logo.svg/40px-Wikidata-logo.svg.png 2x' data-file-width='1050'data-file-height='590' /></a>

- **File:Helmet_logo_for_Underwater_Diving_portal.png** *Source:* https://upload.wikimedia.org/wikipedia/commons/5/5e/Helmet_logo_for_Underwater_Diving_portal.png *License:* Public domain *Contributors:* This file was derived from Kask-nurka.jpg: <a href='//commons.wikimedia.org/wiki/File:Kask-nurka.jpg' class='image'><img alt='Kask-nurka.jpg' src='https://upload.wikimedia.org/wikipedia/commons/thumb/0/0a/Kask-nurka.jpg/50px-Kask-nurka.jpg' width='50' height='70' srcset='https://upload.wikimedia.org/wikipedia/commons/thumb/0/0a/Kask-nurka.jpg/75px-Kask-nurka.jpg 1.5x, https://upload.wikimedia.org/wikipedia/commons/thumb/0/0a/Kask-nurka.jpg/100px-Kask-nurka.jpg 2x' data-file-width='981' data-file-height='1371' /></a>
Original artist: Kask-nurka.jpg: User:Julo

- **File:Henry_Shelton_official_portrait.jpg** *Source:* https://upload.wikimedia.org/wikipedia/commons/5/56/Henry_Shelton_official_portrait.jpg *License:* Public domain *Contributors:* ? *Original artist:* ?

- **File:Hokusai-sketches---hokusai-manga-vol6-crop.jpg***Source:*https://upload.wikimedia.org/wikipedia/commons/7/72/Hokusai-sketche jpg *License:* Public domain *Contributors:*

- Hokusai_sketches_-_hokusai_manga_vol6.jpg *Original artist:*

  - Katsushika Hokusai

  - derivative work: AMorozov

- **File:Holland_cr.jpg** *Source:* https://upload.wikimedia.org/wikipedia/commons/b/bd/Holland_cr.jpg *License:* Public domain *Contributors:* http://www.af.mil/bios/bio.asp?bioID=5834 - Originally uploaded to en:wiki on March 12, 2007 by w:User:Hollandjustin *Original artist:* Unknown<a href='//www.wikidata.org/wiki/Q4233718' title='wikidata:Q4233718'><img alt='wikidata:Q4233718' src='https://upload.wikimedia.org/wikipedia/commons/thumb/f/ff/Wikidata-logo.svg/20px-Wikidata-logo.svg.png' width='20' height='11' srcset='https://upload.wikimedia.org/wikipedia/commons/thumb/f/ff/Wikidata-logo.svg/30px-Wikidata-logo.svg.png 1.5x, https://upload.wikimedia.org/wikipedia/commons/thumb/f/ff/Wikidata-logo.svg/40px-Wikidata-logo.svg.png 2x' data-file-width='1050' data-file-height='590' /></a>

- **File:ISA_Jerry_King.jpg** *Source:* https://upload.wikimedia.org/wikipedia/commons/e/ef/ISA_Jerry_King.jpg *License:* Public domain *Contributors:* http://www.michaelsmithwriter.com/books_special.html *Original artist:* Author's name unknown, member of the U.S. armed forces

- **File:ISA_badge.jpg***Source:*https://upload.wikimedia.org/wikipedia/commons/d/d4/ISA_badge.jpg*License:*Public domain*Contributors:* Image scanned in the book : Smith, Michael (2006).*Killer Elite: The Inside Story of America's Most Secret Special Operations Team*, London: Cassell Military Parperbacks.ISBN 0-3043-6727-3*Original artist:*Unknown<a href='//www.wikidata.org/wiki/Q4233718' title='wikidata:Q4233718'><img alt='wikidata:Q4233718' src='https://upload.wikimedia.org/wikipedia/commons/thumb/f/ff/Wikidata-logo.svg/20px-Wikidata-logo.svg.png' width='20' height='11' srcset='https://upload.wikimedia.org/wikipedia/commons/thumb/f/ff/Wikidata-logo.svg/30px-Wikidata-logo.svg.png 1.5x, https://upload.wikimedia.org/wikipedia/commons/thumb/f/ff/Wikidata-logo.svg/40px-Wikidata-logo.svg.png 2x' data-file-width='1050'data-file-height='590' /></a>

- **File:JCU_badge.jpg** *Source:* https://upload.wikimedia.org/wikipedia/commons/7/77/JCU_badge.jpg *License:* Public domain *Contributors:* http://www.bragg.army.mil/JCU-recruiting/Jcuapp.doc *Original artist:* ?

- **File:JFKSWCS_SSI.gif** *Source:* https://upload.wikimedia.org/wikipedia/commons/2/27/JFKSWCS_SSI.gif *License:* Public domain *Contributors:* Transferred from en.wikipedia; Transfer was stated to be made by User:Nobunaga24. *Original artist:* Original uploader was Nobunaga24 at en.wikipedia

- **File:JSOC.png** *Source:* https://upload.wikimedia.org/wikipedia/commons/b/bc/JSOC.png *License:* Public domain *Contributors:*

- page - http://www.ndu.edu/nwc/nwcCLIPART/COMBATANT_COMMANDS/USSOCOM/0002.html (archive.org copy) *Original artist:* Unknown, US Government / Military

- **File:JSOC_emblem.jpg** *Source:* https://upload.wikimedia.org/wikipedia/commons/4/4c/JSOC_emblem.jpg *License:* Public domain *Contributors:*

- page - http://www.ndu.edu/nwc/nwcCLIPART/COMBATANT_COMMANDS/USSOCOM/0002.html (archive.org copy) *Original artist:* Unknown, US Government / Military

- **File:Landing_on_Queen_Red_Beach,_Sword_Area.jpg**Source:https://upload.wikimedia.org/wikipedia/commons/d/d9/Landing_on_Queen_Red_Beach%2C_Sword_Area.jpg*License:*Public domain*Contributors:*This is photographB 5103from the collections of theImperial War Museums(collection no. 4700-29)*Original artist:*Evans, J L (Capt), No 5 Army Film & Photographic Unit

- **File:MARSOC_Emblem.jpg** *Source:* https://upload.wikimedia.org/wikipedia/commons/b/b4/MARSOC_Emblem.jpg *License:* Public domain *Contributors:* ? *Original artist:* ?

- **File:MARSOC_LOGO.svg** *Source:* https://upload.wikimedia.org/wikipedia/commons/f/f4/MARSOC_LOGO.svg *License:* Public domain *Contributors:* www.marines.mil/unit/marsoc *Original artist:* FOX 52

- **File:MARSOC_parachutist.jpg** *Source:* https://upload.wikimedia.org/wikipedia/commons/a/a9/MARSOC_parachutist.jpg *License:* Public domain *Contributors:* Marine Forces Special Operations Command, United States Marine Corps *Original artist:* Guunery Sergeant E.V. Walsh, USMC

- **File:MH-60_Blackhawk_landing_on_Hercules.JPG** *Source:* https://upload.wikimedia.org/wikipedia/commons/4/49/MH-60_Blackhawk_landing_on_Hercules.JPG*License:*Public domain*Contributors:*DoD Image number DN-SN-88-10165*Original artist:*PHCS TERRY MITCHELL, USN

- **File:MSOSG1-LOGO.jpg** *Source:* https://upload.wikimedia.org/wikipedia/commons/1/15/MSOSG1-LOGO.jpg *License:* Public domain *Contributors:* www.marines.mil/unit/marsoc public domain *Original artist:* USSOCOM

- **File:MSOS_Insignia.jpg** *Source:* https://upload.wikimedia.org/wikipedia/commons/4/4a/MSOS_Insignia.jpg *License:* Public domain *Contributors:* http://www.marsoc.usmc.mil/msos.html *Original artist:* United States Marine Corps

- **File:Marsockunarsvdjp4.jpg** *Source:* https://upload.wikimedia.org/wikipedia/commons/4/47/Marsockunarsvdjp4.jpg *License:* Public domain *Contributors:* MARSOC Website *Original artist:* MARSOC Public Affairs Office

- **File:Members_of_SEAL_Delivery_Vehicle_Team_Two_(SDVT-2).jpg** *Source:* https://upload.wikimedia.org/wikipedia/commons/0/0b/Members_of_SEAL_Delivery_Vehicle_Team_Two_%28SDVT-2%29.jpg *License:* Public domain *Contributors:* ? *Original artist:* ?

- **File:NAVSPECWARCOM.logo.gif** *Source:* https://upload.wikimedia.org/wikipedia/commons/f/f5/NAVSPECWARCOM.logo.gif *License:* Public domain *Contributors:* ? *Original artist:* ?

- **File:Naval_Jack_of_the_United_States.svg** *Source:* https://upload.wikimedia.org/wikipedia/commons/3/3f/Naval_Jack_of_the_United_States.svg *License:* Public domain *Contributors:* Naval Historical Center *Original artist:* Own work

- **File:Naval_Special_Warfare_Development_Group.jpg**Source:https://upload.wikimedia.org/wikipedia/commons/7/70/Naval_Special_Development_Group.jpg *License:* Public domain *Contributors:* R. Wicker - Redesigned Higher resolution of NSW Logo *Original artist:* Roque Wicker 2009

- **File:NavySeal1967Vietnam.jpg** *Source:* https://upload.wikimedia.org/wikipedia/commons/b/b7/NavySeal1967Vietnam.jpg *License:* Public domain *Contributors:* NARA *Original artist:* J.D. Randal, JO1, Department of Defense. Department of the Navy. Naval Photographic Center.

- **File:OA-37B-1.jpg** *Source:* https://upload.wikimedia.org/wikipedia/commons/3/30/OA-37B-1.jpg *License:* Public domain *Contributors:* http://www.dodmedia.osd.mil/DVIC_View/Still_Details.cfm?SDAN=DFST8513142&JPGPath=/Assets/Still/1985/Air_Force/DF-ST-85-13142.JPG *Original artist:* TSGT KEN HAMMOND

- **File:ODA525.jpg** *Source:* https://upload.wikimedia.org/wikipedia/commons/0/0f/ODA525.jpg *License:* Public domain *Contributors:* found in a PDF publication (http://d27vj430nutdmd.cloudfront.net/1448/3252/Spec_Ops_07_flipbook_2008_Mar_13_10_49_47.pdf, p.38, checked on June 28, 2010) *Original artist:* unknown (credited as Special Forces Association in Douglas Waller's book *The Commandos*)

- **File:Operation_Nimble_Archer_DN-SC-88-01042.jpg**Source:https://upload.wikimedia.org/wikipedia/commons/3/38/Operation_Nimble_Archer_DN-SC-88-01042.jpg*License:*Public domain*Contributors:*High resolution download fromhttp://www.dodmedia.osd.mil/DVIC_View/Still_Details.cfm?SDAN=DNSC8801042&JPGPath=/Assets/Still/1988/Navy/DN-SC-88-01042.JPG.*Original artist:*PH3 Henry Cleve-land, USN

- **File:Peter_Schoomaker.jpg** *Source:* https://upload.wikimedia.org/wikipedia/commons/2/2d/Peter_Schoomaker.jpg *License:* Public domain *Contributors:* ? *Original artist:* ?

- **File:Portal-puzzle.svg** *Source:* https://upload.wikimedia.org/wikipedia/en/f/fd/Portal-puzzle.svg *License:* Public domain *Contributors:* ? *Original artist:* ?

- **File:Question_book-new.svg** *Source:* https://upload.wikimedia.org/wikipedia/en/9/99/Question_book-new.svg *License:* Cc-by-sa-3.0 *Contributors:*
Created from scratch in Adobe Illustrator. Based on Image:Question book.png created by User:Equazcion *Original artist:* Tkgd2007

- **File:Ram_air_square.jpg** *Source:* https://upload.wikimedia.org/wikipedia/commons/b/bd/USN_parachute_demo_team_at_Minot_AFB.jpg *License:* Public domain *Contributors:* Public domain released NAVY photo: 040814-F-9208L-008 Minot Air Force Base, N.D. (Aug. 14, 2004) *Original artist:* Air Force photo by Senior Airman Joe Laws, taken from en:wp, uploaded by Dorbie

- **File:Seven_Green_berets.jpg** *Source:* https://upload.wikimedia.org/wikipedia/commons/f/fb/Seven_Green_berets.jpg *License:* Public domain *Contributors:* http://www.flickr.com/photos/soldiersmediacenter/6359212153/in/photostream *Original artist:* U.S. Army

- **File:Shield_of_the_United_States_Air_Force_Special_Operations_Command.svg** *Source:* https://upload.wikimedia.org/wikipedia/commons/c/cc/Shield_of_the_United_States_Air_Force_Special_Operations_Command.svg *License:* Public domain *Contributors:* http://www.af.mil/shared/media/ggallery/other/afg_021220_008.eps *Original artist:* en:United States Army Institute of Heraldry

- **File:SpecialForcesTabMetal.jpg** *Source:* https://upload.wikimedia.org/wikipedia/commons/6/6e/SpecialForcesTabMetal.jpg *License:* Public domain *Contributors:* http://www.tioh.hqda.pentagon.mil/Tab/SpecialForcesTab.htm *Original artist:* United States Army Institute of Heraldry

- **File:SpecialForces_Badge.svg** *Source:* https://upload.wikimedia.org/wikipedia/commons/2/22/SpecialForces_Badge.svg *License:* Public domain *Contributors:* SF RI.gif: <a href='//commons.wikimedia.org/wiki/File:SF_RI.gif' class='image'><img alt='SF RI.gif' src='https://upload.wikimedia.org/wikipedia/commons/thumb/a/af/SF_RI.gif/32px-SF_RI.gif' width='32' height='31' srcset='https://upload.wikimedia.org/wikipedia/commons/thumb/a/af/SF_RI.gif/48px-SF_RI.gif 1.5x, https://upload.wikimedia.org/wikipedia/commons/thumb/a/af/SF_RI.gif/64px-SF_RI.gif 2x' data-file-width='180' data-file-height='172' /></a> *Original artist:* MARKatde.wikipedia

- **File:Special_Air_Service_in_North_Africa_E_21337.jpg** *Source:* https://upload.wikimedia.org/wikipedia/commons/e/ea/Special_Air_Service_in_North_Africa_E_21337.jpg *License:* Public domain *Contributors:* This is photograph E 21337 from the collections of the Imperial War Museums (collection no. 4700-32) *Original artist:* Keating (Capt) No 1 Army Film & Photographic Unit

- **File:Special_Forces_Medic_in_Afghanistan.jpg** *Source:* https://upload.wikimedia.org/wikipedia/commons/e/eb/Special_Forces_Medic_in_Afghanistan.jpg *License:* Public domain *Contributors:* Soldier Magazine November 2009 cover *Original artist:* Steve Hebert

- **File:Special_Forces_commander_meets_with_village_elders_Afghanistan_2007.jpg** *Source:* https://upload.wikimedia.org/wikipedia/c9/94/Special_Forces_commander_meets_with_village_elders_Afghanistan_2007.jpg *License:* Public domain *Contributors:* http://www.flickr.com/photos/soldiersmediacenter/531605513/ (direct link) *Original artist:* Spc. Daniel Love, U.S. Army

- **File:Special_Operations_Craft-Riverine.jpg** *Source:* https://upload.wikimedia.org/wikipedia/commons/1/1f/Special_Operations_Craft-jpg *License:* Public domain *Contributors:* Official U.S. Navy SWCC Information website *Original artist:* ?

- **File:Symbol_book_class2.svg** *Source:* https://upload.wikimedia.org/wikipedia/commons/8/89/Symbol_book_class2.svg *License:* CC BY-SA 2.5 *Contributors:* Mad by Lokal_Profil by combining: *Original artist:* Lokal_Profil

- **File:Tenth_Air_Force_-_Emblem_(World_War_II).png** *Source:* https://upload.wikimedia.org/wikipedia/commons/f/f6/Tenth_Air_Force_-_Emblem_%28World_War_II%29.png *License:* Public domain *Contributors:* ? *Original artist:* ?

- **File:USA-stub.PNG** *Source:* https://upload.wikimedia.org/wikipedia/commons/d/d0/USA-stub.PNG *License:* Public domain *Contributors:* Own work *Original artist:* Bahamut0013

- **File:USAF_CCT_Bart_Decker_on_horseback_in_Afghanistan_2001.png** *Source:* https://upload.wikimedia.org/wikipedia/commons/4/4f/USAF_CCT_Bart_Decker_on_horseback_in_Afghanistan_2001.png *License:* Public domain *Contributors:* http://usatoday30.usatoday.com/news/afghanistan-ten-years-of-war/index.html *Original artist:* Army - although source cites Air Force

- **File:USAF_Pararescueman_Colon-Lopez_in_Afghanistan_in_2004.jpg** *Source:* https://upload.wikimedia.org/wikipedia/commons/b/ba/USAF_Pararescueman_Colon-Lopez_in_Afghanistan_in_2004.jpg *License:* Public domain *Contributors:* http://www.nationalmuseum.af.mil/photos/index.asp?galleryID=529&page=11 *Original artist:* Unknown<a href='//www.wikidata.org/wiki/Q4233718' title='wikidata:Q4233718'><imgalt='wikidata:Q4233718' src='https://upload.wikimedia.org/wikipedia/commons/thumb/f/ff/Wikidata-logo.svg/20px-Wikidata-logo.svg.png' width='20' height='11' srcset='https://upload.wikimedia.org/wikipedia/commons/thumb/f/ff/Wikidata-logo.svg/30px-Wikidata-logo.svg.png1.5x, https://upload.wikimedia.org/wikipedia/commons/thumb/f/ff/Wikidata-logo.svg/40px-Wikidata-logo.svg.png 2x' data-file-width='1050'data-file-height='590' /></a>

- **File:USASOC_DUI_new.jpg** *Source:* https://upload.wikimedia.org/wikipedia/commons/5/50/USASOC_DUI_new.jpg *License:* Public domain *Contributors:* http://www.soc.mil/UNS/Releases/2013/February/130225-04.html *Original artist:* USASOC

- **File:USA_-_10th_Special_Forces_Flash.svg** *Source:* https://upload.wikimedia.org/wikipedia/commons/1/14/USA_-_10th_Special_Forces_Flash.svg *License:* Public domain *Contributors:* File:USA - 10th Special Forces Flash.png *Original artist:* US Army

- **File:USMC_MSOR_logo.svg** *Source:* https://upload.wikimedia.org/wikipedia/commons/1/18/USMC_MSOR_logo.svg *License:* Public domain *Contributors:* [1] *Original artist:* United States Marine Corps

- **File:USMC_logo.svg** *Source:* https://upload.wikimedia.org/wikipedia/commons/2/21/USMC_logo.svg *License:* Public domain *Contributors:* DoD website: http://www.defenselink.mil/multimedia/web_graphics/#mc *Original artist:* U.S. Government

- **File:US_Army_Special_Forces_Command_(Airborne)_Organization.png** *Source:* https://upload.wikimedia.org/wikipedia/commons/8/82/US_Army_Special_Forces_Command_%28Airborne%29_Organization.png *License:* CC BY-SA 3.0 *Contributors:* Own work *Original artist:* Cayman 5-1

- **File:US_Army_Special_Forces_SSI.png** *Source:* https://upload.wikimedia.org/wikipedia/commons/e/e2/US_Army_Special_Forces_SSI.png *License:* Public domain *Contributors:* http://www.tioh.hqda.pentagon.mil/SF/SpecialForcesGroup.htm *Original artist:* US Army

- **File:US_Army_Special_Forces_Shoulder_Sleeve_Insignia.svg** *Source:* https://upload.wikimedia.org/wikipedia/commons/e/e3/US_Army_Special_Forces_Shoulder_Sleeve_Insignia.svg *License:* Public domain *Contributors:* Own work *Original artist:* US Army

- **File:US_Army_Special_Operations_Aviation_Command_SSI.png** *Source:* https://upload.wikimedia.org/wikipedia/commons/1/19/US_Army_Special_Operations_Aviation_Command_SSI.png *License:* Public domain *Contributors:* U.S. Army Institute of Heraldry at http://www.tioh.hqda.pentagon.mil/Catalog/HeraldryMulti.aspx?CategoryId=9478&grp=2&menu=Uniformed%20Services&from=recent *Original artist:* United States Army Institute of Heraldry

- **File:United_States_Department_of_the_Army_Seal.svg** *Source:* https://upload.wikimedia.org/wikipedia/commons/1/19/Emblem_of_the_United_States_Department_of_the_Army.svg *License:* Public domain *Contributors:* http://www.defense.gov/multimedia/web_graphics/ *Original artist:* U.S. Dept. of Defense

- **File:United_States_Department_of_the_Navy_Seal.svg***Source:*https://upload.wikimedia.org/wikipedia/commons/0/09/Seal_of_the_United_States_Department_of_the_Navy.svg*License:*Public domain*Contributors:*Keeleysam*Original artist:*United States Army Institute Of Her-aldry

- **File:United_States_Navy_SEALs_624.jpg** *Source:* https://upload.wikimedia.org/wikipedia/commons/d/d9/United_States_Navy_SEALs_624.jpg*License:*Public domain*Contributors:*This Image was released by the United States Navy with the ID040222-N-3953L-349<a class=' external text' href='//commons.wikimedia.org/w/index.php?title=Category:Files_created_by_the_United_States_Navy_with_known_IDs,< span>,&,,filefrom=040222-N-3953L-349#mw-category-media'>(next)</a>.This tag does not indicate the copyright status of the attached work. A normalcopyright tagis still required. SeeCommons:Licensingfor more information.*Original artist:*United States Navy SEALs

- **File:United_States_Navy_SEALs_81.jpg** *Source:* https://upload.wikimedia.org/wikipedia/commons/0/09/United_States_Navy_SEALs_81. jpg *License:* Public domain *Contributors:*

  This Image was released by the United States Navy with the ID 120109-N-OT964-0062 <a class='external text' href='//commons.wikimedia. org/w/index.php?title=Category:Files_created_by_the_United_States_Navy_with_known_IDs,,&,,filefrom=120109-N-OT964-0062#mw-category-media'>(next)</a>.

  This tag does not indicate the copyright status of the attached work. A normal copyright tag is still required. See Commons:Licensing for more information.

  Original artist: United States Navy SEALs

- **File:United_States_Special_Operations_Command_Insignia.svg***Source:*https://upload.wikimedia.org/wikipedia/commons/1/10/ States_Special_Operations_Command_Insignia.svg *License:* Public domain *Contributors:* http://www.brandsoftheworld.com/catalogue/S/1 html*Original artist:*united states army contributor

- **File:Us_army_air_corps_shield.svg** *Source:* https://upload.wikimedia.org/wikipedia/commons/1/1f/US_Army_Air_Corps_Hap_Arnold_Wings.svg *License:* Public domain *Contributors:* United States Air Force Trademark and Licensing Program *Original artist:* United States Air Force

- **File:Votel_official_photo_USSOCOM.jpg***Source:*https://upload.wikimedia.org/wikipedia/commons/6/60/Votel_official_photo_USSO jpg *License:* Public domain *Contributors:* USSOCOM *Original artist:* TSgt Angelita Lawrence

- **File:Wayne_Downing.jpg***Source:*https://upload.wikimedia.org/wikipedia/commons/6/63/Wayne_Downing.jpg*License:*Public domain tributors: ? *Original artist:* ?

- **File:Working_Diver_01.jpg** *Source:* https://upload.wikimedia.org/wikipedia/commons/0/00/Working_Diver_01.jpg *License:* Public domain *Contributors:*

  This Image was released by the United States Navy with the ID070104-N-3093M-016<a class='external text' href='//commons.wikimedia.org/w/ index.php?title=Category:Files_created_by_the_United_States_Navy_with_known_IDs,,&,,filefrom=070104-N-3093M-016# mw-category-media'>(next)</a>.This tag does not indicate the copyright status of the attached work. A normalcopyright tagis still required. SeeCommons: Licensingfor more information.

  Original artist: Mass Communication Specialist Senior Chief Andrew McKaskle

18.12.3   Content license

Made in the USA
Coppell, TX
16 December 2024

42620091R00118